Googoosh
A Sinful Voice

Googoosh

A Sinful Voice

صدای قدغن

Googoosh
with Tara Dehlavi

Gallery Books
New York Amsterdam/Antwerp London
Toronto Sydney/Melbourne New Delhi

G

Gallery Books
An Imprint of Simon & Schuster, LLC
1230 Avenue of the Americas
New York, NY 10020

First Gallery Books hardcover edition December 2025

Interior design by Hope Herr-Cardillo

Manufactured in the United States of America

10 9 8 7 6 5 4 3 2 1

Library of Congress Control Number: 2025941567

ISBN 978-1-6680-6742-0
ISBN 978-1-6680-6744-4 (ebook)

I dedicate this book to the women, men,
and children of my homeland.

And in loving memory of the one from whom I learned everything—
my teacher, Saber Atashin.

Contents

Part II

Author's Note

This memoir is a reflection of my experiences and the way I recall the events that shaped my life. I am not a historian, and this memoir does not claim to be a definitive historical account.

To protect the privacy of individuals, some names and physical characteristics have been altered. In some instances, composite characters have been used to honor and preserve the essence of multiple individuals whose presence and influence were meaningful in my seven-decade journey, while respecting the inherent length limitations of a memoir. However, these changes do not apply to public figures, who are portrayed as accurately as memory and available records allow.

Conversations have been reconstructed from memory. While the exact words may not always be precise, the substance of the discussions, emotions, and arguments remains true to what was expressed and intended at the time. Every effort has been made to present an honest account of my life and the moments that defined it.

Googoosh
A Sinful Voice

Part I

Chapter 1

The Committee of Vice and Virtue

September 29, 1980

I waited silently as he scribbled on the bottom of a busy page, hoping he would soon release me. His deep frown and tightened lips showed no sign of mercy.

"Who did you sing '*Kooh*' [Mountain] for?" he asked without looking up.

Hours had gone by like this, hours of the same questions, hours of me wishing each one would be the last, hours of Kambiz sitting patiently—an uncommon sight for any eleven-year-old boy—next to my uncle.

"But, sir, I've already answered all of these in Evin Prison," I said. "The interrogator there told me he had everything. I don't understand why I'm here. I even signed the release form, accepting that I'd never again—"

"Answer the question," he said, his eyes piercing straight at me through the dirty lens of his glasses.

"No one, sir," I answered. "I didn't sing '*Kooh*' for anyone in particular."

I knew better than to anger him. He quickly glanced at my hairline before returning to his notes. As he filled the page with black ink, I ran my fingers along my headscarf, making sure it covered every strand of hair. It was still new to me.

An hour before I entered this home with my uncle Farhang and my son, Kambiz, our neighborhood security guard, a sweet older man known as Mansour Khân, had called my mother's home in a state of panic.

"Mrs. Googoosh, some men just came to see me from the Monkarât office!" he uttered, catching his breath between each word. "They said, 'If Googoosh doesn't show up by tomorrow afternoon like she was told to in that letter she got . . .'" He paused to catch his breath again. 'Then we got orders to take her straight to the firing squad!'"

Fear rushed through me like a hurricane, uprooting and destroying the last bits of certainty I had since leaving Evin Prison. This was after all a new government branch designed to eradicate so-called *monkarât*, or societal vices. And as one of the most recognized female pop stars in the Shah's Iran, I was a clear target for the new virtue police.

My uncle, who had stopped over at my mother's for tea, offered to take me. I threw on a coat, covered my short hair with the newly mandatory headscarf, and hopped in his car with Kambiz. I should have left Kambiz with Mama. I wasn't thinking.

As soon as we pulled up to the entrance, my stomach churned. I immediately recognized this extravagant house. It was Mr. Mesbahzadeh's home, the cofounder and co-owner of Iran's most influential newspaper, *Kayhan*. I had heard that his assets, including *Kayhan*, had been confiscated by the Islamic Revolutionary Court, but it was another thing to see his home transformed into a makeshift prison.

Initially, I hadn't paid much attention to the address on the summons letter from the Monkarât. I didn't think I would actually have to go. Saddam Hussein had just started a war with us, and I assumed they had more important matters to attend to.

Now, sitting here, in front of the interrogator and his cluttered desk, I couldn't help but reflect that only a few years ago, I had stood in this same ballroom, in this very house on the exclusive stretch of Vozarâ Street, among Tehran's elite. Men in crisp tuxedos, women in flowing gowns adorned with glimmering jewels, and children dressed in their finest all mingled beneath the dazzling crystal chandelier that sparkled like a constellation above us. Mostafa Mesbahzadeh had personally requested me to perform at his daughter's birthday party, a celebration that rivaled the royal events I was accustomed to performing at, where world leaders and international stars filled the audience. It had never crossed my mind then, as I sang beneath that shimmering chandelier on such a joyous occasion, that I would one day be detained here. Mr. Mesbahzadeh had escaped to the United Kingdom, safe from a likely death sentence. His stunning home was now a bureau of the Revolution's most repressive vanguard.

At first glance, everything looked the same in this grandiose villa, with its white polished stone facade, softened by ornamental flourishes reminiscent of sumptuous nineteenth-century Qajar palaces. The same walls, tall and imposing, still surrounded the property, but now they felt more like the walls of a fortress—not protecting those inside, but trapping them, like prison bars, guarding the world from whatever was hidden within. Their presence, once comforting, now felt heavy and menacing. Even the gate, once elegant, had lost its sense of welcome. And the same windows, those familiar eyes of the house, with the delicate arches above, that whispered of past grandeur, stood as they always had. But today their glass looked opaque, no longer inviting in the warm sunlight. And no one seemed to tend to the once-lush garden anymore. The beautiful rose beds were long gone, shriveled beneath shoots of wild weeds and tangled spiderwebs.

Inside was even more chilling. Revolutionary Guards stood in the former grand foyer with their heavy Kalashnikovs that overshadowed the majestic balustrades. Large desks and stacks of files occupied the former ballroom, which once echoed with joyous birthday cheers and melodies. Gone were the Persian carpets, the crystal chandeliers, and the European antiques, including the elegant Louis XVI chairs and the sumptuous console tables with their heavy marble tops. Even the walls had been stripped bare, ornamented here and there with dusty traces of large frames that had once hung proudly.

Uncle Farhang gently whispered something into Kambiz's ear while placing his hand on my son's little shoulder. I barely looked at Kambiz since we got here. I was terrified. If I looked into his eyes, the fear I fought so hard to bury would show. I couldn't afford to worry about him—not now. I had to stay strong, for both of us. Any sign of weakness would only invite more scrutiny from the interrogator, and I wasn't going to give him that, not even for a second.

"Why did you and Behrouz Vossoughi visit Bourguiba in Tunis, back in 1976?" he continued with a smug look on his face. "What was your purpose?"

I told him the truth. I had performed at the annual International Festival of Carthage, sharing the stage with some of the world's most prominent musical acts. I had also been invited, for the second time, to perform for President Bourguiba's birthday—the first leader of independent Tunisia. He liked my music.

A young armed guard then walked into the makeshift interrogation room. His hands quietly fumbled over his gun in its holster, reminding me of Kambiz playing with a new toy.

"Sir," he said. "Hajj Agha Ansari asks to see you in his office."

He must be referring to the sharia judge, I thought.

"Tell him I'm on my way," the interrogator promptly replied, sending the young guard marching out with his weapon.

His pen barely left the surface of the paper. I couldn't imagine what he was scribbling and underlining over and over. He occasionally lifted his left hand to wipe off the sweat trickling down his temples. The air was stale in this large room, filled with pungent notes of old and new perspiration. Gone were the savory and sweet aromas that had once traveled from the kitchen, and the fresh scent of roses that once breezed in through the large open windows.

"Who did you see at Hotel Râmsar, during President Sadat's last visit with the Shah?" he asked, scratching his stubble that had become the signature look of new regime officials.

"I'm not sure if I was there during his last visit," I replied, giving him the same response I had given during my interrogation in Tehran's notorious Evin Prison seven months earlier.

He looked at his watch before diving back into the file, pen in hand, while the lamplight exposed the grease on his hair and face, as well as the stains on his dark brown suit, one size too big for him. His demeanor and disheveled appearance, typical of most zealous revolutionaries, were a stark contrast to the polished officials of the former regime. He then flipped through the black-ink-filled pages without really looking at them, like an actor shuffling with a prop while trying hard to remember his next lines, hoping not to raise the audience's suspicions. *He has nothing left to ask*, I thought.

Minutes went by before he asked about my current living situation.

"Living with a new husband," he said, referring to Homayoun in a scornful tone.

Homayoun Mesdaghi was my third husband. We had gotten married months earlier to prevent trouble with the Revolutionary Guards.

"But I'm staying alone with my mother these days," I said. "You see, she's terrified ever since those Iraqi jets blasted over the city and bombed Mehrabad Airport."

"How about your father, Saber?" he asked without skipping a beat. "He still in Tehran?"

"Yes," I answered.

Last I heard, Papa was still in Tehran, up to his usual business, without a care in the world for anyone, or any consequences.

Another guard entered the room. He seemed a little older than the last one, bigger, too, with a full beard. He went directly behind the desk and whispered into his superior's ear.

"Abolfazl, tell Hajj Agha I'm on my way," the interrogator responded before dismissing him with a quick hand gesture.

Abolfazl meant "father of virtue" in Arabic. I wondered if his parents had dreamed that he would one day work for something like the Monkarât. Maybe it wasn't even his real name. They never used their real names. The interrogator hadn't even bothered to introduce himself earlier.

The interrogator placed the scribbled pages back into the file, which he then stacked on top of a towering pile of folders. As he got up from his chair, I naturally followed, signaling to my uncle and Kambiz that we were finally free to go—it must've been 7 or 8 p.m. He stopped me.

"You stay here," he ordered.

"I'm sorry?"

"You stay here until this file is complete," he said deliberately.

"But why? On what grounds? What warrant?" my uncle protested as the interrogator walked past him toward the door. "Googoosh will come back whenever you want! I'll see to it myself!"

"I went four times to Evin Prison for interrogations, every time they needed me," I said as my heart pounded against my rib cage. "I can't leave my son and mother alone. I'm all they've got!"

He turned his back to us and called for one of the guards stationed in the main foyer.

My ears started ringing. I helplessly watched as Kambiz cried in confusion, his small body trembling as my uncle begged for my release. The young guard firmly gripped my uncle's arm, paying no attention to my little boy between them. With a rough shove, he pushed Uncle Farhang toward the door, forcing Kambiz to stumble forward along with him. My son's cries grew louder, while the guard, unmoved, continued to push them out into the hallway. My heart pounded as I stood frozen, unable to move, unable to help. Shortly after, two armed Revolutionary Guards entered the room. This time they were here for me. They had been ordered to take me downstairs, to the basement.

The entrance to the stairwell was in the grand foyer, but I had never noticed it before. The sweeping staircases leading upstairs, with their elegant curves and polished balustrades, drew all the attention, making it easy to overlook the understated doorway tucked beneath the grandeur. As I stepped onto the wide, unembellished stairwell leading straight down to the basement, the air grew colder, the stone steps devoid of warmth as they vanished into the shadows below. I could barely see, reaching down cautiously with the tips of my toes, feeling my way into the dim unknown. The ringing in my ears was replaced by a woman's scream in the distance. Her screams, translating an extreme pain whose origin I dared not even imagine, grew louder with each step downward. Then a man began shrieking. My knees were going to buckle any moment.

There has to be a way out, I thought. *Maybe if I ran fast enough, I could make it back to the street?*

There were two dim-lit narrow corridors at the bottom of the stairs. I was escorted into the one on the right. I couldn't see anything, except for shadows, shadows that moved, shouted, whispered, and wept. The air was thick with noise, yet it was hard to tell how many people were down here. The guards led me into a small room with a tiny window just below the ceiling and locked the steel-barred door before disappearing.

It was dark and stuffy. I could taste the mold in the air. The room was very small and bare, with only a carpet to sleep on. It must have been part of the maids' quarters at one time, before the revolution. It had enough space for a single bed and a side table, but they were all gone. My legs shook, but I couldn't sit still. I hadn't felt this terrified since my second interrogation at Evin Prison, when they had first blindfolded me. I wasn't afraid of dying. No. I had accepted that possibility the moment I boarded the plane in New York a year earlier. But I was terrified of torture. You get executed only once, but torture slowly eats away at you.

Everyone warned me not to come back, I thought as the other prisoners' cries echoed in the distance. I wanted to yell for help, but no one would hear me, no one but the shadows. The room started spinning. I couldn't breathe. As I gasped for air, a scene from Bruce Lee's 1973 film, *Enter the Dragon*, flashed before my eyes. Lee's character has just fought off some bad guys in an obscure underground location when he reaches a room where three hidden metal doors come smashing down from above, one by one, trapping him. Seeing that he's trapped, he sits on the ground with his legs crossed and his nunchaku placed around his neck and waits patiently for what's to come. He does nothing. This image suddenly sent a calm wave over and through me. I sat on the ground and breathed deeply from my lungs, something I had learned to do when singing. It was working. I loosened my headscarf and rested against the wall, doing nothing.

Several times, as the cries momentarily subsided, I thought I heard footsteps. Perhaps it had just been a rat, rummaging for scraps of food. An hour or two passed and I looked out the window, hoping for a sign that morning was nearing. But it was still hopelessly dark outside. Beyond these walls people were still asleep in their beds, ignoring this former home and its new tenants. I had been one of them twenty-four hours ago, blissfully ignorant of my fate.

I wondered whether Mama had told Homayoun yet. A part of me was relieved that he hadn't accompanied me here. Of course he would have been worried for me, but he would have been terrified that they would turn their focus on him and his demons. Besides, it was my problem; he had begged me to stay in New York, far from all of this. But I hadn't listened.

I struggled to keep my eyes open, but I couldn't fight off sleep any longer. I had to let go. I drifted off into a semiconscious state, far from these four walls. Names, faces, words, and sentences entered my mind like a train passing through a deserted station.

Loud footsteps jolted me out of my reverie.

"Don't stop!" a man shouted. "Walk faster, you piece of shit!"

The footsteps entered the narrow corridor, accompanied by heavy breathing. The sounds of keys clinking against one another and a woman whimpering echoed all the way to my room. A door was unlocked.

"You think you're tough, huh?" the man said as the door opened. "I'll get you to spit it out soon enough, you *kessâfat* [scum]!"

The door was quickly slammed shut, shaking the ground. I listened carefully, terrified that the footsteps were now coming for me. They didn't. They left behind a new prisoner, who was shouting and moaning in pain, her voice echoing through the narrow corridors.

I tried my best to ignore all the screaming. I covered my ears with my hands. I could still hear them. I pulled on the sides of my headscarf and bunched them into my ears like earplugs. Useless. I moved to the farthest corner of the room, only a few steps from where I had been sitting. There was nothing I could do to shield myself from the bloodcurdling screams. They reverberated all the way to my core, like an electric shock.

When they slowly subsided, the throbbing in my head increased. *If only I had taken my pills.* I had been getting migraines ever since Evin, so I always carried painkillers. In my haste, I'd forgotten them, just like I had forgotten my cigarettes. The more I thought about it, the more excruciating the pain became. I closed my eyes and tried to imagine myself somewhere that brought me comfort: the gray shores of the emerald Caspian Sea.

I tried to imagine the humidity enveloping my skin, the intoxicating sea breeze, often mixed with the scent of wood burning nearby, gently blowing through my hair. I tried to remember how it felt stepping barefoot into the water, how the waves seemed to pull you in, how sticky crustaceans gathered around you, curious. I loved the water. I always had. From a very young age, Papa used to take me with him into the sea whenever we toured across the northern coast. He would take me to the beach and into the choppy water between practices and performances. As soon as we got to the shore, we would run across the sand and jump into the water with all our might. Papa was a child at heart. He never wanted to grow up. Children loved him for that. Back then, I loved him for that.

I didn't know how to swim at first, so I would hold on to Papa's muscular neck and giggle as the waves danced with us. I only had my first swimming lesson when I turned five. Miss Violette was my teacher. She was an Austrian trapeze artist who—like us—was scheduled late nights at Tehran's Cabaret Shokoofeh No. Papa must have run into her backstage before one of our shows and somehow explained to her in his broken English that I didn't know how to swim, possibly with his charming smile that many women found irresistible. He loved women and they loved him back, with his athletic build, warm brown eyes, fair skin, thick arching eyebrows, and contagious smile. His charms must have worked, as Miss Violette offered to take me on as her pupil. Her Persian wasn't good, nor was my English, but by then I was a home-trained acrobat; I knew how to imitate and memorize movements. I followed her every move. I couldn't get enough.

I cherished my time with Papa in the sea. He was all I had after Mama left. And nothing could keep me out of the water, not even a towering wave that came crashing down on me, tearing my right eardrum.

Another painful cry shook me from my daydream and brought me back to these four walls. There was no getting away. I turned to music.

I recalled in my mind the songs that I had learned on the road with Papa. They were the popular traditional songs with melancholic words sung by the greats like Marzieh, Delkash, and Pouran, who, unbeknownst to them, had been my first vocal teachers. They were also the Azerbaijâni folk dances and operettas with lively tempos that Papa and I used to perform together. He loved those folk songs. They reminded him of home, of the western Azerbaijâni province of Iran, where he and Mama had met before they left for Tehran.

I always came back to these songs, from the heart-wrenching ballads to the more upbeat ones. I sang them on my toughest days, when I missed my mother, when I lived under the same roof as my stepmother with her constant wrath, or when I lost my very best friend, my brother, my Fery. It was as though these songs had been ingrained into my soul and spoke directly to my deepest pain, pain that I was otherwise unable to put into words.

Zoya Zakarian's lyrics floated into my mind, lyrics that she had written for me three years ago, in 1977, right after a trip we had taken together to India. The song was going to be called "Empty Stage." It painfully depicted the fleeting nature of fame, from being revered one day to facing an empty auditorium the next. When I first read it, I jokingly told her that it was too early for me to sing it, that I should wait until my retirement. I was only twenty-six then. *The joke was on me*, I thought as her words resonated throughout my body.

"I cannot believe that in the peak of my flight, my wings are withering away."

Chapter 2

Becoming Googoosh

My parents called me Googoosh from the moment I was born. They had made some Armenian friends in the earlier days of their marriage, the happier days, with names like Lidoush, Minoush, and Googoosh. They liked the ring of the two melodious syllables put together and didn't mind that it was a boy's name. When Papa went to apply for my birth certificate, no less than eighteen months later, they told him that they couldn't register a non-Iranian and non-Muslim name. So my first name was officially Faegheh (Victorious), but everyone called me Googoosh. No one ever called me Faegheh Atashin or Googoosh Atashin, just Googoosh.

Mama and Papa were both from Iran's West Azerbaijân province. They were bilingual in Azeri Turkish and Persian like most Iranian Azerbaijânis, but always spoke Azeri Turkish at home. Their Azeri accent was thick when they spoke Persian, which may have limited Papa's acting career in those days. Their mutual love for Azeri language, food, music, and dance served as a bridge connecting two individuals from completely different social worlds.

My mother, Nasrin, came from a family of doctors and engineers, while Saber was born into a humble family that was barely literate. Mama's family lived in the city of Miandoâb, the region's capital, while Papa's family resided in a small village (whose name I can't recall). Mama was spoiled by her parents, especially her father, Gholi Sobhi, a successful mechanical engineer. Papa worked odd jobs from childhood to help put food on his family's table, and his mother died when he was young—I remember Mama, or maybe Uncle Nader's wife, once hinted that my paternal grandmother had likely committed suicide after her husband took on a second wife. Mama's parents were staunch communists, while Papa's were Shia Muslim.

In 1945, at the outset of the Cold War, my grandfather Gholi Sobhi was appointed as a colonel in the Azerbaijân People's Government (APG), a short-lived and unrecognized secessionist state. The Soviet Union, reluctant to relinquish its occupation of northern Azerbaijân after taking control during World War II, supported the creation of this puppet government as part of its broader strategy to maintain influence in the region. When the recently formed APG was defeated by the Iranian army in a bloody battle a year later, my grandfather and other APG leaders were arrested and sentenced to death for treason. Mama was fourteen years old at the time, the oldest of three siblings. A year after his execution, the three siblings and their mother, Mahboubeh, were banished from Iran's West Azerbaijân province, and sentenced to live in exile in Tehran.

Mr. Kousheshi, an old family friend who owned a sugar factory in Miandoâb, promised my grandmother that he would find someone to safely accompany them to the capital—anything could happen to a lone woman traveling more than 385 miles with her three children. He called my father. Papa must have been around twenty years old at the time, having recently returned from the USSR, perhaps Soviet Azerbaijân, where he had been educated and trained as an acrobat, leaving him able to read and write only in Russian. To make ends meet, he worked part-time at the sugar factory while also teaching sports at a local school. Papa had visited Tehran before. His older maternal uncle, whom the family called Dâyi (which literally translates to "maternal uncle"), moved there for its improved economic opportunities like many Iranian Azerbaijânis and members of other ethnic groups. So Papa accepted the task to travel down south with this despairing family. It was perhaps the only selfless thing he ever did in his life.

Papa and Mama had been total strangers, but were to pretend they were engaged in order to avoid any unnecessary trouble—it was socially unacceptable for a man and a young woman to travel together out of wedlock. When they arrived in Tehran after three grueling days on the road, they were greeted by the police on Sepah Street. Mahboubeh and her children were put under arrest in a nearby hotel as part of her punishment. Papa rushed to Dâyi's home and convinced him to speak to the police. The police agreed to free them provided that they would live with Dâyi, their guarantor. Dâyi and his wife and their three children took them in until my grandmother found a job at the Soviet Hospital of Tehran and could afford an apartment. Papa also decided to stay.

Only a year later, the fake couple were madly in love and married. Uncle Farhang once said that their marriage would have been impossible had it not been for my grandfather's execution. After all, Gholi Sobhi always wanted the best for his daughter: the best toys, the best clothes, the best private music instructor, the best education. A struggling entertainer would not have made the cut. But knowing Mama, she would have probably gotten her way.

It was easy to imagine my younger, teenage mother falling for my father's charming youthful smile and his exuberance. Uncle Farhang told me that before I was born, Papa used to take Mama on tour with him and have her sing onstage.

"She had a lovely voice," Uncle Farhang said. "She even seemed to enjoy it."

But all that stopped once they had children. Their first born was a boy named Farrokh. He died when he was about one, from a common illness. I was born not long after, on May 5, 1950, followed by my baby brother, Fereydoun, or Fery, as we called him. In those early days, with an infant and a toddler at home, Papa was either away traveling for work with a troupe of entertainers or out buying rounds of drinks for friends. He was reckless with his money. He barely saved enough to cover our household expenses, including the rent for our one-bedroom apartment on Sarcheshmeh Street, in a middle-class neighborhood. The constant financial stress coupled with all those new responsibilities were just too much for Mama to handle by herself. She was only eighteen years old, and she had been pampered her whole life until then. I suspect that Papa's flirtatious nature didn't help ease matters, either.

I must have been two when Mama left. She took Fery with her. He was six months old, and she was still nursing him. Legally, she couldn't take me, although I didn't know it at the time. Men were automatically granted full child custody until 1975, when the Family Protection Law expanded women's rights to divorce and custody. I never understood how difficult it must have been for her to walk out that door on me, until twenty years later, in 1972, when I would face the same devastating decision to end my first marriage and leave my son.

I can't recall much about Mama from those early days, but I remember how deeply I missed her, all those knots in my stomach. Papa didn't like to talk about her—or anything personal. He must have had enough of me asking for her. One day, a few months after she had left, he told me that she was dead. I never asked about her again.

Papa worked odd hours and toured across the country with various troupes. He didn't know what to do with me. He couldn't depend on his younger brother, Nader, a struggling entertainer like himself. He couldn't call on Dâyi, either, who was busy supporting his grown children and grandchildren. I remember the first day Papa took me to work, not too long after Mama left. It must have been at a cabaret on the buzzing Lâlehzâr Street—one of the city's oldest and most historic streets, once considered Tehran's own Champs-Élysées, a vibrant hub of culture and modernity in the heart of the city, lined with theaters, cafés, cinemas, and shops that evoked the glamour of Paris. We went onstage, and Papa sat me on top of a chair and told me to sit still. Before I knew it, he flipped another chair, placing its backrest on his strong chin. Then, with effortless strength, he lifted me and my chair, and balanced us on the feet of the upside-down chair as he stood up. Papa was a relatively tall man, and my chair was so high up that my head nearly hit the ceiling. But he knew what he was doing. He had carefully measured everything. When I looked all the way down, I saw a sea of wide eyes staring up at me as Papa balanced the weight of both chairs on his chin while I clung to the top one. They held their breath and waited in complete silence. Every muscle in my body tensed. Seconds felt like an eternity. Finally, Papa slowly began to lower me gently toward the ground. When my feet touched the floor, the audience sighed in relief before they erupted into roaring applause. I had survived. And we were a hit.

We left our apartment and lived like nomads, staying either at Papa's friends' places, at some cheap hotel, or with Uncle Nader at his girlfriend's apartment. When Fery was a little older, he sometimes joined us before disappearing again—there must have been some arrangement between Papa and Mama, all while I had been led to believe that she was dead. At some point Papa and I went on tour with a troupe of acrobats, singers, and dancers. For weeks, we traveled across the country, including Shomâl, the northern coastal provinces, where I first saw the sea. Papa would sit me on the chair and amaze the audience with his precision and strength. And I trusted him. One day, I slipped. I don't know if it was me or Papa that had lost balance. As I plunged headfirst toward the ground, Papa magically caught me in midair, grabbing onto my little ponytail. After that, and for the longest time, I refused to sit on that chair. But Papa found other acrobatic acts for me to do. He made sure I learned all the new routines, no matter how long it took. We practiced every day and performed in the evening.

From very early on, I always loved watching the singers perform. Standing behind the curtains, I carefully watched as Mahvash, applauded as the singer of the people in the 1950s, captivated the audience; Ghazaal, whose melodious voice carried the soul of traditional Persian music, mesmerized the crowd; Jebeli, a popular singer who skillfully fused Arabic-inspired singing techniques with the melancholic beauty of Persian lyrics; Delkash, the legendary vocalist with a voice full of longing and passion, sang with unmatched grace; Pouran, a celebrated singer, held the audience in awe with her heartfelt performances; and Viguen, the "Sultan of Pop," whose songs blended Western influence with Persian spirit, lit up the stage with his electric charisma. I was too young to understand what they were saying, but I loved how the lyrics flowed along with the incredible melodies, especially Viguen's upbeat rhythm that was revolutionary at the time—he was the first to introduce pop music to Iran. They sounded like stories, stories that made me feel good. I absorbed everything, including the different rhythms, styles, notes, their dips, and their rises, the breaks in their voices. I learned the songs, the movements and hand gestures, and imitated them.

I was about three years old when Papa first overheard me singing, months after he had made me his stage partner. He placed me in the spotlight that same day, on top of a box so that my mouth could reach the microphone (it was still a little too high). "*Azizam*," he said, "if you sing this song, then I'll buy you a toy." He bought me a baby doll that first time. But he rarely delivered after that.

I would sing alone in most of our acts while Papa accompanied me with what we called a *tempo*, a hand drum. I was nervous at first, receiving all that attention from the audience. But it quickly became natural after performing day after day. I came to see the stage as my playground and the audience as benevolent spectators. I remember a summer night when I was four or five, singing at an outdoor seasonal café-restaurant called Baastaani on Shemirân Road while grasshoppers leapt by my feet under the spotlight. I carefully picked one up in my hand, like it was my tiny pet, all while singing my heart out.

When I was five years old, we regularly performed at night at Cabaret Shokoofeh No. It was a big deal. Iran didn't have large concert venues or music festivals like Woodstock. Instead, performers competed for recurring spots in Tehran's glamorous cabarets, like Cabaret Shokoofeh No, which were akin to the prestigious nightclubs and jazz clubs of 1950s New York City. I would fall asleep backstage until Papa woke me up at around 9 or 10 p.m. I would then find myself standing in front of well-dressed grown-ups in stylish, Western-influenced fashion. They were seated at tables with luxurious arrangements, their dinner plates, and beverages (often alcoholic), with colorful lighting bouncing off the venue's lavish ornaments and through the thick hovering cigarette smoke. At times, I spotted older children fidgeting in their seats or struggling to stay awake at their table. Papa would ask me to sing songs I had learned listening to the radio, songs in Persian, English, Spanish, Arabic, and Azeri. I was barely old enough to pronounce most words in my mother tongue, let alone from another language, so I made up words. I would sing from my belly, not knowing any better without any training, and would quickly run out of breath. That left me no choice but to skip some notes. Back then the audience didn't seem to mind; it was entertaining enough to watch a little girl in a little dress, with a ponytail, standing on top of a box and singing a famous Mâzandarâni song like "*Ranâ Jân*" (Dear Ranâ), about a man declaring his love to a woman named Ranâ.

My career as a child performer began to flourish amid a wave of cultural change. Growing up in the 1950s and '60s, I witnessed the final stages of Tehran's transformation into a cosmopolitan city, fueled by the economic boom—driven by the expansion of the oil industry and the Shah's modernization efforts, including the 1963 White Revolution, which sparked further urban migration from rural areas.

Even before I was born, Tehran—like Isfahan, Shiraz, and Abadan—had already embraced Western influences, from European modern architecture to fashion and music that became popular among the growing middle class. Cinema continued to play a significant role in this cultural shift during my childhood, with films like Federico Fellini's *La Dolce Vita*, Alfred Hitchcock's *Vertigo*, and Billy Wilder's *Some Like It Hot* capturing people's imaginations and opening them up to new worlds. Women dressed as fashionably as those in Paris or New York walked alongside women in traditional, colorful chadors. Intellectuals and artists flocked to the new universities and cultural institutions. The streets buzzed with life, with new shopping centers, cinemas, and cafés. Diplomatic ties and international businesses brought expatriates from abroad, turning Tehran into a global hub in the Middle East. The fusion of traditional Persian culture and modernity not only shaped the city but also deeply influenced my taste, style, and performances.

Yet, despite Tehran's growing cosmopolitanism, it was still scandalous for a child my age to be singing in cabarets—I was the only child in all of Iran doing so—just as it would have been anywhere in the world. Even New

Yorkers would be shocked by a child that young performing late at night in a sophisticated nightclub.

At school, most of the kids avoided me like the plague. Some of the girls would even taunt me: "You work at night!" "You fatherless, motherless thing!" The parents must have told their daughters to stay away. Not only was I in the entertainment business, which was considered lower class, but I also worked in the nightlife, where adults would come to be entertained and drink. These parents might have found me more acceptable if I performed only for children, which I did on Friday mornings (the second day of our weekend) at the cinema, singing for the young audience before the screenings along with other performers, like Viguen's nieces, Alice and Bella, or Hamid Ebadi.

I remember even before school, when I was five years old, some policemen once had some harsh words with Papa. I think we were at the police station. I only recall not understanding why they were so upset, especially since Papa never forced me to do anything. Of course, they were right to be concerned. I wasn't even fully potty-trained the first year of my career—I must have peed myself more than a handful of times, prompting Papa to teach me a code that would let him know it was urgent. I was far too young to be working like that, late at night. But even then, I desperately needed the stage. Music became my everything. It somehow helped me feel less sad about Mama. It made Papa proud of me. The stage was my make-believe world where nothing bad could ever happen.

Around the same period, when I was five, Mama came back in my life without any explanation. It was a different era then. Children only spoke when spoken to, and adults didn't feel the need to explain things to their children, at least not in my family. I don't know how it even happened. Papa was remarried at the time (although this marriage wouldn't last more than a year) and just had a son, Adel. Perhaps this made him more forgiving toward Mama. There is a picture of Mama and me from those days. She's embracing me while we look into the camera. Mama was smiling. I wasn't. I didn't want anything to do with her. She had abandoned me, and Papa had lied to me. But I didn't say a word. I learned to keep it all in, like my father.

After a few months, I let go of the anger. I think it was thanks to my grandmother Mahboubeh, or Bahbah, as we called her. I loved her so much, with her light brown eyes that radiated warmth and compassion. I remember her long, beautiful white hair that she always tied neatly back. She was short with a sturdy build, like Mama, but unlike my mother, Bahbah never held back her affection. She used to shower me with hugs and kisses—I could never get enough of them. Bahbah spoke Russian, Azeri, and some Persian, but always Azeri to Fery and me. I loved listening to her soothing voice, especially as I was about to fall asleep while gently pinching the creases of her smooth neck in lieu of a blankie.

She would bring me empty medical containers to play with from her work at the Soviet Hospital of Tehran, where she was either a dentist or a dental assistant. I didn't have toys, so I cherished these plastic containers. I built a pretend world with them, one with a house, and cars, and a loving family with two parents and their kids. Sometimes I would let Fery play, until he would start smashing them against one another—he was only three and a half years old then.

I think Bahbah's love and affection made it easier for me to let Mama back in. Bahbah taught me a lot about my mother, that she had a good sense of humor but was also direct and often blunt. My mother was a tough-love kind of person. Life made her this way, having witnessed her adoring father's public execution at such a young age. I let go of the past and was just happy to be around her. I remember Papa would drop me off at Mama and Bahbah's apartment whenever I had some time off, or when we got back from touring. I was happier those days. I smiled more. Then Papa married Mouness.

I was seven years old when Mouness entered our lives. She must have been around Mama's age, in her later twenties. She was pretty with big brown eyes that sloped down slightly at the outer corners, thick arching eyebrows, and perfectly coiffed dark hair, carefully pinned behind her ears. She seemed nice enough, too, especially since she looked a bit like our cherished singer Mahvash, who had been very affectionate with me when I was younger on tour with Papa. Mouness came from Rasht, the largest

Iranian city near the Caspian Sea. She had a thick Rashti accent whose melody I greatly enjoyed, at least at first.

By the time I was eight, Mouness had completely banned Mama from our lives. She couldn't even bear to hear my mother's name. Perhaps some part of her sensed how much Papa had once loved Mama, and how heartbroken he was when she left.

I struggled with Mama's absence again. This time, I knew to stop asking for her early on, accepting that this was just my life. I kept it all inside while I was busy with work, touring, school, and all the household chores in between. I enjoyed studying, especially spelling and dictation—I was really good at it—but I hated constantly changing schools. Whether we were on tour, staying for months in Isfahan or Mashhad with a theater group, or moving to a new neighborhood in Tehran, I rarely got to know my teachers or had the chance to form lasting friendships. I also had to quickly adapt to each new class's level, which was challenging, but I managed because I genuinely loved learning.

I wasn't just missing Mama this second time around, I was also dealing with Mouness's violent mood swings and cruelty. As usual, I poured all of my anger, pain, and sadness into my work, including in my first role in a feature film. I was eight years old when Iraqi-born filmmaker Gorji Ebadia hired me as a lead in one of his first films, *Bim va Omid* (*Fear and Hope*). Mr. Ebadia was kind and had an Arabic accent when he spoke. I don't know the details of how he came to hire me. We didn't have the equivalent of Hollywood with film studios and movie lots where you would go to audition in front of casting directors. But I was certainly the only child my age in Iran known for singing onstage and on the radio—the only one to become the family's sole breadwinner through this line of work.

I was nine when I played in my second feature film, also by Gorji Ebadia—he appreciated my professionalism and that I carefully executed all of his directions. *Fereshte-ye Farâri* (*The Runaway Angel*) is about the misadventures of a girl named Mina who runs away from home when she mistakenly believes she has killed her father after pulling on a factory lever she was told not to touch. There's a scene at the beginning of the film where

Mina breaks down, crying alone in her shared bedroom with her father, begging God to return her mother, whom she had never met. Mr. Ebadia asked me to pretend to cry while singing: "*Koja rafti maman? Bia pisham maman* [Where did you go mommy? Come back to me mommy]." But I didn't have to pretend anything. Mina's pain was equally mine.

I loved acting as much as I loved watching films. I played in twenty-nine films in over two decades. It was fun and challenging with all of the required range of emotions and dialogue. But music above all was my refuge. I was driven to become the best singer I could be. My voice was the only thing I had some control over. I always knew I didn't have an exceptional voice, even as a child, listening to some of the greats. From very early on I worked hard to find the best techniques that would complement my voice. I imitated my favorite singers until I was fourteen or fifteen, when I learned how to sing from the throat and from the back of the nose thanks to a couple of private lessons from our beloved soprano Monir Vakili. I was no longer breathless in between notes. A few years later, after signing a music recording contract in Paris with the famous producer Eddie Barclay, I had three lessons with a French vocal teacher. She taught me how to sing from my chest and abdomen, how to control my breathing when singing, and the importance of articulating every single word. I practiced each new technique for days and weeks, from morning to night, just as I did with the acrobatic routines as a toddler, until it became pure muscle memory. Every single performance was an opportunity to sing better than the last time.

My first record, "*Ghesse-ye Vafa*" (Story of Loyalty), a song written for me by Iraj Janatie Ataie, composed by Parviz Maghsadi, was released when I was sixteen. Until then, I had only covered famous songs. I couldn't wait to perform my original song at the next *Honar Barâye Mardom* (*Art for the People*). It was a weekly TV and radio show where famous singers were hired by "Radio Iran" to perform for specific groups—university students, workers, hospital patients and staff, schoolteachers, and others. The crowd booed my song, shouting out names of other songs they wanted me to sing. Clearly, they didn't like the unfamiliar tune. But what if, deep down, they simply couldn't see me as a singer in my own right—someone beyond the echoes of others' hits? The thought broke my heart. Yet, when it aired on the radio, everything changed. People rushed to buy my record, connecting deeply with the heartbreaking lyrics. It became a massive hit and, almost immediately, people stopped seeing me as Googoosh, the child star, and began recognizing me as a serious artist.

With each new song, each performance, I pushed the boundaries. I went bolder. I took from the West. I took from the East. I went for colors. I sang over psychedelic-funk-electrifying beats. I danced and sang the samba. I wore miniskirts and traditional Indian saris. I sported a boyish haircut and the long-feathered hairstyle. I recorded painfully tragic Persian romantic ballads set to pulsating beats, and with each successive release, my fan base grew. Over eleven years, I accumulated more than forty hit records. I frequently sang for the royal family and for visiting foreign heads of state. I headlined numerous music festivals in France, Italy, and Tunisia alongside incredible artists such as Ray Charles, Tina Turner, Charles Aznavour, Sylvie Vartan, Julien Clerc, Peppino di Capri, and Ajda Pekkan.

I became Googoosh, Iran's biggest pop star, not because I wanted to, but because I had to. The stage was the one place in my life where I had full control and where all my pain disappeared. It was my therapy. But none of it mattered now. Sitting in this basement, I knew it was all over. They were going to take Googoosh away from me.

Chapter 3

The New Order

Day 1, Late Night

I could see stars glimmering in the distance through the small window across from the steel-barred door. I could make out branches swaying outside, in the cold night breeze. I wondered if anyone could see this window just large enough for a cat to crawl through—or if anyone could hear the cries.

Footsteps returned, hours after their last visit. This time, they brought someone to my room. A woman. As the footsteps disappeared, she stood in front of the door, her back toward me, sobbing. When she finally turned around, I couldn't see her face, but I could tell she was shaking, just as I had when they brought me in.

She sat on the ground, her back resting on the opposite wall, right next to the steel-barred door; the same spot I had first sat in. The faint light coming through the hallway showed tears streaming down her cheeks. She looked my way without really looking. I did the same, afraid of what I might discover. She then buried her face in her hands, her headscarf slowly slipping off.

I couldn't tell what time it was or how many minutes she had been sitting huddled up across from me. A sudden burning sensation shot down my leg from my lower back, making me nearly jolt up from the ground. It was my sciatica, that's what the doctor called it. The pain was still foreign to me, even though I had been living with it for the past year, ever since I had returned to Iran. I moaned out loud, the pain was too intense to endure quietly.

"Googoosh, is that you?" the woman whispered.

I hesitated as I massaged my lower back. Before the revolution, frustrated and suffocated by my lack of privacy, I sometimes lied to people who would recognize me, saying that I had been cursed to look like her. But times had changed. People now stayed as far as possible from Googoosh, as though she were a leper. Many people I once considered friends ignored my calls, leaving me in silence. Who could blame them? Association with the old world had cost countless lives.

"Is that you?" she insisted.

I recognized that soft voice, its unique pitch and timbre. I looked up. I knew those kind brown eyes, despite the puffiness from all the crying, those arching eyebrows, and her small, chiseled nose. It was Marjan, a singer and film actress close in age to me.

We embraced like long-lost friends even though we had only ever been friendly acquaintances. She sobbed and shivered in my arms.

"What happened to you?" I whispered. "Did they hurt you?"

"They stormed into our house! In the middle of the night!" she said, her voice raised and her body trembling. "They threw all our stuff upside down, looking for something, anything. Our little boy was terrified!" She paused to catch her breath. "They grabbed one of my personal photo albums and said I was under arrest. I don't understand!"

I urged her to sit back down, next to me. She took a few deep breaths and closed her eyes. I could then feel her body relaxing. The room felt a little less cold.

I must have last seen her two or three years ago, on the set of *Rangarang*, a popular television variety show. Or was it for the taping of the Shah's birthday celebration? Or the celebration of Imam Reza? No, it must have been seven years ago, in 1973, at the party held by a trendy women's magazine at Tehran's Intercontinental Hotel. When we had first met in 1972, she was a successful actress, but no one knew about her musical talents. I was stunned when I heard her sing a year or two later. I hadn't expected such a lovely voice. It was soft, but strong.

"What about you?" she asked, her voice trembling a little less. "Why didn't you leave the country when you had the chance?"

"I did," I replied. "But I came back."

"Why on earth did you come back?"

My trip to the U.S. was supposed to last just a couple of months. Instead, it stretched into six—six long months far from home, where I heard of the arrests and executions of friends and acquaintances via BBC Persian radio. Six months of falling deeper into a dark abyss, unsure if I would ever see the people I loved again.

The simplest answer, I told her, was that I had returned because Mama insisted.

"Googi," Mama said, using the nickname all my closest friends and family called me, "you need to come back."

Mama called me in New York City every day like this, ever since the Shah's regime toppled earlier in February of 1979. She was anxious that the newly established Islamic revolutionary government would seize my home, just as they had with all the vacant properties left behind by owners forced to flee. Then one day, sometime in April or May of 1979, she called me in a frantic state. It was 4 a.m. for me.

"They ransacked your house! They took everything!" she shouted into the telephone receiver, her voice trembling with anger.

Her words felt like a blow to my chest. This was my home, the first place I had ever bought for myself, alone, with my hard-earned money.

"Everything but the car!" she added in a defiant tone.

Mama had hidden my new brown Jeep Renegade. I was a little relieved. But more than anything I was worried Mama was going to get her stubborn self into serious trouble.

"Mama, please don't do anything," I pleaded. "You know they couldn't have taken much. At most, they've taken the television, my iron, and vacuum."

No one knew I was broke.

"Googi, come before it's too late!" Mama insisted. "Don't say I didn't tell you so."

All my friends had urged me to stay in the U.S. Wild rumors had spread in Tehran, claiming that I was *sâvâki*, a member of the Shah's feared secret police. They even said that I had once tortured Ayatollah Taleghani, a Shia cleric and one of the leaders of the revolution. Homayoun's mother also heard these rumors. She called him every day, too, begging him to go back without me—she was blissfully unaware of what her son had been doing to himself, and to me, throughout these months in the U.S.

"But they're saying I'm *tâghouti*," I protested. "Everyone's telling me not to come, that I'll be executed."

The revolutionaries were branding anyone they deemed un-Islamic, Westernized, or pro-monarchy as *tâghouti*, satanic. It was like having a target on your back.

"Rubbish!" Mama shot back.

But I didn't return just for Mama's sake, or for my house. I was playing with fire. I was slowly dying in NYC, far from my home, far from my child and everyone I loved, day after day, hour after hour, minute after minute. I decided that I would rather die in my homeland.

Mama was right. They didn't execute me. No. They only summoned me to Evin Prison four times for interrogations and confiscated my passport and the deed to my home. And here I was now, sitting in this basement.

Marjan took my hand, hers were no longer shaking, and said in her sweet soft tone, "Imagine if someone had told us two years ago that you and I would one day be imprisoned, in the same cell."

I never could have imagined, in the early half of 1978, that a revolution was silently brewing, one that would soon engulf the entire country and turn my life upside down. When I left for the U.S. in late September of 1978, right after the Shah's prime minister declared martial law amid the chaos, I naively kept thinking that everything was going to go back to normal. I was also grappling with my own personal turmoil. I had just learned that my manager had secretly cleared my bank account. He stole everything from me. So I was broke, despite being one of the highest-paid performers, even among my male peers. The entire entertainment industry had shut down due to the anti-Shah riots and strikes, and I was out of work. I was desperate to find a way to pay for another year of Kambiz's prestigious Swiss boarding school, Le Rosey. I had sent him there a couple of years earlier with the hope of giving him the best education money could afford—I also wanted to shield him from all the media attention surrounding the breakdown of my second marriage to Behrouz Vossoughi.

I had a little bit of savings left in a French bank account, so I flew to Paris with Homayoun, whom I had been romantically involved with for six months. I then went alone to visit Kambiz in the Swiss Alps. When I got back to Paris, my friend Pouran, the same eminent *pop sonati* singer I grew up listening to, called. She asked that I perform at the upcoming opening of their new Iranian cabaret in Los Angeles, Cabaret Colbeh. I remembered thinking how this gig was a blessing, because I'd make enough to cover the rest of the tuition while things settled back home and the police hunted for my manager.

I was so clueless, I thought before responding to Marjan.

"I would've asked that person what they were smoking—because it's way too strong," I said with a grin, giving my headscarf a little readjustment.

We both burst into laughter. It felt good. I then told Marjan how unsettling it had been seeing many of our peers in Evin Prison, just seven months earlier.

It all started on Wednesday, March 5, 1980, when I woke up in Tehran to the terrifying news that my name had been listed on an official notice from the Islamic Revolutionary Court, published on the front page of the newspaper *Ettelā'āt* (*Information*). There were ten of us summoned to Tehran's notorious Evin Prison. The notice mentioned that noncompliance would "lead to arrest." It had been a year since the Islamic Revolution and almost a year since I had returned home. The possibility of imprisonment and execution had loomed over me since my arrival, but I had tried not to think about it. My denial ended that Wednesday morning.

I didn't sleep the night before my court date. I paced back and forth throughout the house, all the way through dawn of Saturday, March 8, wondering what was going to happen behind those massive concrete walls. Before the revolution, Evin Prison was known for holding the Shah's political prisoners, including members of the Tudeh Party and the People's Mujahedin Organization (MEK), and for the reports of torture by SAVAK, the Shah's secret police force. Under the new government, it became home to members of the Shah's regime, including top officials, military officers, SAVAK members, and others connected to the monarchy, who were often subjected to torture, swift tribunals, and execution.

Several times I walked in and out of my closet. I had no idea what one wore to an Islamic Revolutionary Court, besides the headscarf. By 1980, women were required to wear the headscarf in government offices and public institutions. I was so terrified by the thought of my execution that I barely gave a second thought to the piece of cloth I now had to cover my hair with, let alone the policing of women's bodies. I finally picked some dark loose-fitting pants and a long-sleeve shirt to wear under my coat. I decided not to put any makeup on, but washed my face, desperate to get rid of any sign of fear. I couldn't let them see it.

Homayoun insisted that he drive me down to Evin, trying his best to comfort me with his presence. He always exuded confidence, which stood in sharp contrast to his short and slender build—he was only a few inches taller than me. But that morning his face was even paler than mine. We got to the prison gate before 8 a.m. I had never seen it in person before. The gray concrete walls that stretched upward, with the guard towers placed on the very top, were intimidating, while the minimal signage, other than the prison name, created a sense of foreboding and secrecy. I felt my heart was in my throat. I walked toward the main checkpoint, where a Revolutionary Guardsman carrying a rifle stopped me. He had recognized me.

"Cover your hair," he said with a deep frown. In my haste, a strand of my short hair had fallen out from under the headscarf.

He then directed me to go through the entrance, where another armed guard sent me down the long hallway and into a room on the right.

The courtroom looked more like a classroom with rows of small desks facing two larger ones. There were no juries, no defense lawyers, only a heavyset, middle-aged cleric sitting behind one of the large desks, wearing a brown-colored clerical robe and a white turban. His assistant sat beside him with a pen and paper, dressed in a suit, minus the tie. But the cleric alone would decide our fate. He was our judge.

Sitting behind the small desks were my peers, men and women once revered as the jewels of Iranian film and music industries, including the leading male stars Beyk Imanverdi and Naser Malek Motiee, the singer Nooshafarin, and the actress Pouri Banayi. Some people from the list were missing, including the singer Hayedeh and her sister, Mahasti, who had already fled abroad. I hadn't seen any of them since the beginning of the revolution, after the forced shutdown of national TV and radio programs. Almost overnight, we had found ourselves out of place in a changing world.

Pouri immediately got up from her seat and jumped into my arms crying.

"Look what happened to us!" she said to me.

We hadn't spoken in years, ever since the beginning of my relationship with Behrouz, but I held her tight, forgetting where we were. The mullah's face flushed red in an instant.

"Stop that filthy behavior!" he yelled at us. "This isn't a barnyard!"

I could feel both of us shaking as we pulled our bodies away from each other. I saw my own humiliation and anger in Pouri's eyes. I had a few encounters with revolutionary officials before, but they had never been so vicious.

Seated at our tables, we were each handed a set of written questions to answer in writing. The mullah's assistant would distribute and collect the sheets of questions. I couldn't see what the others were being asked. The questions I was given were not political. They asked who I had seen at particular royal events and private parties. I didn't give names; I wrote down the truth, that I was always focused on my performance and not on the who's who of the attendance list. I wasn't going to lie and give them what they wanted. They were fishing for information on high-ranking officials from the Shah's regime, other celebrities, and foreign dignitaries—names they could use to build their cases or justify their purges. The truth was irrelevant to them; they wanted something they could twist into a confession or a betrayal.

When Naser Malek Motiee, famed Iranian actor and director, asked for further clarification about one of his questions, the mullah shouted at him, saying that he didn't care whether he understood or not. But Naser fought back.

"You speak to us as though we're criminals!" he said, his neck visibly reddened. "I'm proud of my career as an actor and all the love the people showed me. Whenever and wherever we went on location, the people greeted us with so much love. Even in small remote villages they used to sacrifice sheep for me or bring me gifts. And I loved them back. What do you know about what I meant to them?"

I knew what he was talking about.

"Shut up!" the mullah fired back, banging his hand on the table. The clink from his golden ring hitting the wooden surface seemed to linger in the air. "No one cares about you anymore! Sit and answer the damn question!"

Naser stood still. He then asked to be excused from the room for a moment. The mullah reluctantly accepted. When Naser returned minutes later, his eyes were reddened.

The mullah was nasty like this with every single one of us, while his assistant was busy taking notes. My turn came at the end of the day when all of my peers had left after signing a release form. He asked me why I had sung the Turkish upbeat song "*Sakine Dåygezi.*" I told him that I thought people would enjoy listening to an uplifting song after a long day of work.

He looked at me and said with disgust, "How dare a piece of shit like you decide for others?"

"You're right, sir, I wasn't thinking," I said to him, remembering how I used to handle Mouness when she got in one of her moods.

"Why did you play in *Dar Emtedåd-e Shab* [The Night Never Ends]?" he asked.

Well, I would have never agreed to participate half-naked in an intimate scene in 1977 had I known there would be an Islamic Revolution the next year, I thought. But before I could answer, he continued with bulging eyes, "Why did you take your clothes off in that film, like a whore?"

He briefly paused to catch his breath.

As a practicing Shia Muslim, I had never met a cleric with such a foul mouth, so much animosity from someone supposedly pious. I hadn't thought clerics like him existed. Then again, as a woman, my interactions with mullahs were limited to traditional wedding ceremonies and funerals. As a child, when I went to the local tekyeh (Shiite holy shrine) with Dâyi and his wife, I only saw the clerics from afar—there was always some degree of gender segregation. "What do you have to say for yourself?" he shouted.

"It was a mistake, sir, a mistake," I said, looking down at my feet. "I didn't think."

"Clearly, you don't have two thoughts in that corrupted brain of yours!" he puffed as he straightened his thick beard.

I was released not long after, with instructions to return at a later date.

"I forgot to tell you the best part," I said to Marjan. "He asked me in all seriousness, 'What's your relationship to Shaban Jafari?'"

Marjan bursted out in laughter before covering her mouth. It was funny in its absurdity, as I had no ties to Shaban Jafari, famous for calisthenics training once used by Persian warriors and for his outlaw reputation. He might as well have asked me about my relationship to Sylvester Stallone's fictional character Rocky Balboa. The meaning of his question was clear, though; in his eyes we were both outlaws.

Marjan and I quietly laughed some more, releasing some of our tension, but our moment of levity was cut short when shrieks of pain echoed down the corridor. I had never heard such agony. Nothing came close, not even the cries of a mother weeping at her child's burial, nor the sound of her heart breaking as she says goodbye. These cries were different. They were bloodcurdling.

"What've they done to her?" Marjan asked as her body shivered.

I didn't want to think about it. I looked up toward the window. Rosy hues of dawn had chased away the darkness, casting a gleam of light onto the leaves of what looked like a cherry tree swaying in the distance. I remembered that last day in Evin Prison. It was sometime after Nowruz, our Iranian New Year. I was all alone with my interrogator, Ali Tehrani, in a room somewhere below the courtroom. The window, much larger than this one, was also ground level. Mr. Tehrani went over my file with a fine-tooth comb, looking for any unanswered questions. *Impossible*, I thought. I had been asked every imaginable question, sometimes twice. As he carefully shuffled the documents, I noticed the light coming in from the window behind me. The sun was still shining over Tehran on that spring afternoon. The smell of blossoming hyacinths and daffodils permeated the air, momentarily giving back the city a sense of normalcy. *Any time now, I'll be free to go and live a quiet life*, I thought.

He handed me a sheet of paper, the same one I had been prevented from signing at the end of the three previous interrogation sessions.

"Sign this and you can go," he said, placing the pen in front of me.

Four times I had walked through that gate, sat in that cold room, answered those questions, waited in vain for my turn to sign. It was finally happening.

Black ink ran across the page, from right to left. The words spun in my mind, letters detaching from one another, morphing into incoherent shapes. I couldn't make any sense of it. My heart pounded. Slowly, the letters and words stopped moving and a sentence emerged. It read something like this:

"I, Faegheh Atashin, also known as Googoosh, declare that from this day onward, will not sing or engage in any artistic endeavors, will not attend or participate in any social or political gatherings, and will be forever loyal to the principles of the great Islamic Revolution."

They want my voice, I thought. I hesitated for a moment, feeling my heart lodge in my throat. I then signed my name with big strokes at the bottom of the page.

I left Evin Prison shortly after, thinking that they were now going to leave me in peace.

Chapter 4

Mouness

I tried not to dwell on my fate in this basement, beneath the shadows of this new dawn. I was scared and helpless, yet somehow not surprised by the upheaval in my life. Darkness, after all, had always been there, lurking just beneath the surface, ever since my childhood, ever since the day my stepmother arrived.

I was seven years old and Fery must have been five and a half. I don't know how Papa and Mouness met. She wasn't a performer. All I know is that when Papa first told Fery and me that we had a new stepmother, I was ecstatic. I thought we were finally going to have what other kids had—a real family. I was hopeful, even though it hadn't worked out between Papa and Mama, or with Adel's mother. Shortly after the big announcement, Papa took Fery and me to his maternal uncle Dâyi's home, just south of Tehran's Grand Bazaar. This was the same uncle who, back in 1946, had taken in my grandmother Bahbah and her children when they first arrived in Tehran.

Papa didn't tell us how long we were going to stay or where he was going—the newlyweds wanted to be alone. My brother and I lived with Dâyi and his family for about a year. Papa would come by twice a week to take me to perform in the afternoon at the theater, and later in the evening, at Cabaret Shokoofeh No. By the time he brought us back to live with them, in their newly rented house, Mouness was a few months away from giving birth to my half brother, Fariborz.

Very quickly, she had Fery and me doing all the house chores, while her pleasant smiles morphed into menacing frowns and her gentle demeanor turned violent. There was no disobeying her. I had to make the beds, sweep the floors, clean the kitchen, the dishes, and the toilet, while Fery, who by then was six and a half, scrubbed the cold stone floors. I didn't mind scrubbing the toilet as much as I hated doing the laundry. We didn't own a modern washing machine so we handwashed the dirty clothes, towels, and heavy bed linens in the courtyard *howz*, the small shallow pool in most Persian homes. We washed the pots and pans in there, too. Fery and I were so little that we had to stand in the water to do the washing, since we didn't have the proper reach from the outside. The fabrics doubled in weight when they were submerged. Our arms and shoulders would tire easily from all the heavy lifting and twisting. It was even worse in the winter when the water became freezing-cold. I hated it, but I took on as much as I could to spare Fery from the pain.

Fery was catching so many colds and infections. He was later diagnosed with rheumatic heart disease at around thirteen or fourteen, after years of excruciating pain in the joints of his feet. I've often wondered whether he might have been spared from this disease had it not been for all the scrubbing of the wet cold stone floors or standing in the freezing *howz*. All those times I watched him helplessly as his body shivered, praying that Papa would just walk in and save us, while a heavy sense of dread weighed on me, as if I already knew these hardships were quietly sealing his fate.

Papa never saw anything. Mouness made sure he didn't, just like she made sure we kept our mouths shut. Papa was mostly out with his friends, avoiding Mouness's mood swings that worsened after Fariborz was born—she seemed even more eager to smack us or shove us to the ground. When she wasn't hitting or yelling at us, she directed her venom toward Papa. She insulted and yelled at him almost daily, calling him a "good-for-nothing dumb Azeri Turk." And sometimes she would hurl things around, plates, glasses, anything that she could lift. Papa was a calm person, but he could only put up with so much. One time, as they argued in the living room, Mouness kept screaming into Papa's face. As the insults poured out of her mouth and the objects flew at him, his face turned a flaming red—even his ears were as red as a tomato. Then, suddenly, he snapped. Papa grabbed a chair and swung it at her. Blood gushed out of her head.

There was another incident in the car, not long after, in Papa's white Volkswagen. It was nighttime. Papa was driving silently as Mouness uttered every known insult at him. The tension was palpable. Fery and I watched nervously from the back seat—I can't remember where Fariborz was. I must have been eight and a half, and Fery, seven. Papa stopped the car by the side of the road. He turned off the ignition. He grabbed her head and smashed it against the stick shift. When she slowly lifted her head back up, a bulge appeared under her left eye.

Once, when I was nine years old, Mouness screamed at me for the way I had made her bed—it was no different than all the other times. I could see the rage blazing in her eyes before she kicked me down a flight of stairs. My head slammed against the edge of the bottom step and cracked open. As usual, Mouness threatened me not to say anything to Papa, who came home not long after and rushed me to the hospital. The excruciating pain magically disappeared later that afternoon when I started singing onstage in the city of Qazvin for an audience of children from the local orphanage. Standing there with my newly stitched and wrapped head, I told the kids that I was so excited to perform for them that I had slipped and hurt myself. The room roared with laughter. When I finally dug up the courage to tell Papa some weeks later, careful that Mouness wasn't around, all he did was ask why I hadn't said anything sooner. Nothing changed. It didn't matter. I felt betrayed.

Papa was all I had after Mama left. He was my stage partner and my buddy. I trusted him with my life, even during the riskiest acrobatic maneuvers. He used to make me giggle with his jokes and all his silly made-up stories. He used to take me to the sea. All that stopped when he married Mouness.

Mouness was also just as impatient and cruel with Fariborz. I often threw myself on top of him to shield him from her wrath, just like I did with Fery. I couldn't understand how she could bring herself to hit a toddler like that. I knew her mother had been hospitalized at a psychiatric ward, but I couldn't connect the dots back then. Her mother had stayed about a week or two with us in between two hospitalizations, before Fariborz was born. She constantly yelled, her voice rising and falling in nervous, rapid bursts. I couldn't understand a word she was saying, since she spoke a dialect of Gilaki, a northern Iranian language, from her hometown of Rasht. She sounded frantic, and her eyes darted around the room, wild and unfocused. Mouness tried to calm her down, with no success. She was taken back to the psychiatric unit. Looking back, I wonder whether Mouness inherited some underlying anxiety or condition that could have explained her erratic behavior.

One day, after Fariborz turned one, Papa and Mouness told us they were expecting a second child. I never recalled them mentioning they wanted more kids. I was around ten years old when Farâmarz was born. I wasn't upset that my workload had increased. I loved taking care of him, just as much as I loved taking care of Fariborz. Holding an innocent newborn, showering him with love and kisses, was healing for me. I couldn't get enough of that baby smell around his neck and head, that soft powdery scent mingled with a hint of milk and a whisper of sweetness. For two months, I took care of all of his needs. I was with him every second when I wasn't at school or work. I came home from school one early afternoon, and as I was getting prepared to feed him and Fariborz, I noticed he was gone. I looked frantically all over the house. Papa stopped me. He explained that he and Mouness had decided that I couldn't do everything. He said I didn't have enough time to work, attend school, and take care of both an infant and a toddler—he left out all the house chores. So they decided to give Farâmarz away. I felt like I had been sucker punched.

How could they? I didn't understand. Adoptions were not rare in Iran, but it didn't make sense for a family with our means—my growing income—to give away a child like that. When I pressed Papa for more details, he explained calmly, "You see, this lovely couple couldn't have their own children, so we gave them one of ours." He was right about the couple being lovely, as I discovered later. But Papa and Mouness were not the selfless kind. I still don't know if they got anything in return. For years, I kept my mouth shut when we visited Farâmarz in his new home. I called him by his new name, Mehrdad, and pretended we were never related, that everything was normal. I still loved him, though. He eventually learned the truth many years later.

After a year or two, Mouness told Papa that she'd had enough of taking care of three children, even though she barely lifted a finger. She said that Fery had to go. He was only ten or eleven years old. Again, I couldn't understand why. Fery was an easy child, he often babysat Fariborz and regularly helped me with the chores. Maybe the real reason was because Mouness didn't want to "needlessly" spend another penny from my earnings. By this point, Papa had stopped performing onstage and focused on managing my career. His once-athletic body grew soft and round, weighed down by all the heavy eating and drinking. Mouness loved shopping more than anything. She was constantly buying herself the latest outfits, shoes, and accessories. To her, Fery was simply another mouth to feed. So, just like that, my dearest Fery was out. He was passed around like a football between Dâyi, Uncle Nader, and Mama, who was remarried and had two little children, my half siblings Roya and Joseph. I missed Fery so much. He was my best friend.

I wasn't only missing Fery. I also missed Mama. I only ever spoke about it to my school principal during my last year of school, at the all-girl Pishro school on Khâjeh Nasir-e Toussi Street. I was twelve or thirteen years old then, in the sixth grade, and Dr. Jalali was my school principal. He was also a trained psychologist. He routinely invited me to his office during recess to ask how I was doing. Everyone knew about the child star Googoosh, about my workload—I had one amazing teacher in the third grade at my previous school, Delshâd, Mrs. Ahmadi, who would kindly let me sleep at my little desk during the first class of the day and catch up during recess or lunch. But Dr. Jalali must have detected something deeper, my silent depression.

In the first few sessions, he mostly asked about me and my classmates. It seemed like the more famous I became, the meaner the other girls seemed to get. I fought back only once, when I was about nine years old. Without even thinking I wrestled a loudmouth to the ground after she insulted me and my work. Some of our classmates pulled us apart and took us to Mrs. Nazem, who whipped my hands with a wooden ruler in front of the entire school, while the other girl got to play victim. I stayed away from my classmates. I was often alone. I did make some friends, but the friendships never grew, as I constantly changed schools because of the constant traveling for work. Dr. Jalali would mostly listen, though he did suggest that jealousy was part of what was fueling their animosity toward me. It didn't help improve things between me and my classmates, but it did make me feel a little better.

In the following sessions, Dr. Jalali asked about my home life. By then, I knew speaking up wouldn't matter anyway. The only thing that I dared to bring up was that I missed my mother. I told him how I hadn't seen her in years and how much I wished I could see her again. It felt good to say it out loud. I don't remember what he said, but I remember always feeling a little more peaceful after leaving his office, so much so that I decided I wanted to become a psychologist. Then one day, after the school bell rang, as I rushed out in a hurry to get home to get my chores done before going off to work, I caught a glimpse of a silhouette standing across the street. I recognized that silhouette. I tried to catch a better look by zigzagging my way in between my huddled classmates and their mothers. Once I made it past them, I saw Mama standing there. I darted across the busy road straight into her arms.

It had been more than five years since I felt her arms around me, five years since I felt that silky smooth skin, five years since I heard her voice. I couldn't say anything; I just wept and emptied my sadness in her arms. It was like a scene from a Bollywood film. She cried, I cried, and the entire school staff cried on the other side of the street. Dr. Jalali must have warned his team ahead of time—I would be forever thankful to him for reuniting us and for having taken a special interest in me.

Mama was aware of my hectic work life, but she couldn't do anything about it. She had her own problems with her second marriage and raising two little children. We both understood this without having to say a word. She had come alone, secretly, without her husband's approval. All the pain and fear melted away that day as Mama held me close to her chest and stroked my hair with her delicate fingers. It was our secret meeting, ours to savor alone. For a couple of months, she showed up like this, standing beside the other mothers, several times a week. We would catch up, without ever discussing Mouness. Then one day, at the end of sixth grade, Mouness decided I didn't need to go to school anymore. She must have told Papa that I had already learned how to read and write, and that I needed to focus on work, being the sole breadwinner of the family. Just like that, she took my mother away from me again, as well as my short-lived dream of pursuing a career in psychology.

Mouness didn't know about my meetings with Mama. I think she felt threatened, thinking that more education would inevitably lead to my emancipation from her and Papa. They couldn't afford to lose their cash cow. But she was wrong. It made me even more determined to get the hell away from her.

My escape from all the pain was through the stage, music, movies, and books. One day, when I was thirteen or fourteen, I went to the Moulin Rouge Cinema on Shemirân Road, with Fariborz, who was five at the time. We went to watch John Lee Thompson's film adaptation of Nikolai Gogol's *Taras Bulba*, starring Yul Brynner and Tony Curtis. I had to see it, especially since Tony Curtis was my Hollywood crush—he was so dreamy! The film was great (as was Curtis), and I knew I had to buy a copy of the novel when I saw a young street vendor selling the Persian translation outside the movie theater. It was the first book I ever bought. And without thinking, I hid it in my pants before returning home—no one ever told me I wasn't allowed to read.

Every night, for weeks on end, I secretly devoured its pages. Once I finished performing at Cabaret Shokoofeh No, usually around 10 p.m., I'd rush home alone in a taxi while Papa and Mouness often stayed out. When I arrived, I'd check on Fariborz—when Fery was still with us, he'd be the one watching over him—who was usually fast asleep. Then I'd quietly settle onto my mattress on the floor of the small room near the storage space, light a candle, and carefully retrieve the novel hidden beneath my pillow. Mouness would never find it there. She never made our beds. For an hour or so I would completely lose myself in Gogol's fictional world filled with love, battle, loyalty, betrayal, and exile. I had to stop myself from reading too fast, so desperate to stay in that world, far from under this roof. I even began rereading it as soon as I reached the final word on the last page. Then, one night, I made a clumsy mistake. A terrible mistake.

I was in a deep sleep when someone kicked me. Hard.

"What's this?" Mouness spat, her foot slamming into my chest with brutal force. I was more shocked and confused than in pain, however great the pain was—she was a fairly tall woman with an average-size build, much stronger than a young teenage girl. She sneered down at me and hissed, her voice shaking with fury but barely above a whisper so Papa wouldn't wake in the other room, "You stupid child! What the hell are you doing with this? And with a candle, no less? You worthless piece of shit!"

I had fallen asleep after a long day of school, work, and house chores, and had forgotten to put everything away. She tore my prized possession out of my hand.

"May you die! May you die so that I can get some peace!" she hissed before storming off.

Papa never found out, just as I never found out what she did with my book. I don't know why she was that upset. She never said that I shouldn't read books. She never said anything about the films I watched, either. Maybe she thought the candle could have started a fire, killing Fariborz and me. Or maybe she just didn't like that I had something all to myself, something that I treasured. She had taken everything from me, everyone that I loved: my mama, Bahbah, Papa, Farâmarz, and Fery.

One day, when I was fifteen years old, Mouness came to pick me up from Uncle Nader's home, where I had gone to see Fery and my cousins for lunch. Before she turned on the car ignition, she asked in her usual paranoid way if Papa's relatives had said anything about her, anything negative, or if they had talked about Mama. When I answered no, she accused me of lying and raised her hand to smack me. I grabbed her wrist. I didn't let go. I could see the shock in her eyes. I was still much shorter than her with my five-foot build. But I felt stronger than before. I felt more confident through my work; I worked every day, with all kinds of gigs (cabarets, weddings, and new film roles), and with barely any time off since I was pulled out of school. Mouness never laid a finger on me after that—though her questioning never stopped.

By then, I understood that I was earning Papa and Mouness a lot of money, though I never saw a penny of it. It wasn't uncommon for families to rely on their children working, despite child labor laws, but it was rare for a child like me to be earning so much, thanks to the spotlight. I was Iran's first child star, and in a way, I had been conditioned to think it was normal to be my family's breadwinner. But I did stop doing all the chores—Mouness hired a housekeeper—believing that I had at least earned that right. I also stopped feeling the need to reassure her with her paranoid thoughts. She only grew angrier. Since she could no longer intimidate me, she turned her frustration on Papa, pressuring him constantly. He couldn't stand her endless nagging about me, so when I turned sixteen, he rented me a small one-bedroom apartment near the center of Tehran, on Bahar Street, in a vibrant upper-middle-class neighborhood, right above a flower shop. It was unusual in our culture for a teenage girl to live on her own, but then again, nothing about my life was normal. Papa would lock me in there, late at night after work, then pick me up the next morning for more work. Not seeing Mouness as often was a relief.

Mouness left Papa the moment I got married at seventeen—she had always warned him that she would leave the day I did. And though Papa had already let himself go by that point, undoubtedly in part because of all the turmoil, it only worsened without her nagging him about eating right or drinking less.

I could never understand why Papa put up with her for as long as he did. Maybe it was because he saw another side of her, a playful side that she kept far from me. I had caught glimpses of fun Mouness from time to time when she was out with Papa and friends at Cabaret Shokoofeh No. There were also those two summers, when Mouness seemed the happiest.

For two years in a row, Papa had arranged for me to perform all summer long at Jamshid Javanshir's Motel Ghoo beach resort, the first resort of its kind in Iran by the Caspian Sea. I must have been thirteen or fourteen that first summer. Mouness was busy the entire time with other guests she befriended. Her vibrant and infectious laughter rang out as they played cards, gossiping, exchanging jokes, and teasing each other over the game. She barely had time to look at us, let alone order us around. Those two summers I was allowed to be a child. And Fery was there! I was so happy they allowed him to join us, both years—it didn't cost them a dime to board and feed him.

At night, I sang at the resort's discotheque, Neptune, for the guests, accompanied by a live band of young male musicians, future renowned singers including Aref, Shahram Shabpareh, and Siavash Ghomayshi. Later in the evening, all of us youngsters, including my band mates, would partner up and dance to rock and roll hits by artists like Chuck Berry, Elvis Presley, and Little Richard. During the day, we would swim, bowl, and play ping-pong together. Even Jamshid Javanshir's children, Sâghi and Amir, joined us—they introduced me to the Beatles with their single "She Loves You" and became two of my true lifelong friends. Everyday Fery and I would jump into the emerald water, instantly forgetting everything we were going through.

I've often wondered what my life would have looked like had Mouness not been a part of it. Maybe I wouldn't have needed the stage so much. Maybe I wouldn't have rushed to get married so young. Maybe I wouldn't be sitting in this basement. Certainly, I wouldn't have been as prepared for such dark days.

Chapter 5

Meeting the Other Women

Day 2

Morning had finally come, filling the permanently dim-lit basement with even more cries, chatter, and banging sounds on the iron-barred doors. Marjan and I were up. We barely slept. It didn't help that the city's howling sirens went off early in the morning, signaling the possible arrival of Iraqi jets on a bombing raid. Luckily they never came. One of the guards had quickly switched off the only light in our narrow hallway, as if the Iraqi fighter pilots could somehow spot us down here, hidden away in this basement.

It was still hard to believe that just a year and a half after the Islamic Revolution had toppled the Shah and the monarchy, ushering in a theocracy that unleashed waves of political purges and cultural upheaval, we now found ourselves at war with Iraq. It was one week ago, on September 22, 1980, when out of nowhere the distant roar of engines filled the sky, followed by the terrifying whistles of falling bombs. The sound of explosions ripped through the air, sending shock waves that could be felt throughout the city. At first, it was hard to comprehend what was happening. The piercing wail of air-raid sirens added to the chaos. Panic spread quickly as the news confirmed the bombings of Mehrabad Airport and military installations around Tehran by Saddam Hussein's forces, reigniting old territorial disputes. We all knew Mehrabad well—it was our main international airport. Now it was under attack. Though the physical damage to the airport was rather contained, the psychological blow was immense.

People poured into the streets, afraid and confused. I took Kambiz straight over to Mama's that day, while Homayoun went to his parents. In a matter of seconds, everything had changed. We were at war, and whether or not you supported the new regime, everyone was united for Iran. This was why I hadn't taken the notice from the Committee of Vice and Virtue that seriously. I was wrong. Clearly I was still perceived as an enemy.

For a second after the siren began, I couldn't shake the terrifying thought that it might only be a matter of time before there was no Iran left. But talking to Marjan helped fight off these dark thoughts. It must have helped her, too. We talked all night.

"I've got to tell you the funniest story," I whispered to Marjan as the pale morning light now seeped through the small window. "A few months ago, I saw Delaram Keshmiri at a Komiteh station. You won't believe what she said to them!"

Marjan smiled and urged me to go on.

I told her how I had been summoned to the Komiteh station of the Haft Howz-e Nârmak neighborhood, months after my last interrogation session at Evin Prison. Young revolutionaries and overzealous students mostly made up the Komiteh (short for the Islamic Revolution Committee). These young men eagerly enforced the new Islamic laws by interrogating and intimidating civilians into submission, often with violence and terror. But despite their zeal, they were also clumsy, untrained enforcers, at times behaving as ridiculously as armed teenage hall monitors. I'd had many run-ins with them ever since I returned. Armed with their Kalashnikovs, they would knock on my door and raid my home with just about any excuse, as if to remind me that they were watching Googoosh. I was living in constant fear and anxiety, even though they never laid a finger on me. That was one of the main reasons why I decided to get married to Homayoun, at the end of 1979 or early 1980. I was too afraid to live alone, and with the

Islamic government enforcing laws based on sharia, we would have faced punishment for living together out of wedlock.

There were three of us at the station that day: me, Pouri Banayi, and Delaram Keshmiri. Pouri, the same Pouri who had hugged me at Evin Prison months earlier despite our complicated past, was a beautiful and cherished actress who first gained fame in the 1960s for her roles in Iranian cinema. Delaram was the most beloved TV host and actress, known for her role as the witty assistant to the fictional character "Billy the engineer" on the hit TV show *Shabakeh-ye Sefr*. None of the Komiteh members would tell us why we had been summoned. But deep down, we knew the real reason. They were targeting entertainers, actors, and singers because we were seen as symbols of the old era—Western culture and what they deemed to be moral corruption—that the regime wanted to eliminate. They wanted to control cultural expression, suppress dissent, and enforce strict Islamic values.

They interrogated us separately for hours, asking us about other artists we knew or had previously worked with—they were fishing for information on our peers. Finally, when they brought us into the same room, their chief told us that they had received damning information on all of us. He claimed, with the most self-righteous tone, that we had been illegally smuggling people out of Iran in return for 1 million toman (about 140,000 U.S. dollars then).

"Guess what Delaram said to him," I asked Marjan, struggling to keep a straight face.

"What?"

"She looked at him, dead in the eyes, and said, 'Sir, if I may? If I smuggled people out, I would've made sure Googoosh was the first one out!'"

We both laughed.

"You should have seen his face. Complete shock! I had to bite down on my lip to stop myself from cracking up."

It felt good to see Marjan's face light up again.

"The whole thing was a mess from the start," I continued. "They didn't want to begin the questionings until Leila Forouhar was present."

Leila, who was about nine years younger than me, became a child star nearly a decade after I did, and later, also transitioned into a famous actor and singer. I secretly knew that she was on her way to the Pakistani border—her aunt had boldly told me over the phone, despite the real risk of our conversation being intercepted. I thought we would be stuck there for days. All I could think about was how I was going to share this with Pouri and Delaram. Luckily, the Komiteh gave up waiting.

We were there all day until they rather casually decided that we were free to go. As we got up to leave, the chief asked us if we wanted to know who had ratted us out. To his greatest disappointment, none of us cared. We knew he was going to lie, his goal being to divide and demoralize us.

"How was Pouri?" Marjan asked, her eyes fixed on the concrete wall below the window.

"Maybe a little better than in Evin."

We were all getting a little more accustomed to living in this permanent state of fear.

Right then a guard appeared at our door. Marjan and I immediately sat upright and tucked our hair under our headscarves. My heart raced.

It was the same one from yesterday, the one who had whispered into the interrogator's ear, the one with that name—Abolfazl. He was younger than what I had first thought, perhaps just a bit younger than my thirty years. He unlocked our door and let in an even younger guard. I immediately recognized him. He was the one who couldn't keep his hands off his revolver. His hands now, however, were busy carrying a tray. It was just food.

The younger guard looked barely eighteen years old with his week-old patchy stubble. I wondered how he had ended up here as he placed the tray on the filthy carpet, whose original colors were indistinguishable. I wondered whether he was the sole provider of his family, forced to take any job to put food on their plates. I wondered whether he had finished school. He reminded me of Komiteh members I had seen, disadvantaged young men who found an opportunity to gain more power. He looked at me right then, as though he heard my thoughts. His baby face suddenly took on a reptilic air as he contorted his mouth into a sinister smile. My flesh crawled. I quickly looked away.

"Hurry up," Abolfazl ordered. "Go to the other rooms, and then the men's side."

The young man obeyed, not before glaring at us one last time before disappearing in the hallway. Then Abolfazl, who had been standing by the door, took one step into the room. His eyes remained focused on the tray with its two glasses of tea and the small plate of dried dates for us to share.

"Normally Zahrâ will be the one delivering and collecting your food," he said in a softer tone.

He then paused briefly.

"Each room gets ten minutes to use the bathroom, shower and everything," he continued. "Women go first, then the men. I would eat quickly if I were you."

He looked at us with his brown timid eyes and added, "The bathroom is just here," pointing to side of the door.

He swiftly left, leaving the door wide open.

Marjan and I first sat quietly, looking at the metal tray, not moving an inch. Moments later we made our way to the bathroom.

He was right, it was just next to our cell, in the entrance of the corridor. The one toilet and two showers were separated by a curtain. Unfortunately, the squat toilet wouldn't flush properly. Despite the repulsive stench and the battalion of flies feasting on human waste, we considered ourselves lucky to be there before everyone else.

Neither of us could stomach anything when we got back to the cell, even though it had been more than a dozen hours since either of us had eaten. We just had a few sips of the lukewarm tea to hydrate our dry mouths as we waited for them to lock our door. Then a woman dressed in a black chador marched in and collected the tray without even glancing at us, before locking us in once more. She was Zahrâ.

One by one the other rooms were given their allotted time for the bathroom. When it came to the men's turn, Abolfazl quickly pulled on a curtain I hadn't seen before and covered our steel-barred door from outside. We sat quietly, listening to the tired footsteps of the shadows walking past our door. We couldn't see them. I tried to count them, but my mind wandered, imagining who they were, how long they had been here or what they had been through. I wondered which ones had shrieked from pain throughout the night. Marjan must have been doing the same.

The routine was repeated several hours later for lunch. This time, Zahrâ brought in two trays instead of one, all while ignoring us as before. I managed to get a better look at her face. She couldn't be much older than me, I thought, though she was much taller. She had pale skin, dark bushy eyebrows, and a trace of a mustache. She wasn't unattractive, though her cold brown eyes contributed to an overall mean look.

"*Adas polo*," Marjan said with a small grin as soon as Zahrâ left the cell.

The trays contained a plate of white rice topped with about a dozen lentils and a greasy glass of water. We only ate a spoonful of the lukewarm rice. It wasn't *adas polo* without the caramelized onions, raisins, and spices, but it didn't matter. We still had no appetite. We just wiped the rims of the cups with our sleeves and gulped down the water.

Hours tediously went by following lunch. Marjan and I would sometimes stand up to stretch our legs and arms and then get back to sitting in our same spots. Neither of us felt comfortable lying down, fearing it would make us even more vulnerable. Each time the footsteps came back to the corridor, my heart raced, mostly from fear, but part of me was also secretly wishing that they were coming to release us from this cold, humid room. They didn't. It seemed like the guards were too busy with the other rooms, opening and closing the screeching steel-barred doors.

I wondered how the room looked and felt when it was still just the maids' quarters—properly ventilated, with a single bed and a side table in place. It was hard to imagine this cramped, musty room once being a simple yet functional living space. The carpet was likely never so filthy. Just as I was nudging some dust balls away from me with my foot, I felt a sudden tingling sensation in my left leg. Worried that it would turn into that sharp pain, I got up and stretched.

As I balanced myself upright, careful not to step on Marjan, I let out a chuckle. Marjan looked at me as though I had gone mad.

"What is it?" she asked.

I couldn't stop laughing. And her inquisitive smile and confusion only made it worse.

"What?"

I remembered that one particularly absurd rumor involving me, Hayedeh—one of the greatest female Iranian singers—and Ayatollah Taleghani. Rumors had always followed me like shadows I couldn't escape. They started early, with claims that Papa had beaten me as a child and forced me to sing onstage. But this one? It was so ludicrous it could have been the plot of a bad satire. They said that, back in the day, Hayedeh and I had somehow managed to torture Ayatollah Taleghani in the SAVAK headquarters by singing and dancing on his chest. Even in its absurdity, it was hard not to laugh.

When I finally managed to tell Marjan, she let out a boisterous laugh. Tears rolled down both of our cheeks as we hopelessly tried to control ourselves and failed miserably several times. We needed the laughter. Then Abolfazl marched to our door.

I hastily sat back down next to Marjan and wiped my tears as he turned the key in the lock. He took one step into the room and then stopped.

"It's four o'clock. You have an hour to use the bathroom and stretch your legs in and around the hallway," he said matter-of-factly.

He only glanced in our direction, almost timidly. I was confused. I had seen people act shy around me before the revolution, but there was no way that Abolfazl was a fan—none of these zealous guards were.

"But careful," he continued, this time in a cautious tone. "Some of the girls know that you're both here. I won't be too far."

Who had told them? Marjan and I had been very careful, whispering all this time. I glanced at her. She looked as dumbfounded as I did. He left again, leaving the door wide open. Then, one by one, the doors of the other cells were unlocked.

Soon enough footsteps rushed to wait in line to use the bathroom. I didn't move. Marjan and I sat silently.

A woman, waiting by the entrance of our cell, peered in. The shadows had faces.

"I can't believe it! It's true!" she said as she put her hands on her head, covered by a colorful headscarf. "The guards weren't lying!"

She was in her early twenties, yet her face bore the unmistakable signs of exhaustion, with dark circles shadowing her eyes. She took one step toward us, her eyes sparkling as she glanced back and forth between Marjan and me. Before we could say anything, she turned around and called for the others.

"It's them!" she whispered loudly.

Marjan and I glanced worriedly at each other. Dozens of footsteps rushed to our cell. Six or seven women walked in, mostly young, also in their twenties. A few tried to follow, but there wasn't enough space for everyone.

"Is it really Googoosh?" one of them asked, stuck behind in the narrow corridor.

"Yes!" replied the first woman.

"Let me see!" one of them demanded, pushing her way to the front of the group.

She wore a black-and-white polka-dot headscarf that was barely hanging over her ample wavy dark hair. She had long eyelashes with heavy mascara that appeared days old and thick black, slightly smudged, eyeliner that accentuated the fierce look in her dark brown eyes. She took a drag from the cigarette tucked between her lips and then crouched down in front of us, studying our faces. Her own face was wrinkled beyond her years, with traces of old scars, straight cuts—the work of a sharp blade.

"It's them," she finally said in a deep smoky voice.

"I wanna see!" another woman cried from the corridor.

"I love you both!" one woman said.

It was surreal to see all these women in good spirits, gathered in this dimly lit basement, especially after the heart-wrenching cries we heard since our detention yesterday. I then remembered Abolfazl mentioning that he wouldn't be too far. My heart raced, fearing that he might have overheard the commotion and was already marching toward us. Or worse, that he might send in the young guard, this time with his hands free to use the gun.

"I love your song '*Gol-e bi Goldoon*' [Flower Without a Vase]," one of them said to me.

"I love your song '*Kavir-e Del*' [Desert of the Heart]," one of the voices said to Marjan.

"Googoosh, I collected all your pictures since I was a little girl, four albums full!" someone said in the corridor.

"What are you doing here?" the woman with the colorful headscarf asked us as she crouched beside the woman with the polka-dot headscarf and heavy eye makeup.

"Googoosh, I've copied all of your hairstyles!" another voice said from the corridor.

I had always enjoyed experimenting with all sorts of cuts and colors on my naturally straight dark hair, though lately I had stuck to the easily manageable short cut and hazel color.

"My boyfriend loved the Googooshi!" the voice from the corridor continued. "What does it look like now?"

The magazines ignored that my short boyish haircut, which they dubbed the "Googooshi," was a direct result of my feelings of hopelessness toward the end of my first marriage in 1972. I just got up one morning and shaved my head, shedding all my long locks. It was my way of punching a wall.

"I loved you in the film *Hamsafar* [Fellow Traveler, or Companion]!"

"Give 'em some room!" the deep, smoky-voiced woman ordered in a typical curt southern Tehran accent as she sat down across from Marjan and me.

No one listened. She then raised one of her thin eyebrows and smiled mischievously, visibly sharing their excitement, as she offered us a cigarette, which I couldn't refuse. Marjan didn't smoke, but my body was shaking for nicotine. I took a long puff, filling my lungs as much as I could.

"Zari, can I have one, too?" one of the women asked.

Zari counted her cigarettes and then tossed the woman the pack.

"What's your sentence?" someone asked.

The room went silent, but Marjan and I didn't know what to say to the seven women staring at us.

"Haven't you seen Afshoun?" they asked.

"They mean the interrogator," Zari clarified.

It was an ironic nickname. The word *afshoun* ("the scattering" or "sprinkling of") is often used in poetic or literary contexts to describe something beautiful or elegant being scattered or spread, like petals or light. The interrogator upstairs in the stained, oversize suit was anything but beautiful and elegant.

Marjan and I nodded.

Everyone had something to say about Afshoun.

"He's a despicable man!"

"The worst!"

"So dirty, too! He reeks! He thinks rose water can hide that sweaty—"

"They all do!"

"Just breathe through your mouth, like I do when I'm up there."

As the ladies chimed in one by one, Zari muttered his name under her breath.

"Watch out for him," one of the girls said. "He's a snake!"

The girls nodded.

"What about the sharia judge, Hajj Agha Ansari?" someone asked. "You seen him yet?"

"He sentenced me to sixty lashes!" one of the women blurted out.

Chills ran down my spine.

"Me too!"

"He gave me sixty-four!"

Some of the girls explained how they had been rounded up and arrested some weeks ago, including Zari. Once prostitutes in Tehran's famous red-light district, Shahr-e No, they had lost everything when the brothels were burnt to the ground shortly after the revolution. And now, they were here, paying for their old sins.

"I got thirty-four lashes," another woman sullenly said. She then turned around and pulled up her coat and sweater, revealing cuts and purple stripes all over her back.

I could almost feel her back throbbing. I wondered whether she had been the one crying from pain all night long.

Her name was Fahimeh, an office secretary. She had received her punishment some days ago. She explained that she had never experienced anything like it, the stinging sensations that lingered for days. But the humiliation, she said, was even worse. She had been arrested for walking in public with a man who wasn't her husband.

"You should've worn more layers," one of the girls blurted. "Isn't that right, Zari? We told you to put on some jeans."

Fahimeh paid no attention.

"You can't walk down the street with a friend anymore?" Fahimeh tried to whisper, but her trembling voice grew increasingly louder. "They called me a whore in front of everyone! How did we get here?"

Zari smirked to herself as she exhaled smoke, blowing it as far as possible.

"I know he tipped them off!" Fahimeh continued, her eyes reddened. "My husband! He always hated that I had close male friends, guys I'd grown up with. But I'm not gonna take it! I'm leaving him!"

"Keep your voice down," someone whispered.

The room went silent again.

I remembered how things weren't this bad just a year ago, in the months following the revolution. At first, if you weren't on the growing arrest list, or if you weren't tied to the previous regime in any way, you could still enjoy some normalcy, as long as you were able to avoid the overzealous Komiteh agents. I remembered that pool party I attended in the summer of 1979, a couple of months after I had returned from the U.S.

Amir, my dearest childhood friend from those summers at Motel Ghoo, invited me to a friend's small pool party in a northern Tehran villa. I agreed, needing the distraction from the uncertainty about my future in this country. Lying by the pool, I soaked in every sunray while the children splashed away with their games and the adults played cards and discussed the latest news. Emotions went up and down, even more so with the help of alcohol, while the children passionately argued over who was the fastest swimmer. Later that night, we were all inside, listening to music, some with a glass of vodka with lime in hand—I didn't like alcohol—pretending everything was normal, just like the children pretended that they were cops and robbers in the room next door.

When the children were finally sent to bed, one of the guests offered Homayoun LSD, which he gleefully took. He could never pass on drugs; I had seen him try almost everything, everything but heroin. I had done LSD before, curious about that altered state, but I didn't want to anymore. I didn't want to take anything, not after what I had gone through in New York with those little yellowish rocks. Thirty minutes later, pupils dilated, Homayoun and his new friend raved about the vivid colors on the carpet, the patterns twirling like they would in a kaleidoscope. The other guests were slightly amused, but they quickly returned to their conversations while I worried, hoping that he wouldn't have another bad trip. Amir noticed me from across the room and came to cheer me up with his wittiness—he was quick to whip out a sarcastic quip, often faster than me.

Like many other men who feared the revolutionaries targeting them for their family business or ties with the monarchy, Amir had joined the Komiteh in Motel Ghoo. It was the only way he could ensure the protection of his family's resort—or so he had thought. Amir told me how he had recently gotten drunk one night in Motel Ghoo when his fellow Komiteh brothers (which they called each other) came knocking on his door, warning him about a young drunk couple they had arrested; they had been found fooling around on the beach.

"I told them, '*Hold on* a minute—sssssecond," Amir said as he pretended to slur his words while waving his finger in every direction. "Let me handle those *infidels*!"

The men obeyed, surprised by their superior's determination to deal with the drunk couple.

"You had drinks with the couple, didn't you?" I asked.

He laughed.

"Of course. They were very good looking."

Just as he had me folded in two with laughter, blasting sounds of gunshots pierced through the walls.

Everyone froze. Everyone but Homayoun. He decided he would have a look outside. Amir and several other men held him back as another round of gunshots cracked nearby. We moved to the back rooms, far from the windows. When the shots stopped ringing, some of the men looked out the window.

"The Komitehs are coming!" one of them shouted.

Amir and the host grabbed my arm and pulled me to the floor, urging me to crawl to the bedroom, where I would hide among all of the slumbering children—after all, no one would be able to tell in the dark with my five-foot height and thin frame. I quietly tiptoed into their room, and without waking anyone up, found a small corner of the bed to lie on. Meanwhile, the Komiteh members stormed into the house. Their voices were muffled and distant, barely audible above the silence—so much so that even the children, both guests and hosts, remained fast asleep. I learned later that they were looking for two men, without saying more. Amir quickly identified himself and assured them he hadn't seen anyone enter the house. They didn't care. They examined the guests one by one and then searched every nook and cranny. My heart thumped like a beating drum as the armed men peeked into the bedroom, only a few inches away from me. But they didn't see me. They didn't even notice Homayoun's bizarre rants. They were more concerned about the alcohol and the record player after they couldn't find the two people. The armed men took down everyone's name, including mine, Faegheh Atashin. Then they left as swiftly as they had forced their way in. Everyone knew Googoosh, but no one knew Faegheh. Not even here, in this basement.

We would have all been arrested had the party taken place this past summer, just a year later. Everything changed as new laws began cropping up overnight—whether it was the banning of alcohol, pop music, or public strolls for unmarried couples, along with the execution of drug addicts and homosexuals. Within less than six months, sharia was woven into the country's judicial and legal framework, impacting every aspect of public and private life. The freedoms we once took for granted had vanished. And here we were now, locked up in a basement, in an unofficial makeshift prison run by the new Committee of Vice and Virtue.

"They've sentenced me to thirty-four lashes!" a young, slight woman murmured before sobbing uncontrollably.

Those standing closest to her tried to comfort her, but their eyes showed their horror. It was impossible to hide it.

Her name was Niloufar, she finally managed to tell us. She was nineteen years old, studying to be an accountant. She had been arrested at a small party.

"The Komiteh broke into my classmate's house and swarmed around us, hitting us like a bunch of animals!" she said, her voice shaking as much as her hands. "Then they separated us from the boys and threw us into a bus and took us to the station." Niloufar began weeping again. "I didn't even do anything! I wasn't dancing or drinking—"

"They don't care," Zari abruptly interrupted. "They don't. You think that they don't drink? They don't party?" She paused, looking for her pack of cigarettes, which had made its way back to her. She lit another with the dying one while Niloufar stared at her with a clouded gaze.

"I know these types," Zari continued with smoke pouring out of her nostrils. "They'd come to me, to the other girls, stinkin' of alcohol and sweat, with no money, threatenin' to beat us up if we didn't sleep with them."

While some of the women nodded, others turned their focus to the yelling in the corridor.

"That son of a bitch Afshoun," she said, flicking the ash to the side of the carpet. She chuckled, unfazed by all of the heads now turning toward the cell door. "He thinks he can fool us? Sittin' up there behind that desk in that shitty brown suit?" She briefly paused before continuing, oblivious to the growing raucous in the corridor. "For years I'd seen him around the block, always at the same spot with his—"

She stopped midsentence, realizing her audience was fully absorbed by the yelling outside the door.

"Nahid's at it again!" one of the women said with a big grin.

"Don't worry," Mojgan, the woman with the bright-colored headscarf, tried to reassure Marjan and me.

She explained that this was a daily occurrence, ever since two guards had fallen in love with Nahid, a beautiful fifteen-year-old girl, who wouldn't have any of it. I wondered what a fifteen-year-old was doing here.

"She insults them and Khomeini to their faces, and they don't dare say a word," Mojgan explained.

It was surprising, given that you could get killed for speaking ill of Ayatollah Khomeini, the leader of the Islamic Revolution and crowned, so to speak, as the country's Supreme Leader.

"She has them wrapped around her finger," another one added as the chanting continued. "Even Zahrâ, Her Holiness, keeps her smug head down around Nahid."

"The little one has fallen hopelessly for her," another woman whispered. "He's down here day and night, any excuse to see her."

I wondered whether it was the same young guard who couldn't keep his hand off his gun.

Nahid continued her chanting, although her words were now muffled by our guests, who bombarded Marjan and me once more with questions. Niloufar, meanwhile, stood absentmindedly with fresh tears in her eyes.

One of the young women then pointed to the small window and said, "Can I take a couple of those? We're out of 'em."

Marjan and I looked up as she carefully reached high above Zari's head and grabbed a filthy slab of cotton fibers resting on top of the windowsill. They were using them as menstrual pads.

"*Dâdâsh* [Brother] Abolfazl said Zahrâ will bring us some, but that was two days ago," she said.

I couldn't believe they were using those slabs, just as I couldn't believe they liked Abolfazl—calling him *dâdâsh* was a sign of closeness.

"Zahrâ must've taken 'em home for herself, that bitch," she added as she put the dirty cotton in her coat pocket.

"I told you, that's going to make you sick," Fahimeh insisted.

"What else do you want me to use?" she argued as she pulled out the slab of cotton fiber from her pocket and began picking off specks of dirt.

The women started asking us about old rumors involving singers and actors we knew or had worked with. They wanted to know the juicy details, anything fit for the gossip columns. Had that actor left his pregnant wife for that actress? Had that actress cheated on her husband? Who was the real father of that singer's child? Wasn't that actor homosexual? They assumed we knew everything, that everyone in the business openly shared their darkest secrets with one another. Some of the things they mentioned I had never even heard of. After all, I was always so busy with work and my own personal problems, problems that were dissected in magazine columns for the whole nation to see, that I had no energy left to inquire about others. Of course, I knew a few secrets, but they were not mine to share. Unfortunately for this group, I was taught early on how to keep my mouth shut tight.

The glimmer in their eyes faded a bit more each time we couldn't answer. They weren't just looking for gossip, I realized, seeing the heavy dark circles around their eyes and their growing nervous ticks. They were looking for stories, distractions from these four walls. And we were failing them, like two novice performers onstage paralyzed by stage fright. These women were looking for Marjan and Googoosh, not Shahla Safi Zamir and Faegheh Atashin.

Marjan and I took turns sharing stories, each one bringing a little more light into the dim-lit room. We laughed together, recounting funny moments and inside jokes about our peers, savoring these brief escapes from the grim reality around us. I told of my short-lived feud with the famous singer Elaheh from my late teens in the 1960s. Elaheh, much older and much more established, seemed to dislike me for reasons I never understood. Whenever I performed after her, she would extend her set, cutting into my time onstage. Finally, one night at a wedding where we were both performing, fed up with her antics, I told the guests that I didn't understand why she didn't like me—then took a jab at our age difference by saying she could be my mother. She called the cops—they didn't do anything, of course. The feud didn't last long after that, and we eventually enjoyed working and traveling together. It was a reminder of a time when my biggest worry was getting the stage time I felt I deserved.

The women listened intently, smiles reappearing on their faces. Even the pain in Niloufar's eyes seemed fainter.

I told them about that summer at Motel Ghoo, when I first met Pouri Banayi. It must have been in 1965, when I was just fifteen and she was in her twenties. She had come to the beach resort for a few days of rest with her family, and I was completely starstruck. Pouri was everything I imagined a movie star to be—beautiful, elegant, and humble. One afternoon, as we kids were splashing around in the pool, she came over to say hello. She stood by the edge of the water, looking every bit the star in her lovely dress, her hair perfectly styled. The temptation was too great to resist—I had already managed to push a few people into the water that day. So, without thinking, I crept up behind her and gave her a playful shove.

Papa was horrified, worried about what this glamorous film star would do to a scrawny teenager like me. Pouri surfaced with her makeup and hair entirely ruined. She surprised everyone with a heartfelt laugh, promising to get me back. That playful response, her easy laughter—it was one of the things I admired most about her, besides her humility. She was a true movie star. That moment marked the beginning of our friendship. I stopped my story there. I didn't go into how our friendship was wrecked less than a decade later, when I fell for Behrouz Vossoughi. Everyone knew.

When my marriage to Mahmoud Ghorbani hit rock bottom in 1972, Behrouz appeared as my knight in shining armor. He and Pouri had already called off their engagement—they were nicknamed "the eternal fiancés" by gossip magazines after being engaged for so many years—and had gone their separate ways nearly two years earlier. But it didn't matter. Everyone believed that I had broken them up, and I knew Pouri still felt betrayed by me, even though she never said a word; I had broken an unspoken rule of sisterhood by falling for her ex. But that was the problem; I had fallen madly in love with Behrouz, and I couldn't do anything about it.

"I've got your poster with Behrouz Vossoughi in my bedroom!" said one of the women from Shahr-e No with a thick *pâ'in-e shahr* accent, a tough working-class accent, commonly heard among residents of the poorer neighborhoods of southern Tehran.

I smiled, not knowing exactly what to say.

"I've also got a poster of Sattar and one of Dariush," she quickly added.

"I love Dariush!" another woman interjected. "I've got all his records. I cry every time I hear his soulful voice."

Niloufar nodded.

"Fardin's my favorite actor," another one said, standing somewhere in the middle of the crowd.

"But Behrouz is such a hunk! And that body!" the woman with the posters continued. "I watched every film you starred in together. I loved *Mamal Amricayi* [*Mamal the American*]. Shame you two split."

Everyone hushed, as though they were waiting for a reaction, a confession, perhaps a declaration of love. I smiled again.

"I loved that last scene in *Mamal Amricayi*! So romantic!" someone interjected. "Can you sing us that song? What was it called?"

"'*Komakam Kon*' [Help Me]," one woman answered. "That song got me through the worst days of my life, after my boyfriend tossed me aside like an old pair of worn socks."

Heads once more turned toward the corridor. It wasn't Nahid this time. It was one of the guards, coming to lock the doors. As the girls got up to leave, they whispered to us, "Will you please sing it for us tomorrow?"

Chapter 6

Mahmoud

I couldn't tell how much time had passed since our visitors were sent back to their cell. Time seemed to stand still, while gravity seemed to press the basement deeper into the earth. To keep myself occupied, I cleaned up the slabs of cotton fibers that I had pulled down from the windowsill. They were unusable—grayish and brown, the filth appearing to seep into every filament—yet I needed something to do, even if it got my hands dirty, anything to distract me from this place.

I told Marjan about the first time I got my period. I was thirteen years old. It was supposed to be another ordinary weekday where I would wake up in the morning, dress, and feed Fariborz before rushing off to school, where I would struggle to keep my eyes open in the early classes, and then head over to the Pars Theater on Lâlehzâr Street in the afternoon, where I sang, danced, and performed acrobatic routines, and did my homework during breaks while sitting in a small wooden armoire, using a candle for light, before having to get back home, feed my brother, and perform all of the house chores, and then finish my homework just in time to get back on the cabaret stage at 9 or 10 p.m., before finally passing out on my little mattress. But on that afternoon, my routine seemed meaningless, because in the theater bathroom I discovered that I was dying.

I was terrified when I saw the bloodstains. No one had ever told me about puberty; they didn't teach it at any of the schools I had attended. Mama wasn't around to tell me about these things, and Mouness had no interest in any interaction beyond giving me orders or pouncing on me. What was I going to do? Who was I going to tell? Could people tell by just looking at me? I tried my best to keep calm, hopelessly trying to focus on something other than my impending death. I was relieved when Farrokh-lagha Houshmand came backstage. Mrs. Houshmand was an actress in her early thirties, with high cheekbones and a defined jawline that gave her an elegant look. She had always been kind and warm to me. I rushed over to her as she was taking off her stylish coat, and in a moment of panic, I blurted out to her that I was dying.

"Why? Why do you say that?" she asked in a worried voice with her coat half removed, her eyes examining me from head to toe. "What happened?"

"I'm bleeding!"

She scanned my whole body again, wondering how she could have missed the gushing blood.

"No, you can't see it," I tried to explain to her.

I told her about the state of my underwear. She paused and then quietly finished removing her coat. She then raised her hand and slapped me across the face. Twice.

As I nearly burst into tears, Mrs. Houshmand quickly took me in her arms, and said, with a smile, "I'm so sorry *jigaram* [my dearest]. I had to do it. It's part of our custom. When a girl gets her first period, it means she's becoming a woman, so we do this so that she may always have healthy and pretty red cheeks."

She explained that I would have my period every month, for about a week, and that my body was preparing for the possibility of becoming a mother one day in the distant future. She also taught me about wearing pads during this time of the month. I was just relieved to hear that I wasn't dying. I also felt some pride in knowing that I was now a woman, with permanently red cheeks after those slaps. I went home that day and never said a word about it to anyone. Though I will always appreciate what Mrs. Houshmand did for me, I would have much preferred for Mama to have been the one to give me that talk.

"It must have been hard not having your mother around," Marjan said sympathetically.

"Had she been around, maybe I would've become a psychologist, who knows," I said.

"We wouldn't have had Googoosh then," Marjan quickly replied.

"Maybe. But more than anything, I'm pretty sure I would've had the sense not to marry Mahmoud!" I said half jokingly.

When I was seventeen, in 1967, Papa must have felt bad that my life was all work. He started taking me to the Western-style *thé dansant*, afternoon dancing tea parties, at various upscale venues. It was like the fancy British afternoon tea, but with dance music and all kinds of refreshments, from tea to champagne. It was an upper-society affair. In retrospect, I think Papa was looking for a potential suitor for me. Problem was that none of the young men would ask to dance with me. None, except for Mahmoud. At the time, I thought these eligible bachelors from good families were not interested in me because I was an entertainer, from a lower social class. They all knew who I was, after all. Now I wonder whether they were intimidated by my fame. Or perhaps they were deterred by my two large bodyguards, Papa and Uncle Nader, who watched the boys closely like a hawk.

It's funny how Papa only started to worry about my safety when I reached my teenage years. He stopped sending me home alone in taxis late at night, as he did so often throughout my childhood. I remember once, when I was five, I woke up in some bed, in some lodge, in some city or village where Papa and I were touring with a troupe. I was scared, not knowing where I was or where Papa had gone off to—he often left me, sometimes days on end, with mere acquaintances as he took off on a romantic pursuit. I was crying and yelling frantically for Papa when a stranger appeared at the door, a tall man. He entered the room with the strangest look in his eyes that sent a cold chill running down my spine. I wanted to scream. He stood there for the longest time, staring at me until something abruptly shot out from the front of his pants. Like spit. Then he left. I didn't understand what happened, but my heart raced, and my body shivered. I cried until one of the troupe members found me in a state of terror. I never spoke of this to Papa. I didn't know what to say. I suppose it never crossed Papa's mind that an adult would want to hurt a child in any way.

One afternoon, my two protectors, Papa and my Uncle Nader, took me to the *thé dansant* at Hotel Miami. I was busy dancing the jitterbug with Uncle Nader (he was a great dancer) when I noticed Mahmoud Ghorbani looking straight at me. I knew who he was. His brother owned this glitzy hotel, along with its in-house Cabaret Miami and trendy discotheque, the 007—they frequently had famous international singers perform, like the Italian pop star Peppino di Capri. I had noticed Mahmoud before. He was in his mid-twenties, tall, good looking, with fair skin and brown eyes with long lashes, and impeccably dressed in a tailored suit. He reminded me of the handsome Italian actor Vittorio Gassman. As my uncle and I spun across the dance floor to some electrifying rock and roll music, our eyes locked. He walked over to us at the end of the song.

"Your father said I could dance with you," he said suavely as my uncle stepped aside.

I was surprised, but I just smiled and nodded. At first, I tried hard to avoid looking into his eyes, though I felt his gaze on me, like a warm spotlight. I could feel my cheeks heating up. Mahmoud started asking me about my favorite songs to dance to, his voice gentle and his eyes filled with tender curiosity, as if he wanted to uncover every detail that made me who I am, making my heart flutter with each question. He had a way of making me feel like I was the only person in that large room. He wasn't a bad dancer, and his self-confidence gave him some allure that most young men my age lacked.

After that first dance, Mahmoud showed up a few times at the Cabaret Moulin Rouge, where I was performing nightly. He would sit at a table alone, drinking a soda. Papa was not very keen on him. In fact, he was against our courtship and articulated this to him. A few employees instructed by Papa attempted to prevent Mahmoud from entering the cabaret, telling him he wasn't welcome. But he never gave up. Night after night he was there.

He persevered, and on one occasion he managed to convince my father to accept his invitation for the both of us to attend a trendy restaurant discotheque called Couchinie. I don't know why Papa accepted. Maybe he had thought it was a business meeting. At Couchinie, Mahmoud once more asked my father's permission to dance with me. Papa reluctantly agreed. In the middle of our dance, he looked at me and asked if I would be his wife. I couldn't believe it. It all happened so quickly, just weeks, maybe a month after our first dance.

Papa sat me down the next day and talked to me like he had never done before. He said that he never wanted me to see bad things in life, or to get hurt in any way. My blood boiled, thinking of everything I had been through right under his nose. He warned me that the man I wanted to marry had tremendous debt, and that everyone in our small entertainment industry knew that. Papa didn't elaborate. I didn't want to believe Papa. Mahmoud appeared well-off, always well dressed in his slick suits. And he never mentioned anything about his finances other than expressing how busy he was as the acting director of Cabaret Miami. I didn't know better. I was a child, only seventeen.

"Open your eyes," Papa said.

How many times had I wished he had opened his? That he would have seen what was happening to Fery and me right under his own roof?

"This is what I want, I'm going to be his wife," I replied with my voice choking.

I barely knew Mahmoud. But I was attracted to him and the life I thought we could build together, away from Papa and Mouness.

Not long after I said yes to Mahmoud at Couchinie, I went one evening with Papa to Hotel Miami after work to see him. I was shocked. He was dancing with a young woman. I was desperate to find a logical reason. *Maybe it's a close family member*, I thought. As soon as he saw me, he brought the woman over and introduced her as his wife. My heart sank. She quickly added that it had been an arranged marriage organized by her father and Mahmoud's older brother and that neither of them was ever happy about it. They both insisted that they were getting a divorce.

"I wasn't able to make him happy, but I'm sure you will," she said to me with a smile.

I felt nauseous. Then the nausea was replaced by anger. When I asked Mahmoud why he hadn't mentioned it earlier, he said that he had wanted to, but that he never found the right moment. I felt trapped. I didn't want to marry him, but I couldn't back down after what I said to Papa. They were officially divorced a few weeks later, only two days before our wedding.

There were so many signs for me not to go through with it, besides the glaring fact that he was already married. A few weeks before the big day, Mahmoud and I borrowed Papa's car to deliver our wedding invitations. No sooner had I started the car than I hit the back passenger door of a taxi—luckily there had been no passengers. I had run a red light. After a moment of shock and disbelief, I saw the taxi driver get out of his car and storm toward us. I didn't have a driver's license yet, so I urged Mahmoud to switch seats with me, since he had once boasted about getting his a while back.

"What for? I don't have one, either!"

Another lie. I didn't have time to get angry at him as we jumped out of Papa's car and sprinted away from the taxi driver.

The accident was a sign that I was rushing into this marriage. I became a more cautious driver after that. If only I had given a second thought to sending out those invitations.

The final sign was at the actual wedding celebration at Hotel Miami, where we had invited more than a thousand guests, including relatives, friends, and the crème de la crème of the Iranian cinema and music industries. Fery was there, Mouness was there, but Mama couldn't make it to the dinner with two young kids at home—she promised she would come to see me once the kids were in bed, later that night.

Everything was going seamlessly. Our guests were enjoying themselves, Mahmoud looked dashing in his elegant tuxedo, and I felt good in my wedding gown designed by a lovely woman named Firouzeh, who had sewn all of my stage outfits since I was a little girl. It was made of gorgeous white chiffon and handsewn pastel-colored floral patterns that matched the base of my veil and hat, handmade by a Mrs. Pouran Daroodi. All my doubts about this marriage vanished by the time we cut into the Western-style wedding cake.

After dinner was long over, I watched dozens of guests rush out of the main room, almost simultaneously. Panic spread quickly, and soon guests were frantically running toward the bathrooms, their faces pale and stricken with fear. More guests then followed, some clutching their stomachs in agony. As I observed this strange pattern unfold, a wave of severe nausea washed over me. I ran toward the same exit, desperately looking for the closest restroom. I found one in time before I started heaving in my wedding gown.

The party ended and the police were called in. They conducted an investigation that same night and concluded that the food had been tampered with, though they couldn't identify the exact chemical used. The culprit had poured whatever it was on the dishes before they were served. Thankfully it wasn't a lethal dose and everyone recovered. The police didn't identify the culprit, either. Many believed it was Mouness. She had reportedly been seen in the food-preparation area. I wouldn't have put it past her. She didn't want me to get married, and when I did, she followed through on her threat to leave Papa as punishment.

My woes didn't end there that night. Mahmoud's parents still expected us to perform the old custom of *hejleh*, whereby both families wait outside of the honeymoon room to encourage the married couple to consummate the union, as well as to make sure the bride was in fact a virgin. It was odd that his family, who were big players in Tehran's nightlife, insisted that we do this old tradition associated with more religiously conservative families, which had become increasingly rare in Tehran in the late 1960s. Both of my parents were mortified by the idea. Of course, Mama only made it to this part of the nuptial festivities, after Roya and Joseph were finally asleep.

As soon as we got home that night, to our rented one-bedroom apartment in the heart of Tehran, Mahmoud and I both collapsed on the bed. Meanwhile, everyone including my mortified parents, my father-in-law and his two wives, and Mahmoud's aunts, uncles, and siblings sat in the barely furnished and unheated living room, waiting in the cold for the nuptial verdict. But there was no way we were going to have sex. I still felt sick, and Mahmoud was exhausted from all the socializing. I couldn't even sleep, unlike Mahmoud, who snored away beside me. It didn't help that I could hear laughing and arguing through the thin wall.

"The worst were those knocks on our door!" I said to Marjan.

Every so often Mahmoud's female relatives would knock on the door, waiting for the green light to start the celebration. And then, at one point, I heard howling sounds. Mahmoud's old aunt accidentally poured scorching hot tea onto her lap.

Mahmoud and I walked out of the bedroom into a battleground the next morning.

"How dare you insult us and our daughter's integrity!" Mama shouted at my in-laws. "Who the hell are you to question her virtue?"

I was heartbroken when Mahmoud stood silently by his family, who continued to question my virginity. When I saw the doubt in his eyes, I started boiling with rage and suggested to his sister that we go to their family doctor—it wasn't that uncommon in these situations for a physician to verify whether a woman's hymen was intact. At first, everyone protested, saying I still looked ill. But with one serious glance I shut everyone up. I grabbed my bag and rushed to the doctor with my sisters-in-law. Their doctor confirmed I was indeed a virgin and wrote an official document upon my request—it wasn't his first time. Mahmoud and his family were quickly reassured and acted as though they never had any doubts.

I was hoping that the wedding was just a rough start to the happy life we would build together. I was wrong, as I learned seven months later—when I was six months pregnant with our son, Kambiz. I was supposed to pick up Mahmoud at work that afternoon at Hotel Miami, but he wasn't in the lobby or the office. His adult nephew, nicknamed Bozy (Little Goat), helped me look for him. I suggested we look in the cabaret, thinking Mahmoud was probably overseeing the table settings and other preparations for that night's show. We entered the dim-lit balcony area overlooking the stage, and there he was, on top of another woman on one of the couches. I felt a violent surge of nausea, as if my insides were twisting and I was about to vomit any second. When he looked up and our eyes met, he jumped under a nearby table, leaving the woman scrambling to pull her skirt back into place. I pretended not to see anything. I didn't want to believe it. I told Bozy in a shaky voice that no one was there, before storming out the back entrance. Just as I was about to get in my car, I saw Mahmoud rushing the woman out of the same door. Our eyes locked once more. I ran as fast as possible with my pregnant belly and pounced on the woman. Mahmoud had already scurried back inside like a scared rat. Poor Bozy was the one to pull me off her.

Mahmoud's infidelities went on and on. The final straw came five years later when one of his affairs landed me in the hospital with a humiliating medical issue.

"If it weren't for Kambiz, my marriage to Mahmoud would've been my life's biggest regret," I said to Marjan.

Looking back, the one thing I appreciated about Mahmoud was how he genuinely believed in Googoosh and her potential for becoming an international star. As my acting manager, in 1970, he got me a recording deal with the legendary French producer Eddie Barclay, who was known for discovering and promoting major artists, including Dalida, Charles Aznavour, and Jacques Brel. During my time with the Barclay record label, I recorded a 7-inch record titled "*Gougoush*," which featured two songs in French, "*Retour de la Ville*" and "*J'entends Crier Je T'aime.*" "*Gougoush*" was selected for the gold record at the 1971 Marché International du Disque et de l'Édition Musicale (MIDEM) festival in Cannes. I performed both songs at the festival, which that same year also showcased young artists like Ike and Tina Turner, Elton John, and Cat Stevens.

Back in Tehran, I was earning a lot, but in Paris I hadn't made a penny for months, as we hadn't sold enough records to meet the terms of my contract. We gradually spent whatever money we had brought from Iran on our substantial living costs, including our stay at Hôtel Élysées. I even reached out to the office of the Shahbânu, the queen of Iran, Farah Pahlavi, as she was a patron of the arts who had studied architecture in Paris. I was told to contact the Maison de l'Iran, where they had emergency funds for Iranian artists working in France. It was helpful, but not sufficient. At some point, Mahmoud made multiple trips back to Tehran to scrape together more money—this after selling off most of our belongings, something he could have avoided if he hadn't mismanaged my past earnings so badly. He left me alone with Kambiz, just two years old then. I didn't have enough money to hire a nanny. So I took Kambiz everywhere, including my recording sessions. It was tiring for us both.

One morning, as I was getting us ready to go to the recording studio, five French policemen forcefully entered our hotel room. I froze with Kambiz screaming and sobbing in my arms as they threw our stuff in the air, searching for something. They took us to the police station. I was terrified. As my French was very limited, I only knew that it was about Mahmoud, since they kept saying his name. I understood that they were carrying out an investigation on the whereabouts of a French female artist who had once worked at Cabaret Miami in Tehran. They wanted to question Mahmoud about the nature of his relationship with that woman, but I kept telling them in my broken French and English that I didn't know anything. They refused to believe me. I was afraid they were going to lock me up. Several hours later, to my relief, they finally let us go.

I couldn't handle it anymore. I had all the fame and help back home, while in Paris I was struggling financially and apparently under criminal investigation for Mahmoud's extramarital activities. I immediately packed our things and went straight to the airport with Kambiz, abandoning my career in France after just over a year. I was furious at Mahmoud. He had secured this once-in-a-lifetime contract for me, but his reckless behavior ultimately drove me to the point of no return, and sent me packing back home.

Chapter 7

Behrouz

It must have been 9 or 11 p.m. Marjan and I lay side by side on the filthy carpet for the second night in a row. Neither of us had been taken upstairs for further questioning yet. With the hallway quieter at night, the shrieks of pain seemed even louder. This time, I thought of Fahimeh, the office secretary, now turned unofficial prisoner. I could almost feel my back throbbing and swelling as though the same garden hose used on her had pounded against my skin. How can anyone do such a thing? Purposely tearing someone's flesh like that? I thought of Afshoun and what the girls had said about him. I wondered whether he had gotten a hold of my file from Evin Prison. If so, he would see that I already answered all of their questions and even signed that release form. *But what if he's had it all along and still won't let me go?* I tried not to think about it, just as I tried to forget the horror in Niloufar's eyes. As usual, Marjan and I turned to our past to forget the present moment.

Marjan also shared a little about the breakdown of her first marriage, from which she had her daughter, Poopak. She, too, got married young—she was fresh out of high school. As her acting career gained momentum, the demands of her rising stardom, combined with the pressures of married life, strained her relationship. I knew exactly what she went through. The glare of fame, the constant spotlight, magnifies flaws and insecurities, while public scrutiny erodes trust and privacy. Even the greatest of love stories couldn't escape its destructive force, whether it was Romy Schneider and Alain Delon, or Marilyn Monroe and Joe DiMaggio. Behrouz Vossoughi and I never stood a chance. I was head over heels in love with him, the kind of all-encompassing love that only the greatest poets have ever truly captured.

I first met Behrouz in 1966, at my sixteenth birthday party—I told everyone I was turning eighteen, eager to escape Mouness and step into adulthood. Papa threw me a big classic Hollywood bash. He invited all the celebrities, movie stars, and singers. And it was a great publicity stunt, whether or not that was his original intention. Pouri Banayi, whom I had become close to since the pool incident, attended the party with Behrouz. He was twenty-nine years old then, three years older than her. They went well together. She was a beautiful woman with almond-shaped eyes and a delicate nose, while he was tall, broad-shouldered, and ruggedly handsome. Behrouz seemed very nice, and funny despite his initial serious demeanor. But I didn't think much of him, other than he was Pouri's fiancé and a struggling actor—he hadn't yet played in Masoud Kimiai's iconic film *Qeysar* (1969), where his portrayal of the eponymous hero, Qeysar, would cement his status as a legend of Iranian cinema. My admiration was for Pouri, who was an already-renowned movie star. It wasn't just her talent and grace that captivated me, but also the way she carried herself with poise and confidence. She gradually became an older sister to me, an older sister who I leaned on heavily and turned to with all my marital troubles after I married Mahmoud in 1967.

I remember rushing to her house a year and a half after that birthday party, six months pregnant, trembling with shock after I had caught Mahmoud that time with another woman at Cabaret Miami. When Mahmoud arrived at Pouri's place, he started swearing that I was mistaken, that I hadn't seen what I thought I had seen. As the argument escalated, Behrouz stepped in, pulling him aside to try to defuse the situation. Mahmoud kept insisting that he loved me, that he had married me and wanted only me. I went back home with him that night. But our marriage was already broken, like a mirror smashed into countless shards.

In 1970, Behrouz Vossoughi and I costarred in Jalal Moghadam's film *Panjereh* (*The Window*), which was based on George Stevens's *A Place in the Sun* (1951). The film was centered around a fatal love triangle, with my character, Leili, as the wealthy socialite who Sohrab, a young and poor factory worker played by Behrouz, falls in love with, mirroring the tragic dynamics of the original story. I was looking forward to working with him after seeing his amazing talent in *Qeysar*, and I was not disappointed. It was a great experience collaborating with someone of his caliber and strong work ethic.

When Behrouz and Pouri called off their engagement a year and a half later, I was on Team Pouri. She was my friend. She had previously confided in me her concerns of possible off-screen relationships with certain female costars. The mere mention of his name stirred such anger in me that I found myself incapable of speaking about him with kindness to our mutual friends in the entertainment industry. Certainly, it was immature of me. But I was young, twenty-one years old, and brimming with confidence. Not long after I had started bad-mouthing Behrouz, I unexpectedly ran into him at Cabaret Vanak, where I had been invited to a party thrown by the famed producer Ali Abbasi, who had produced our film *Panjereh*, for his latest movie. I didn't look at Behrouz once that night. I was ignoring him in a very noticeable way. When I got up onstage to perform at Ali's request, Behrouz immediately stood up from his front-row seat and left the room in such an obvious manner that it caused some murmuring among the confused audience.

Behrouz and I didn't speak again until we met by chance one afternoon in Rome, in 1972. I was twenty-two years old then. Behrouz must have been thirty-five. I was there for my new record deal with RCA Italiana, while Mahmoud was stuck in Paris, having gambled away my hard-earned money that was supposed to cover our hotel bills and other expenses. I was returning to my hotel on Via Veneto with Kambiz in my arms when my flutist, Khosrow, exclaimed, "Look! It's Behrouz Vossoughi!"

Everyone in Iran loved Behrouz. He became an icon with his mesmerizing screen presence and his manly good looks, which were defined by his strong jawline and high cheekbones, dark, brooding eyes, and thick, slightly tousled black hair. Men wanted to be him, while women wanted to be with him.

"Turn around," I muttered to Khosrow. "Quickly, before he sees us!"

Khosrow, Kambiz, and I dashed into the hotel elevator. The mechanical doors were about to close when Behrouz stepped in.

"Hello, Googoosh jân," he said in his typical charming way, adding the term of endearment *jân* before kissing my hand to show respect.

"Hi, Behrouz jân," I said, acting surprised to see him, while ignoring his gesture. "What are you doing here?"

He explained briefly that he had some time off between two film projects, and so he was visiting a friend. He invited me to join him for lunch the next day. I tried to find an excuse. Any excuse would have worked. And I had plenty. But my mind froze. I politely accepted, all the while wondering why he was being so nice to me.

I couldn't remember where we went, or what we ate, but I remember how quickly I felt comfortable with him. He had that gift of making everyone feel at ease and important. We briefly exchanged some pleasantries about the beautiful city of Rome, but Behrouz was eager to share his side of the story, denying he ever cheated on Pouri. I listened, although I was still on Pouri's side given my past experience with men—Papa and Mahmoud. When Behrouz finished, I felt compelled to share my own grievances concerning Mahmoud.

Mahmoud and I had just recently returned from a successful tour in the U.S., where I performed for Iranians abroad. On our way to Rome, we stopped in Paris for a few days. Mahmoud was in such good spirits after that fruitful tour that he decided to reward members of my orchestra with their own individual rooms at the prestigious Hôtel George V.

"But he lost everything at a gambling club on the Champs-Élysées the next day," I added.

When the hotel realized we couldn't pay the bill, they seized all of our personal belongings and instruments until the account was paid for. Mahmoud and the musicians couldn't go anywhere until the bill was settled, but

I had to leave since my recording sessions with RCA were going to start. I wasn't going to miss this second chance to build an international career.

So I flew to Rome with Kambiz, and my flutist. Once in Rome, I did as Mahmoud asked. I called a wealthy acquaintance of his, and he flew to Paris to pay off the balance, freeing my husband and my band.

I also told Behrouz about Mahmoud's family business debt, which was weighing on me. Papa had been right all along. Hotel Miami owed money everywhere, and he and his brother's checks were bouncing left and right. So they had opened a bank account in my name and had me sign blank checks, six of which they gave to one rich poultry farmer named Hajji Dorfeshan as a security deposit before he paid off all their debts. At the time, sitting at that table with Behrouz in Rome, I didn't know yet that a year later, in 1973, after my divorce from Mahmoud, Hajji Dorfeshan was going to fill out and deposit one of the checks for 1 million toman (around 145,000 U.S. dollars at the time), and then take me to court after it bounced. I refused to pay him this incredible sum, knowing fully well that I had never filled out that amount. Luckily, the court agreed with me and declared my innocence. As if things couldn't get any better, the court's decision became jurisprudence, unofficially carrying my name, to be used in similar cases to render void any check that displays handwriting different from the account holder.

I was surprised by how good of a listener Behrouz was. The more he listened, the more I felt like sharing. There was a kindness in his eyes, softening his otherwise rugged appearance, that made me feel like I could tell him anything. I even admitted to him that I had repeatedly asked Mahmoud for a divorce, and that he ignored me. Mahmoud's infidelities, along with his reckless financial decisions, had taken a heavy toll on me, deepening the resentment and frustration I already felt toward him. Behrouz didn't seem too surprised. He was aware of our marital problems from back when he was with Pouri. He even recalled that night I arrived tearfully at Pouri's house, six months pregnant and heartbroken.

I remember thinking during our lunch how much talking to Behrouz helped. Until that moment, Fery was the only man I felt I could talk to this way, the only man who really listened. Sitting at that table across from Behrouz, I felt as though some weight was lifted off my shoulders. I felt more peaceful. I also forgot how funny and playful Behrouz was, despite his tough-guy exterior. He was Azeri Turkish, just like me. We shared the same mother tongue, though we spoke in Persian together, and shared the same cultural and comedic references. Sitting there, just the two of us, for the first time, it felt like we had always known each other.

Lunch flew by. After Behrouz paid the check, he smiled and asked me if I remembered when we were filming that scene of us driving along the coast in *Panjereh*.

"Googi," he said as he twirled his straw in his half-finished Italian soft drink, "do you remember when the floor of my car suddenly got soaked?"

I remembered that we had used his car in that scene—props and clothing were usually our own, since producers didn't have the budget—but that was it.

"I'll never forget how you rushed to dry it," he said with a playful smile as he gazed into my eyes—that same captivating gaze that drew in his viewers, conveying a depth of emotion and thought without any need for words.

"Why did you do that?" he asked.

"I don't know," I replied, looking away from his soft brown eyes, my cheeks blushing. "I can't remember."

"Whenever you come back to Tehran," he said as we parted ways, "call me if you need to talk. I'm here for you."

I thanked Behrouz and wished him a safe trip home.

As soon as I got back to Tehran I called him. He invited Mahmoud and me to a private viewing of his movie *Baluch*. Mahmoud didn't want us to go. His friendly attitude toward Behrouz shifted after I told him about our lunch. I would have gone by myself, but I felt that my life was in shambles. Having lost all of our money, all my hard-earned money, Mahmoud had no choice but to give up our rental apartment. Kambiz and I started living out of a suitcase at the Sheraton Hotel in Tehran. After a while, I couldn't stand it anymore. I couldn't stand Mahmoud anymore. I told him I wanted a divorce and went to stay at my mother's with Kambiz. Mahmoud acted as if nothing had changed. I felt on edge. Then one night, while attending a dinner at my old friend and mentor Pouran's house, I collapsed and was rushed to the hospital. It was a panic attack.

I was first taken to the Jam Hospital, where Pouran's friend, Dr. Solhizadeh, a renowned addiction specialist, administered some very strong medication to help manage my pain and distress. Unfortunately, my anxiety came back quickly as the media began reporting that I was hospitalized for an alleged opium addiction. When the head of the National Iranian Radio and Television (NIRT), Reza Ghotbi, and his chief of staff, my friend Lila Fouladvand, read these headlines, they came to my rescue and transferred me to Mehr Hospital (which had a contract with the NIRT). I wasn't surprised that they intervened. Googoosh was now Iran's number one pop star, and with that amount of fame came a loss of privacy. My life was no longer just my own; Googoosh belonged to the public.

Mr. Ghotbi quickly decided that the best way to end the rumor was for me to take a drug test. No one thought to tell him that it was a bad idea, not even the nurses or the doctors. No one around me thought it was shortsighted, either. Unfortunately, when the test came back positive—for opiates—no one at Mehr Hospital thought to check with Jam Hospital for a list of the medications or sedatives Dr. Solhizadeh had administered to me. And I was too sick and exhausted to think clearly, let alone challenge their conclusion.

The drug test results were all over the news and magazines. Reporters kept showing up at my hospital room door, pressing me for more information on my supposed drug addiction. When did I start opium? Who got me addicted? Did I like heroin, too? The nurses would ask them to step away, to give me space. All this added humiliation contributed to my resolve to divorce Mahmoud. But Mahmoud wouldn't give up.

Just like the reporters, Mahmoud kept showing up. He kept begging that I move back in with him. I would ask my brothers to keep him away, just like they did with members of the press. But my brothers weren't always around. When Prime Minister Amir-Abbas Hoveyda heard about the commotion, he called my room one day.

Prime Minister Hoveyda had been in his role since 1965. I had met him at various royal events where I had performed. Unlike some of the other ministers or heads of state I had encountered, he was approachable and humble, despite his polished suits, scholarly appearance, and sharp intellect. He was always kind to me, making our interactions both comfortable and respectful. As he asked me how I was doing, I wondered whether he believed the drug test results. I told him everything—from the false test results to the press, and, of course, Mahmoud. Without going too deep into the details, I explained that Mahmoud was refusing to grant me a divorce. I then hopelessly asked the prime minister if he could help me with the situation. Less than an hour later I saw a security guard standing outside my room, pushing back Mahmoud and members of the press. I don't know what Prime Minister Hoveyda did, or if he even got involved at all, but not long after, Mahmoud reluctantly agreed to sign the divorce papers.

I was in the hospital for a few weeks. As I lay on my hospital bed, the only thing I looked forward to each day was seeing Behrouz. He came by nearly every day—he knew better than to believe the rumors. At night, he called to tell me he'd be stopping by soon. I got up and walked over to the window, and there he was, standing across the street by the lamppost. We just waved to each other, a simple hand gesture. That was it. But to me, that was the epitome of romance—all he was missing was a guitar.

I went back to Mama's briefly after I was discharged. My feelings grew more intense with each call from Behrouz. I felt butterflies in the pit of my stomach as soon as I heard his name. I tried my best to act cool, but even Mahmoud had noticed a change in me from our brief exchanges about our ongoing divorce. He immediately started feeding the media stories that I was leaving him for Behrouz. He didn't mention the countless other women or how I had been asking for a divorce for more than a year, long before Behrouz came into the picture. He whipped the media into a frenzy, convincing them that I was a selfish mother, eager to ditch my five-year-old son. Magazines published pictures of a tearful Kambiz on the cover, along with words like "Mama don't leave me!" They would also publish letters they received from the public, mostly concerned mothers, and some fathers, admonishing my behavior, like a disappointed parent. They asked, "Why is Googoosh repeating her mother's mistakes? Doesn't she remember her own childhood?" I pushed back in multiple interviews. But no one cared to know the truth. No one cared that Mahmoud wouldn't grant me the divorce unless he got full custody of Kambiz; I only agreed because I knew he couldn't keep me away from my son. The public was upset with Googoosh. They had made up their mind, and there was nothing I could do about it.

As soon as I regained my strength, I left for Paris, where Fery had moved a few months earlier. I needed to get away from all the noise. I stepped away from whatever was blossoming between Behrouz and me. I didn't want it with all this pressure. I didn't want to feed that false narrative and create more scandalous headlines like "Googoosh Abandons Husband and Little Child for Behrouz Vossoughi." I told Behrouz over the phone that I was going away for a while. I didn't have to explain further. He understood.

I spent a month with Fery, a magical month. He was twenty years old then. He went to Paris for a year to learn French at the Alliance school while training in wine cultivation, all at his own expense. Several times a week, after his classes, Fery would drive to a local vineyard outside of Paris, where he would roll up the bottom of his pants and crush grapes for hours at a time for six francs an hour. I was so proud of him. He had moved in with his girlfriend and her roommate in a tiny *chambre de bonne*, once the maids' quarters, in an Haussmann-era building on the Boulevard Saint-Germain. I will never forget the narrow flights of stairs we had to climb all the way up to the seventh floor. Four of us slept in there, packed like sardines, with no room to turn. I slept like a baby every night. I didn't think about Mahmoud, the media, and all the hate Googoosh was getting. I didn't think about Behrouz, either. I was just enjoying the moment with Fery—we even did some traveling across Europe, just the two of us.

Fery knew me better than anyone. He didn't pry, he just let me be. He talked eagerly about the new life he was building for himself. He had always been optimistic and resilient no matter what obstacles he faced. I shared his happiness and took pride in the confident and mature man he had become. I wanted to stay in Paris with him indefinitely. And I would have stayed, had Hajir Darioush not come looking for me, hoping to persuade me to attend the Sepâs Film Festival back in Tehran, where I was nominated for best actress for my role in his film *Bitâ*.

I was stunned when I won the Sepâs award. *Bitâ* was a dark, avant-garde film, unlike anything I had done before, so I was never entirely sure of my performance. The black-and-white film was based on Goli Taraghi's original story about a young woman's struggles with her father's mental illness, unrequited love, social barriers, and self-destruction. For some reason Hajir Darioush started off the film shoot with a very emotional scene that comes near the end. I remember feeling nervous just before we began shooting that scene, where my grieving character, Bitâ, silently enters an empty home dressed in black. She lays a cloth on the living room floor, sets out three empty plates, and then begins drinking vodka. It was the first time I started a movie with such emotional intensity. I wasn't convinced that I had delivered the right notes until I was quickly reassured by Hajir, Goli Taraghi, and Houshang Baharlou (the cinematographer). We had filmed *Bitâ* when I felt most hopeless in my marriage to Mahmoud. I felt at times that there wasn't much separating my character's depressed feelings from my own, even though we were very different people with very different lives. I found myself experiencing the same emotions Bitâ felt, blurring the line between fiction and reality. For a moment, receiving the Sepâs award almost made all that pain and struggle feel worthwhile.

I called Behrouz after the award show. The media had moved on from Mahmoud and me by the time I had gotten back, and Behrouz and I started a romance free from media scrutiny. We quickly became inseparable. Every time I was four blocks away from his home in Amir Abad—a rapidly modernizing neighborhood near the centrally situated University of Tehran—my heart fluttered uncontrollably. He was so different from Mahmoud, athletic, playful, and funny; we spent hours giggling together like children. I loved him. I could have never imagined in those early days that our love would eventually consume us, like a wildfire destroying everything in its path.

Several months into our relationship, I was performing at the birthday celebration of the Shah's twin sister, Princess Ashraf, where Behrouz was attending as a guest—his fame, charm, good looks, and wit earned him a spot within her mostly male entourage. He seemed surprised to see me there—then again we both had such busy schedules that it was hard to keep track. He came up to me after my performance, dressed in his perfectly fitted tuxedo, and said that he didn't like his woman to be singing in public.

I was stunned. I was Googoosh. He had seen me perform many times before—even a couple of days earlier. *Why did he feel different about it now? And as a true artist, how could he even say such a thing?* Mahmoud, despite his many flaws, always believed in Googoosh, and encouraged my singing. I was livid. Perhaps Behrouz was testing me, asking me to choose between him and my career. Or perhaps his family had pressured him, asking him to leave me, a previously married woman with a child, and an entertainer, what they called a *motreb*. I couldn't blame them. It was all still new. It was only a few decades earlier that a woman named Qamar-ol-Moluk Vaziri had been the first to dare to sing onstage in public, unveiled. But music was my life. I wasn't going to give it up for anybody, not even Behrouz. I didn't go back to his apartment that night or the following nights.

Weeks later, we were separately approached by Mehdi Mosayyebi and Shapur Gharib to star in their movie *Mamal Amricayi*. The story was interesting. A man named Mamal—nicknamed Mamal the American because of his lifelong dream to move to the U.S., the land of opportunity and Hollywood—desperately schemes a plan for his big move. But everything seems to go south after he encounters a young woman named Nasrin, who isn't exactly who she appears to be. As soon as I found out Behrouz was going to play Mamal, I wanted nothing to do with the project. I was so angry with him. But Mehdi, the producer, was persistent. He insisted that the director had envisioned the roles only for us; Behrouz was one of the highest-grossing male actors and I had just won my Sepâs prize, Iran's highest film award.

For weeks, Behrouz and I didn't exchange a single word off camera. As soon as the director yelled, "Cut," I would rush back to Pouran's house, where I had been staying since returning from Paris. Since Mahmoud had drained all my money, Pouran and her husband kindly offered me a place to stay. The public had no idea that Googoosh was broke. They helped me save my earnings from the film and my nightly performances at the cabarets and other gigs, lifting me out of financial ruin—this made Pouran's later betrayal in Los Angeles in 1979 even more devastating.

Back on set, Behrouz and I would ignore each other, walk past one another without a glance, and as soon as the director yelled, "Action," we would switch into characters that were falling in love. I was furious at him, and furious that I still loved him. In the very last scene, we were asked to engage in a heartfelt embrace and cry from joy. Something happened as I gazed into his warm brown eyes. Genuine tears rolled down our cheeks. I was no longer playing Nasrin, and he was no longer Mamal. The entire film crew, including Shapur Gharib, choked up. Behrouz never asked me to give up singing again.

The following months felt even more magical as my hard work began to pay off. In just nine months, I had saved enough to purchase a house. So when Mr. and Mrs. Tehranchi, a kind couple I had met, told me about the new properties they were developing in Velenjak, known as the "Roof of Tehran," I didn't hesitate to visit. Located in the affluent Shemirân district, home to foreign embassies and the Niâvarân and Sa'dâbâd palaces, it was farther north than I had ever lived.

I drove up there one late spring afternoon—it was a fifteen-minute drive from Pouran's, where I was still staying, unprepared to move in with Behrouz just yet. I remembered thinking the air was always fresher on the foothills of the Alborz mountains as I followed the address onto Kambiz Street (coincidentally sharing a name with my son). Before all of the new luxurious houses were built, people used to come up here for the day in the summer to escape the heat.

From Kambiz Street, I turned onto a quiet cul-de-sac still under construction, the road little more than dirt. On one side, new villas stood, each one bordered by tall, imposing walls and gates, while the other side was lined with empty lots. Behind one of those walls, shielded from the gaze of passersby, I came upon the house—a modern two-story villa, its architecture a perfect blend of traditional and contemporary Iranian design. It had a small garden, neat and understated, with a swimming pool that sparkled beneath the warm light.

Walking toward it, I could feel the cooler air up here in the foothills. I loved how the bustling city sounds of speeding traffic, honking cars, and heated arguments slowly faded into the distance, replaced by the soft, melodic chorus of sparrows, the gentle rustling of leaves, and the rhythmic chirping of crickets. I felt peace.

The villa was pristine, its light-colored stone facade glowing in the late-afternoon sun, as if freshly polished. There were no vines here yet, no creeping plants to soften the structure's modern lines. The curved metal railings on the large windows, newly installed, echoed the geometric patterns of Persian art, a subtle nod to tradition. Sunlight glinted off the railings, casting shadows on the untouched stone floors of the terrace.

Above me was a small balcony. I imagined standing there on a cool evening, the breeze carrying the scent of blooming jasmine and roses, watching the sun disappear behind the trees, painting the sky with hues of gold and orange. It was a perfect moment of quiet beauty, and I felt a wave of pure contentment.

The front door was tucked in a shaded alcove. It felt like an entrance to something more than just a house—a sanctuary. I could feel a warm sense of calm settle over me as I walked in. Inside, the layout was spacious, with the rooms bathed in natural light from the many windows that framed views of the garden. I walked through five spacious bedrooms, all on the second floor, and selected right there and then one for me (and Behrouz), one for Kambiz, and one for overnight guests like Fery, Fariborz, Adel, or some close friend. I chose right then which bedroom would be converted to a TV den. After all, cinema was not only my passion, but it was also my school, where I would study and learn from the greats, dissecting their every move on-screen, every glance, and the way their lips quivered with a certain emotion.

The villa was nowhere near as grand or lavish as Parvaneh's sumptuous mansion in *Dar Emtedâd-e Shab*—no extravagant marble columns or gilded accents existed. But its simplicity, unpretentiousness, made it all the more inviting. It was comfortable, yet elegant. I felt at home.

I knew Pouran and her husband would be happy for me, and secretly relieved to have their house back after months of hosting me. The asking price was just shy of 1 million toman—about 145,000 U.S. dollars in 1973—just within reach after all those months of hard work. Signing the deed, I was overwhelmed with an incredible feeling, thinking to myself, *I've made it on my own! Without Papa, without Mahmoud, or any man managing my life!* On some level, this made me appreciate Behrouz even more for never interfering with my financial decisions, allowing me the independence I had worked so hard to achieve.

Behrouz and I were together for three years before we got married. He was happy the way things were, living together in my new house in Velenjak, spending the little free time we had at his villa by the Caspian Sea, sometimes with Kambiz, who Behrouz adored. He said he didn't want our relationship to be in the public eye and asked that I deny it to reporters. But deep down, I knew he didn't want to make the commitment. And in 1974, a year before our marriage, I got pregnant.

I remember the day I told him like it was yesterday. It was after one of those very busy days of long hours on set for Behrouz and my usual running between performances on TV, radio, and cabarets. We sat down on the couch in the living room, a rare moment of quiet. Our schedules were usually so hectic that we hardly ever had the chance to unwind together like this. But I couldn't wait any longer. My heart raced with nervous excitement as I prepared to share the news that I knew would change everything. His eyes lit up. He spoke about how he always wanted to be a father—he was great with kids, with Kambiz. We talked names, and imagined what our child would look like. I went to bed that night feeling like everything had finally fallen into place, that we were now going to go public with our relationship. I fell asleep with a smile on my face, our future feeling so bright, so full of promise.

But the next morning, everything changed. His excitement was gone. He told me he spoke with his mother, and together they had decided that it was best for me to have an abortion. He didn't explain further. There was no discussion, no consideration of what I wanted. They had decided for me, about me, without me. I was devastated. I wanted to cry and scream at him and his mother. But the words caught in my throat, strangled by the fear of losing him. And so I didn't fight. I didn't argue. I just nodded while I fought back my tears.

I tried to convince myself that it was the right decision, that otherwise I would have been subjected to another nasty media campaign for having a child out of wedlock. I called my manager. He took me to this couples' house in the Yousef Âbâd neighborhood, where I was kept half-awake the whole time—abortions on demand were not legalized until 1977. Behrouz and I never spoke about it again. He acted as if nothing happened, as if we had just made a minor adjustment to our plans. I kept quiet and buried my feelings in my work, like I always did.

Behrouz would talk about marriage, but he never actually wanted to go through with it. I pushed him. I didn't want to get a reputation for living with him as an unmarried woman—a stigma that would never apply to him, or to men in general. Even though it was growing more common in elite circles, the broader public still frowned upon Iranian women who lived this way, though it was not illegal. The societal expectations weighed heavily on me. It felt like I was walking a tightrope between the modernity seeping into our lives mostly through international cinema, and our deep-rooted customs. It was perhaps similar for women living in European cities in the 1950s or '60s, though Iran being a Muslim country added another layer of scrutiny.

But what bothered me even more than societal pressures was that Behrouz didn't want to tell everyone that I was his. After all, I was young and madly in love with him. I naively thought I could change him, that he would ignore all the countless women that were throwing themselves at his feet. So I pushed him. And eventually, I got what I wanted.

We got married in 1975, in my home in Velenjak, in the presence of a dozen people, including a mullah to officiate the marriage, Mehdi Mosayyebi as our witness, some close friends and Behrouz's mother. I didn't invite Mama and Papa, or Fery, or any of my brothers; I didn't want to make a big fuss, since Behrouz and I had already been living together for several years. It was a very simple *aghd*, the legal and spiritual marriage contract ceremony preceding the wedding celebration, with a very simple *sofreh*, or wedding spread—it was nothing like the sumptuous reception Mahmoud's family had thrown for us at his brother's home days before our wedding celebration at Hotel Miami. Our friends helped set up the *sofreh*, adorning a decorated cloth with the usual key items, including a mirror, a Quran, candles, wild rue seeds, *naan-e sangak* bread, nuts, honey, fruits and sweets, gold coins, sugar cones, and rose water. Everyone was dressed more casually, compared to my first wedding.

Behrouz's mother was visibly unhappy, repeating that this was not how her son's first marriage was supposed to be, on the fly, and in secrecy. But the truth was that she never liked me, a divorcée with a child. She had mentioned in front of me many times over the years how her son deserved better—Behrouz was her first son, out of five, and her prized jewel. I ignored it, just like I ignored the fact that Behrouz hadn't even bothered to get me a ring.

When his mother asked him to show her the ring, Behrouz replied that he hadn't known that he was supposed to get me one. I told them not to worry, that I had something that looked like a wedding band that he could put in a box and then on my finger during the ceremony.

"But I didn't buy anything for Googoosh, either," his mother quickly added.

I told her not to worry again and placed a golden necklace from my safe in the box. I didn't let her get to me. Besides, deep down, beneath the smiles, I was struggling with my own contradictory feelings. I was happy that I was finally marrying the love of my life, but I was also angry at Behrouz. We had gotten into a huge argument two days earlier, when he got cold feet, and I chucked the wedding ring I got him into the toilet. When he heard the ring clink in the toilet bowl, he ran over and we both dug it out with our bare hands. We never mentioned the fight again, pretending that it didn't happen.

We didn't go on a honeymoon. Behrouz traveled instead to the U.S. with Princess Ashraf and her entourage not long after the wedding, while I went to the city of Bandar Pahlavi, in Gilân, a region north of Tehran on the Caspian Sea, for the shooting of Alirezâ Davood Nejâd's film *Nâzanin* (1975), in which I played alongside my new brother-in-law, Changiz Vossoughi. I found out a couple of weeks into the shooting that I was pregnant again. I had another abortion, this time without waiting for Behrouz to say anything. I knew he was going to have mixed feelings about the pregnancy, just like he had about us getting married, and the media was already saying things like "Behrouz married Googoosh because she's pregnant." Perhaps a part of me realized in that moment that our relationship was destined to fail, and I couldn't bear the thought of bringing another child into this world under those circumstances. The character I was playing, Nayer, was also grappling with having an abortion. It's a big decision after all, if not the biggest in one's life. Each abortion was painful, leaving a mark on my body and my soul. I've wondered who those children could have been. But at the same time, I knew I wouldn't have been able to provide them with a traditional, stable life, just as I hadn't for Kambiz. I knew my shortcomings as a mother, with all the pressures of fame, with all my childhood emotional baggage. But still, every so often I think about them. I told Behrouz about it when he got back from the U.S. He seemed fine with my decision.

From the outside, our relationship seemed perfect: two young famous artists, costars in romantic films, in love. Glossy pictures in magazines captured our chemistry, comparing us to Hollywood dream couples like Elizabeth Taylor and Richard Burton. But they didn't tell the whole story. Like most relationships in the spotlight, our hectic schedules, long stretches of time apart, and the constant rumors got the best of us and brought out our worst. The magazines didn't know about all the women swarming around Behrouz, including his rumored ex-lovers, nor his extreme jealousy over me that bordered on paranoia. Several times I caught him going through my clothes, checking my pockets for evidence, or sniffing for another man's cologne. I would get so mad. It felt like a slap in the face. I loved him so much and I couldn't understand how he could doubt my loyalty. But then it also made me wonder whether he was simply acting out of guilt. My suspicions about him and some of his female friends were confirmed only after our separation. I kept everything bottled inside, never wanting to upset him, never wanting to risk him leaving me.

We had many happy moments, too many to count, throughout our relationship. In those times, we were like young, playful teens in love. But those moments were fleeting, often overshadowed and forgotten amid the arguments and tensions that plagued us. The drop that overflowed the glass occurred on Monday, October 11, 1976. Behrouz was away on location in Mâku, a city in Iranian Azerbaijân, for his new role in Khosrow Haritash's *Malakout* (*The Divine One*), and I was busy with my daily fasting and praying for Ramadan—prayer had become an important part of my life since I learned how in Dâyi's home. I was in the middle of the afternoon prayer when Behrouz first called. His friend Ari, who was openly gay and who had befriended me over the last few years, was at my home when the phone rang. He picked it up. As soon as I was done praying, he told me that I had missed Behrouz's call. I knew right then that this was going to cause another headache. Behrouz called again thirty minutes later. He was angry.

"Why the hell is Ari there?" he started without even saying hello.

I couldn't understand why Behrouz felt so threatened by Ari, as if he had forgotten that he was homosexual. But he was that paranoid.

"He's kindly stopped by to see if I'm okay," I replied in a cool manner, hoping that Ari hadn't overheard him.

Behrouz immediately asked me to pack all his things and to send them to his mother's. I asked him to calm down and to think things through.

He called again a few hours later, asking why I hadn't sent over his stuff—I knew right then that he was back in town, calling me from his mother's home. I hung up. I gathered all of his belongings and stuffed them in the back of my manager's car. We sped down to the National Iranian Radio and Television building on Pahlavi Street—Tehran's most iconic and prestigious avenue, stretching from the northern foothills to the city center, with its tree-lined sidewalks—where I had a scheduled recording for a television program. *I don't have time for these childish games*, I thought as I furiously puffed on a cigarette. But it weighed heavily on me, as it always did, like a ton of bricks. When we got there, I pushed back against the crushing weight, as hard as I could, so that Googoosh could smile for the cameras and sing upbeat love songs.

Behrouz had called the NIRT while I was recording and asked that I go over to his mother's when I was done. We argued as soon as I stepped foot in his family home, until we were interrupted by a phone call. It was one of his friends, a high-ranking air force general. Behrouz told him about our argument before passing me the phone.

"What's Behrouz doing there?" the general asked.

I had no idea what he was doing there. Had he flown back to Tehran in a fit of jealousy in the middle of a film shoot and gone straight to his mother's? But that didn't seem like him—he was always so professional when it came to work. Still, I was too angry and fed up to ask him directly.

"I don't know, General," I replied. "He wanted his things, so I've brought them over."

I passed the phone back to Behrouz, eager to get back into my manager's car and out of there. But just as I was about to leave, Behrouz said, in an obviously dramatic tone, "Okay. General, I'll do as you wish. I'll go back just for you!"

I knew he was too proud to admit he wanted to come back home, but this was too insulting. I didn't say a word as my manager piled Behrouz's things back into the car. I had to get to Cabaret Vanak, where every night I performed the last act—it was a big deal to perform the last act at places like Cabaret Vanak, Cabaret Shokoofeh No, and Baccara, which were as prestigious as Paris's Moulin Rouge in its heyday. We dropped Behrouz off at my house in Velenjak before making our way to the cabaret.

When I finally got to Vanak, my head was throbbing with pain. But as Papa had always taught me, the show must go on no matter what, ever since that night in Qazvin after Mouness kicked me down the stairs and cracked my head open.

Before I got onstage, Eric, a French musician and composer, informed me that he had finished rearranging the music for "*Khalvat*" (Uncrowded). He suggested we head straight to Studio Pop on Lârestân Street after my performance to record it. It was almost midnight. I agreed. I didn't want to go home.

I was so thrilled when I heard his composition, an uplifting samba-like melody. It was exactly what I had asked of him. I stood in that booth, put on the headphones, and sang into the microphone. My migraine disappeared, along with the heavy weight of fatigue and anxiety, as I sang my heart out. Music always made my pain disappear, including that time I performed for an hour or so with a nearly ruptured appendix without a worry in the world, only to collapse backstage. I sang in that booth for hours, refusing to settle for anything less than perfect. It was around 5 a.m. when my manager's wife called, saying that Behrouz had been calling around, looking for me.

When I got back home an hour later I found Behrouz sitting in the living room, all dressed up, next to his packed belongings. He barely looked up. I walked past him and headed to the bedroom upstairs. As soon as I collapsed in bed, fully dressed, the phone rang. No one ever called me in the morning. Friends, family, my manager, and film directors, they all knew that I couldn't be reached before noon. I grabbed the phone with the last bit of energy left in me. It was my brother's wife.

My heart sank to the pit of my stomach before she could even utter the words that I had been dreading all these years.

"He's dead!" she shouted over and over.

"He" was my Fery.

I couldn't believe it. Fery was only twenty-five. He wasn't supposed to go this young! I always worried for him, ever since those early dark days with Mouness. But I never believed he would go so soon. Just four months earlier we were celebrating his wedding with a reception I had thrown for him at the Intercontinental Hotel in Tehran, surrounded by my famous peers. How could this be? He wasn't supposed to go before me.

When Fery's wife finally calmed down, she managed to explain that he had died from heart failure in the hospital in Shiraz—they had moved there for his new job with a French petrochemical company, coincidentally several years after his time abroad in France. His rheumatic heart disease had finally gotten to him. As she spoke, I felt like the ground was being pulled from beneath my feet. He was gone. But how? He seemed as good as ever when I last spoke to him just a few days earlier. I had no idea that would be the last time I'd hear his voice. I could still hear his excitement, the way he sounded hopeful about the future. When the surgeons told him a year earlier that they couldn't repair his heart valves due to the risks of anesthesia, he refused to seek help from a renowned surgeon in Texas who had successfully operated on patients with the same condition. He kept insisting that his medication was going to take care of it. I should have pushed harder.

My best friend, my little brother, my Fery—the only one who fully shared the pain of our childhood—was gone. I couldn't breathe. I collapsed onto the bed as the world came crashing down around me.

It no longer made any difference whether Behrouz left or stayed. Nothing mattered. He stayed and stood by my side for Fery's funeral, for the seventh-day and the fortieth-day commemoration ceremonies.

A few months later, in January 1977, Behrouz told me in the middle of a small intimate gathering thrown for Princess Ashraf by Prime Minister Jamshid Amouzegar that he had gotten permission from Her Highness for us to get divorced. I didn't protest—I didn't even bother to ask why he needed her permission. I didn't want to play these stupid games anymore. I was willing to let go of the man I had been madly in love with because I couldn't handle the jealousy, the arguments, the betrayals, the disappointments—it all felt trivial now that my Fery was gone. I was ready to say goodbye, even if it meant facing more heartbreak. The following day, on a Thursday afternoon, when most places are closed in Iran, the Ministry of Justice, which usually didn't handle personal matters such as divorces, opened its doors. They bypassed the standard court procedures and granted us a divorce immediately.

I found out I was pregnant yet again shortly after. I never told Behrouz. I didn't want him to think I was trying to win him back. So I had an abortion—my third and last. This time it was different. I had gone each time before with a heavy heart and a head filled with doubts. But this time, I felt nothing. I was numb, like a part of me had died with Fery.

After the numbness, all I could feel was rage. I was enraged at Behrouz for the way our marriage ended. I was enraged that Fery had left me so soon. I was enraged at Mama, who wept at his grave, remembering how she had left us when we weren't old enough to beg her to stay. But most of all, I was enraged at Papa, for not having protected us from Mouness. Even Mouness, who was also present at the burial, sought my forgiveness that day, just as she claimed to have asked for Fery's forgiveness a year earlier—I told her I'd forgive her, but I'd never forget. The rage was eventually replaced by a vast feeling of emptiness. I was barely mentally present for Kambiz, whom I eventually sent, for his own good, to the exclusive Swiss boarding school, Le Rosey. Singing and performing barely helped. I did everything mechanically, devoid of meaning. I lost all purpose. That's when Homayoun walked into my life.

Chapter 8

Homayoun

I first noticed Homayoun when I was fifteen years old, at Couchinie, the same restaurant-discotheque where Mahmoud proposed to me a couple of years later. I saw a young man with hypnotic dance moves from across the room. He was maybe a few years older than me, and only an inch or two taller. His body moved in unison with the infectious beat and rhythm of some groovy song—maybe it was the Rolling Stones's "(I Can't Get No) Satisfaction." I was awed by his performance. Nothing more. Ever since I was a little girl, I loved dancing, especially to pop music—it had an electrifying effect on me, with its pulsating rhythm vibrating all the way to my core. I could unleash the pain and the anger I kept inside out onto the dance floor, where nothing mattered but the music. Homayoun was doing just that. I later discovered that one of his idols was Fred Astaire, with his effortless grace and one-of-a-kind steps, gliding across the floor as if he were weightless, every movement a perfect blend of elegance and precision.

Over the years, I saw him again and again at various discotheques. He was hard to miss with those incredible dance moves and his uniquely stylish sense of fashion. Sometimes he would wear traditional Iranian handmade shoes from wool or cotton, instead of the latest trendy leather boots or loafers, paired with his lightly flared trousers. He tucked in one side of his shirt, another small rebellious gesture that set him apart from the crowd.

Our paths really crossed in the winter of 1978, when I was twenty-eight years old, twice divorced, and still deeply heartbroken from Fery's passing. I was at a party, and for some reason unknown to myself, I got angry seeing him—a man I never spoke to before—smoking opium with a couple other people.

"You're destroying yourself!" I snapped at him.

I was moodier in those days, sometimes even short-tempered with friends and family. My patience and tolerance level had dipped with Fery's passing. It didn't help that I detested opium ever since that time I was falsely accused of being an opium addict after collapsing at Pouran's house in 1972.

He seemed puzzled, perhaps surprised that Googoosh, Iran's biggest pop star—someone he had never personally met—was interfering in his life this way. Then, with a mischievous smile, he replied, "This body needs to get fucked up. If I return it to the earth in one piece, then I've lost."

That was Homayoun. I learned more about him through our mutual friends that night; he came from a very respectable family (one of the noble "thousand families," as they were called) and he co-owned an insurance franchise. Aside from dancing, he was also a talented disc jockey.

A few nights later, I threw a little get-together at my home in Velenjak and Homayoun showed up with our mutual friends. He brought me a gift. It was a perfume bottle by Yves Saint Laurent, "Opium." *He's cheeky*, I thought. He was lucky that I loved collecting perfumes. For a long time since my early twenties, I wore Guerlain's Chamade. But I was always on the lookout for something new.

"I love it," I said to him after discovering its smoldering spicy notes, with a hint of sandalwood, against my skin.

"I thought you would," he replied with a sparkle in his eye.

The men I was usually drawn to—smart, charming, and effortlessly blending sophistication with masculinity—often seemed a little insecure, maybe even intimidated by all the fame that surrounded Googoosh. They kept their distance, just like at the *thé dansants*. But not Homayoun.

Later that night, after Homayoun said goodbye and walked out the front door, he turned one last time in the garden and said with a teasing smile, "I've got a feeling we'll be seeing each other again soon."

A soft smile crept onto my face before I could stop it. He didn't have the kind of looks that would turn heads instantly, but there was something quietly magnetic about him. His features were balanced, carrying an understated charm that drew you in the more time you spent with him. But it was that smile—warm, genuine, full of confidence and a hint of daring—that really got to me. It lit up his face, and in that moment, something stirred inside me, a pull I hadn't felt since those early days with Behrouz. I couldn't help but want to see him again.

A week or two later, some friends and I headed to Dizin, Iran's largest ski resort. Growing up, I'd had no time for leisure or sports, so as an adult, I made sure to carve out time for them, including skiing. I learned to ski in my late teens and loved the feeling of gliding through powder, leaving my troubles behind in Tehran. I frequently took Kambiz, though he was initially terrified of the idea of sliding down a mountain. Dizin, just fifty miles north of Tehran, was close enough to drive up early, ski the day away, and return home by evening.

We stayed at our favorite hotel, nestled 1.65 miles high in the majestic Alborz mountains. After two full days of skiing, I caught a cold that quickly worsened. My chest ached, my throat was raw, and even drinking water was painful. I drank endless tea with honey and lemon, but nothing helped. One night around midnight, I woke to the sound of clanking against my window. It was some friends I'd invited to the resort and completely forgotten about. Homayoun was with them, in his brown leather jacket.

They waved up at me, signaling they were coming upstairs. When they arrived, they were shocked by how sick I looked—pale, disheveled, dark circles under my eyes. "Don't worry, it's fine," I said. "I could use some company."

I called reception for an extra room and more tea. When the tea arrived, Homayoun, who had been quiet as I coughed through most of the conversation, stood up and said he'd make me a special tea for my cough. I didn't know what to say. I had never had a man take care of me before; I was the one who always looked after others—Papa, Mahmoud, Behrouz. But now, as Homayoun carefully handed me the cup, he smiled and said, "You're about to feel much better, real soon."

Homayoun was right. The tea miraculously healed my cough. It also brought back my appetite. I was famished. We ordered some room service, and I ate everything in my sight. I couldn't remember having ever eaten this much. I felt alive again, and an hour later, we were dancing downstairs in the hotel's discotheque. As we moved together on the dance floor, our bodies close and swaying in sync with the rhythm of the music, I looked at Homayoun and realized I might have been wrong. Maybe love isn't just about passion and butterflies in the pit of your stomach; maybe it's about giving to one another. Homayoun was nothing like Behrouz. He wasn't tall, famous, or ruggedly handsome, but he was a great dancer—and more than that, he seemed to be a giver. After that night, we became inseparable. Only months later would Homayoun reveal that he had made his special tea with *shireh*, concentrated opium.

Homayoun told me who he was that very first night we met. I should have taken his word for it and kept my distance. But my broken heart had given up on the idea of true love. And Homayoun appealed to the part of me that was shattered by Fery's death and haunted by my unresolved childhood traumas. It was the part of me that was desperately searching to feel alive again, even if it meant flirting with destructive forces. We were together for less than six months when the whole country fell into chaos.

Chapter 9

The Revolution

The revolution swept across my homeland like a raging storm, unraveling the delicate fabric of a world once interwoven with tradition, modernity, and poetry. Almost overnight, the shimmering parties, the premieres of daring, boundary-pushing films, and the intoxicating rhythm of music and freedom were replaced by fear, uncertainty, and darkness. For me, the days surrounding the revolution—spent mostly thousands of miles away—marked not just the end of an era but also my own painful descent into rock bottom.

I would never forget that one night during the month of Ramadan in the late summer of 1978 when I heard the horrific news that sent shivers down my spine. It was a Sunday evening, August 19. Four men had locked the exits of the Cinema Rex in Abadan, poured gasoline around the theater, and set it on fire. Four hundred and seventy people, including women and children, were horrifically murdered that day, most of whom had gone to watch Masoud Kimiai's latest film, *Gavaznhâ* (*The Deer*), starring Behrouz. Like millions of Iranians, I was sick to my stomach from this scene of pure evil.

In the days and weeks that followed, we heard of other attacks, including one on Tehran's famous restaurant, Hatam, on Pahlavi Street, and another on the discotheque Darvish—both establishments viewed as symbols of

Western influence and decadence, where alcohol flowed, dancing flourished, and men and women mingled freely. What was happening? I couldn't make sense of it. I had never heard of attacks like these before. Growing up, I had always witnessed a kind of harmony between those who were more religious and those who embraced modern, Western lifestyles. They lived side by side, coexisting peacefully, whether in Tehran or in other cities or small towns across the country.

By August 27, the Shah's new prime minister, Jafar Sharif-Emami, ordered the closure of bars, casinos, discotheques, and liquor shops, hoping to restore order. But anti-Shah riots soon erupted around the holy city of Qom, as well as in the capital, near the southern Tehran mosque. The annual Shiraz Festival of Arts, the Kerman Traditional Music Festival, and the Tehran International Film Festival were all canceled. With the closure of the cabarets, and the strikes leading to the shutdown of entertainment programs on television and radio, I, like all my peers, was out of work.

It all happened so fast. One minute I learned about my longtime manager's betrayal, and the next, the whole country was in chaos. I didn't know what to think. I was never political—I didn't have time to be. Of course, I knew that intellectuals, and some artists, criticized the Shah and the idea of an absolute monarchy. I also knew about political groups like the communist Tudeh Party and the People's Mujahedin Organization (MEK) fighting the system. I learned later that the pro-Soviet Tudeh Party focused on underground activism and spreading Marxist ideas, while the MEK took a more direct approach with armed resistance and attacks on key government and foreign targets. I knew there were political prisoners. But at that time, I hadn't yet heard or seen large crowds of thousands chanting, "Death to the Shah!" or "Death to America!" I had never sensed any underlying rage before, all those times I traveled across the country, including to the most remote villages, or when I visited my relatives in more conservative parts of Tehran. I had no idea then that the world I had grown up in was slowly falling apart.

I was out of work, devastated by my manager's betrayal, and frantically searching for a way to pay off the remainder of Kambiz's boarding school tuition. I didn't feel comfortable asking for money, even from Homayoun. Maybe it was because I never had that support and was always the one carrying my family financially, so it didn't feel right to ask someone else to help carry the burden. And Mahmoud wasn't going to pay for it—he was grappling with his usual debt. I became restless. Besides, I'd barely had any time off since I was three years old. I couldn't sleep. So Homayoun insisted that I try freebase cocaine with him, that it would help me relax.

Just a couple of months earlier, his dealer in Tehran had given him several yellowish rocks, each the size of a piece of popcorn, and told him it was the purest form of cocaine (unlike crack cocaine). I don't think more than a few people in Tehran had ever heard of freebase cocaine when Homayoun smoked it for the first time. He experienced such an intense and euphoric rush that he spent the following months learning how to convert the white powder into those little rocks. I was reluctant to try. I had never even tried regular cocaine, despite it being easily available in Tehran at the time, just like in many cosmopolitan cities around the world, and considered chic in some circles. The idea of snorting it repelled me. But freebase cocaine stirred the same curiosity I had felt when I first tried LSD a few years earlier. One day, I sat down on my chocolate-colored carpet in my living room floor in Velenjak as Homayoun placed one of the tiny rocks onto a piece of aluminum foil. He handed me a straw, also made of aluminum foil, and told me to inhale the smoke once he lit the fire beneath. I never experienced anything like it. I was overwhelmed by an intense feeling of love, from the tips of my toes to the top of my head, followed by a longer-lasting feeling of complete numbness that swept over my mind and body, soothing me like a mother's warm embrace. Homayoun was right. It was the "best high" I had ever experienced. I smoked a couple more times with him, but I often found myself saying no. Deep down, I feared a part of me might never want to leave that state again.

The government declared martial law and imposed a 9 p.m. curfew some twelve days later, on September 7, 1978. That's when I remembered I had some savings in a French bank account in Paris. When Homayoun and I left Iran in late September, I never imagined I would return less than a year later to an Islamic Republic.

Los Angeles, fall 1978

Los Angeles always reminded me of home. Perhaps it was the mixture of hills, the warm weather, or even the heavy traffic. Perhaps it was also because Hollywood played such a large role in shaping my childhood—maybe just a tiny bit more than French and Italian cinema—introducing me to a world of glamour, drama, and adventure. While French and Italian films brought a certain artistry and sophistication, Hollywood's grand narratives and larger-than-life stars captured my imagination. Working in the theater on Lâlehzâr Street ever since I was six or seven, I spent my time in between performances watching American films featuring legends like Charlie Chaplin, Anthony Quinn, Audrey Hepburn, Gregory Peck, and Elizabeth Taylor. I used to collect the film rolls the theaters and cinemas threw away, cutting and gluing the frames in albums I kept secretly under my mattress. Luckily Mouness never got to them. I must have been eight and a half years old when I had first snuck into an editing room, where I quietly watched Gorji Ebadiah precisely cut and paste the positive copy of the film negative, carefully stringing the film *Bim va Omid*. Some kids collected stamps or dolls, I collected film frames.

I was fifteen when I first visited Los Angeles, in 1965—it was my first time traveling abroad. Papa, my orchestra, and I embarked on a tour that took us to London, then New York City, followed by L.A., and finally San Francisco, where I performed for Iranian students studying overseas. As we drove along the highway into L.A., I gazed out the window of the American car and thought of all the Hollywood films I had loved. The magnificent actors and actresses whose outstanding craft had fueled my passion for cinema filled my mind as the city stretched out before me. I looked up to those artists; I wanted to learn how to act on-screen just like them. I even wondered if I would get a chance to see them and ask for their autographs. But that feeling of familiarity and awe disappeared that fall of 1978.

When Pouran first contacted me about doing the opening of their new Cabaret Colbeh in Los Angeles, I remember thinking that I was being given a lifeline. The opening was terrific. The energy in that room was palpable. Both the crowd—made up of Iranians living in or visiting the U.S.—and I instantly forgot all the uncertainty and chaos back home. Pouran and her business partners were thrilled seeing their new business launch with such enthusiasm. As soon as I got offstage, they asked that I perform one more time that week. I agreed, as I needed the money, and I was in no rush to return home, where it was still a mess despite martial law. I performed again later that week, in the overcrowded cabaret, as though we were back in Tehran, forgetting that outside of those doors we were in the U.S. I was just as happy to be back onstage, my comfort zone. One week turned into a couple of months as the situation in Iran continued to deteriorate. Pouran kept her distance from me, and I plunged headfirst into the rabbit hole.

At first, I didn't think much of it when Pouran welcomed us at LAX with a small plastic pouch containing several grams of cocaine that she placed in Homayoun's hand. She had heard from our mutual friends of his newfound interest in freebase cocaine. She was just trying to be hospitable to my boyfriend, I thought. She was my friend, after all. She and her husband, Habib Roshanzadeh, had been so nice in taking me in for those nine months after my separation from Mahmoud in 1972 and had helped me put my life back in order. I trusted her. I asked her to store my prized emerald ring and necklace along with our passports in her L.A. home's safe. I should have known something was wrong when they continued to deliver the same small pouches of cocaine to the apartment hotel they had us staying in, while repeatedly asking me to do another show before they could pay me—it was cheaper for them to put us up in an apartment hotel and to give us these small pouches of coke than to pay my performance fees in full.

Homayoun would freebase the entirety of the small pouch in one stretch and was always desperate for more. Eventually, Pouran's business partners stopped delivering them. Instead, they gave us a little sum, once a week, to cover our basic food needs, which Homayoun mostly used up buying coke from their dealer—one of the sound engineers called Aper was nice enough to bring us food. Twice a week, they would pick me up from our apartment hotel, which was not within walking distance to anything, and drive me to the cabaret, where I was expected to perform. The rest of the time, Homayoun and I stayed in our room. And soon Pouran was nowhere to be found. I knew she was in town, through Aper, and was purposely avoiding me. I had no idea what she did with our passports or my jewelry. At first, I tried to calm myself with my deck of cards, playing solitaire for hours. There was something soothing in the ritual of shuffling the deck, arranging the cards into seven neat piles, and flipping them one by one. But as the days dragged on, stranded in L.A., the turmoil and uncertainty back home began to eat away at my core.

We listened to BBC Persian religiously in our room. We learned that there were more bloody riots across Tehran, despite martial law still being in place—even the news segments in the U.S. closely followed the turmoil. On November 6, a military government was appointed. I was saddened to hear of the arrest of former Prime Minister Hoveyda. He was arrested by the Shah's government—less than two months after I had left for Paris—along with other government figures in what seemed like a desperate attempt by the regime to show that they were aware of the public's growing discontent, and that they were willing to make changes. I couldn't believe that kind man was arrested.

Work hadn't resumed in the entertainment industry and there had been a succession of general strikes, including in the bazaar, universities, banks, and among government workers. By October, the strikes spread to Iran's petroleum industry—the backbone of our nation's economy. Weeks later, BBC Persian reported that millions wept tears of joy across the country after seeing Ayatollah Khomeini's face on the moon—I couldn't make sense of any of it. He emerged as the leading opposition figure to the Shah. I had only heard of Khomeini's name once before, on a work trip in Iraq, several years earlier.

"Do you know Ayatollah Khomeini?" one of the event organizers had asked me. "He's been living in exile in Najaf."

I told him I hadn't, like many Iranians at the time, and he continued with the rest of the local tour.

The more the situation grew increasingly uncertain, the more I became overwhelmed by a sense of helplessness and dread. The cards couldn't distract me from my growing anxiety and restlessness. I needed to get away from everything. But I was like a fish out of water in L.A., with no one to turn to for help. Homayoun was barely holding it together. I didn't know how to call the American police, or what to even say—they would've thought I was crazy. Without money or passports, it felt futile to make a run for it. I couldn't call my brothers, Papa, or Mama. They wouldn't know how to help. And all of my friends back home were busy with their own worries. I felt helpless. So one day, I sat alongside Homayoun in our remote apartment hotel living room, and with nothing to look forward to, I started smoking freebase cocaine. I had already been using sleeping pills to calm my nerves, but only freebase would give me that feeling of numbness that drowned out my pain and anxiety. At first, I was careful not to smoke in the hours leading up to my performance. I could go long stretches without it, since my body wasn't dependent on cocaine, and unlike Homayoun, I never smoked alone—only when I was with him. But as time went by, even onstage I gradually performed more on autopilot mode. I smoked more. Gradually, I lost my appetite and desire to sleep, slipping deeper into the rabbit hole. I stopped listening to music, and singing on my own, something I had always done naturally, like breathing. I only smoked and played solitaire. I was barely alive.

One night, about two months into our stay, as I was getting changed in the back room of the cabaret before my performance, I noticed a cold breeze coming in through the small window. When I tried to close it, I pushed too hard, and my hand went straight through the glass pane. I saw the blood gushing everywhere, but I was expected onstage, so I grabbed a white table napkin that lay nearby and tied it around my wrist. A few songs into my performance I felt my knees were about to give in, so I sat on the edge of the stage and continued to sing, something I never did before. After one of the guests saw the large bloodstains on the napkin, I was rushed to the hospital—some people said that I had attempted suicide. When my friend Jaleh Khajenoori heard about this incident all the way in New York City, she had her friends come to my rescue. I had met Jaleh through Behrouz, they were good friends, and we always got along because of her terrific sense of humor. Her friends, Bahman, a powerful businessman, and Parviz Kohan, owner of the NYC discotheque called Darvish, immediately hopped on an L.A.-bound plane and came to my rescue. Bahman wasted no time in demanding our passports and my earnings from Pouran's business partners. They knew better than to mess with Bahman. They immediately handed over our travel documents and part of my earnings to him. Bahman even managed to retrieve my jewelry from their cocaine dealer.

I felt a wave of relief the next day on our flight to New York City, grateful that the nightmare was finally over. Or so I thought.

New York City, late December 1978

It was a cold winter morning. I left the bedroom as Homayoun was busy mixing his latest batch of coke with ammonia. I was smoking a little less these days, relying instead on my deck of cards and cigarettes to get by. Even though I still didn't know when I was going back home, I felt a little better in NYC, where at least I had my passport, a real fixed income, and a friend, Jaleh, whom I could count on. As soon as we got here, Jaleh and Bahman helped us book a suite on the twentieth floor at the Sheraton Hotel, on Seventh Avenue between 55th and 56th Streets—Jaleh was also staying in the same hotel.

I lit my third or fourth cigarette of the morning and wandered over to the living room window, watching snowflakes gently drift down twenty stories onto the busy streets of NYC. The city hadn't changed much since my first visit on my world tour at fifteen. I remembered that first time, walking in between the city's towering skyscrapers, through Central Park, and past the various public landmarks, feeling the vibrancy and sophistication of NYC that I had seen in films like *Breakfast at Tiffany's*, starring one of the greatest, Audrey Hepburn. Each corner of the city seemed almost magical and full of promise, which the film captured so well in all of Holly Golightly's adventures across Manhattan. But I had no energy to go for a walk or leave our hotel suite, except for that one night a week when I performed at Parviz Kohan's discotheque. I had taken Parviz's offer to perform there once a week, and whatever money was left after we paid the hotel bill and other basic needs, Homayoun spent on cocaine.

Below, cars drove swiftly along the snowy avenue, while a few pedestrians bravely pierced through the cold. I wondered who they were, what their lives were like. As I looked at the tiny figures below, my mind drifted thousands of miles away to home. Listening to BBC Persian and speaking to my mother, I knew the situation wasn't improving, with more violent riots during the month of Muharram (which this year, 1978, fell on the month of December). There were reports that more than 2 million people marched in the streets of Tehran on Tasu'a and Ashura, the two most ceremonious days of Muharram, calling for the Shah to step down. Some claimed Ayatollah Khomeini was the rightful leader. No one knew what was going to happen, but everyone knew the growing tension wasn't going to disappear. It was still unclear when I could return and start working again. But I didn't want to think about it. Kambiz was going to land at JFK in a couple of hours.

Kambiz was joining me for his two-week Christmas vacation. There was too much uncertainty to send him to Tehran to be with his father or with Papa. And even though I knew this wasn't the healthiest environment for him, there was no other choice. I convinced myself that if I kept him busy outside, then at least he wouldn't be exposed to the drugs and chaos that defined life with Homayoun.

I had always wanted to be the best mother I could be to Kambiz, but it was very difficult. Like many other women around the world, I worked all the way through the ninth month of my pregnancy. I worked as a TV host during the day and performed at the cabaret late at night. When he was born, on November 13, 1968, I was only eighteen years old and struggled, like many women, with the challenges of being a young mother while also pursuing a demanding career. Even Mahmoud and his brother were adamant that I start performing as soon as possible at their Cabaret Miami. My act brought them more guests and they needed the added revenue to pay off some of their larger debt. I had no other choice but to leave my two-month-old baby in the hands of his nanny and my mother-in-law. I breastfed Kambiz for a couple of months until I wasn't producing milk. After that, I worked nonstop. Everyone depended on me.

I was away for most of his first year, and even missed his very first birthday. Mahmoud and I were frequently traveling to Paris, hoping to launch my career there. In our absence, the entire family had thrown Kambiz a birthday party in Tehran, showering him with love and attention. Everyone adored him, not to mention he was my parents' first grandchild. But whenever I looked back at the pictures of that day, it hurt to see the little frown on his face. I could tell he was upset I wasn't there.

I would never forget my first terrifying experience as a mother. His first nanny was an older provincial lady we had met through a mutual acquaintance. When I returned for a few weeks from Paris, Kambiz appeared weaker than usual. I went to the pharmacy to pick up some medication and the pharmacist told me, "Your nanny came last week to pick up your medication." I didn't know what he was talking about.

"You know, the sleeping pills."

Suddenly, my heart dropped. The nanny was giving Kambiz sleeping pills to avoid any hassle. I ran home and fired her immediately. She denied everything, but weeks later, Kambiz was back to his old energetic self. After that terrifying incident, I would only entrust Kambiz with my mother-in-law when I was away. When I got the record deal with Eddie Barclay in Paris, I took Kambiz with me. He was only two years old.

As he got older and more mischievous, I found myself losing patience with him more often than when raising my half brother Fariborz. Trouble was, I was often exhausted from work and usually irritated by something Mahmoud had done (his philandering). And after Mahmoud and I divorced, I did my best to be around Kambiz as much as possible. I even accepted

Mahmoud's offer to perform nightly at Cabaret Miami while he was still trashing me in the media just so I could see Kambiz before he went to bed.

But between my singing and acting careers, my hectic schedule made it hard for me to be there for him most of the time. Mahmoud was also busy, so Kambiz was often with my mother, and sometimes with Papa, who absolutely cherished him. Papa would make Kambiz laugh, and he spoiled my son like he had never done with me or any of my siblings. Despite all of the love around him, at times I felt Kambiz needed more stability. So when my neighbors spoke highly of their children's boarding school in Switzerland, one of the world's most prestigious and expensive, attended by future kings and world leaders, including our own Shah, I knew I had to send Kambiz there. I wanted to offer him the best education money could buy, and I thought that he would benefit immensely from that environment, away from all of the media gossip around me and Behrouz. He was eight or nine when he started at Le Rosey.

When I last visited him in Switzerland—shortly after I left Iran in September and weeks before I went to L.A.—I was so happy to see all the progress he was making. He was ten years old. He looked just like me at his age, with his big brown eyes and his arched eyebrows—but luckily he was a tall boy.

"Mama, look, this is my bed! I make it every morning!" he said, running to the side of his dormitory bed.

His room that he shared with his classmate was neat and orderly, something he refused to do back home. Back home, Kambiz always had someone doing everything for him. He was spoiled, and even famous in his own right, as the good-luck charm of one of our top national football teams—Taj, later known as Esteghlal—since the team often won their games whenever he attended the matches. I could see how much he had grown and matured over the past two years. Later that day, I joined him and his little classmates in their cooking class. They had a professional chef teaching them basic cooking skills. I felt a lump growing in my throat as I watched him follow the instructions. I was so proud of him, but also filled with guilt at the same time, as I didn't know how I was going to pay the rest of his tuition.

Luckily I now had enough left from my earnings from Colbeh to pay for the entire school year.

Before I picked up Kambiz at JFK, I needed to clean the mess in our suite. Homayoun wouldn't let the housekeeper do her job, convinced that she would steal his cocaine. A couple of times, when the housekeeper knocked on the door, he locked himself in the bathroom, yelling that the police were here for him. There was also one time, several weeks earlier, when his behavior really puzzled me. After one of the hotel's staff members slipped a bill in an envelope under our door, Homayoun jumped up from the couch and said:

"Who are these people sneaking into our garden and leaving letters?"

"What are you talking about?" I asked.

"Go see who they are!"

He gazed at the door as though he could see through it. I picked up the envelope and showed him the bill.

"See, it's just our bill," I said as Homayoun sat back down, all the while keeping a wary eye on the door. "Someone from the hotel staff brought it for us."

He hadn't hallucinated since.

After I cleared the trash and crumpled aluminum foil from the living room table and hid the pipe in the bedroom, Aper showed up. He was the same kind, Armenian sound engineer from L.A. who was accompanying me to JFK airport. We arrived just as the air hostess was bringing Kambiz through the gate.

"Mama!" Kambiz cried, running into my arms.

I held him tight, fighting back my tears, hoping that he wouldn't notice his mother's pain. "Let me have a look at you!" I said. "You're almost my height! Come, we have so much to see!"

This was Kambiz's first trip to the U.S. and I wanted him to enjoy himself. He had learned English while attending Rustam Abadian International School in Tehran, so I thought he would get some good practice speaking it on this trip.

We dropped off his suitcase at the hotel, where he quickly met

Homayoun for the first time. Homayoun greeted him before retreating into the bedroom, where he would spend most of his time during the next fourteen days. Despite my exhaustion, I took Kambiz outside almost immediately.

Kambiz was amazed by the city, the honking yellow taxis, the skyscrapers that seemed to touch the clouds, and the New Yorkers who rushed past us in every direction. His eyes shined as we walked around, entering stores filled with toys and gadgets, and stopping somewhere for some good old-fashioned American fast food—a slice of pizza, a hot dog, or a hamburger. That was just the first day.

During his entire stay, Kambiz didn't say a word to me about Homayoun, about this new man in my life. Kambiz was like me in many ways. He kept everything inside. He must have wondered why Homayoun stayed in the bedroom all the time. Perhaps he could tell that this man wasn't doing well. Perhaps he could tell that I wasn't doing very well, either, despite all the efforts I made to act normal. Perhaps he worried for me as he sat quietly in front of the television—children are aware of everything, even when they choose to keep quiet. He must have known something was going on. He must have caught a glimpse or two of Homayoun smoking freebase when the bedroom door was left wide open. But I didn't know what to say to him. I couldn't even understand what was going on myself. I simply tried to keep him away from our suite as much as I could. We would only come back after dinner. And before going to sleep, the two of us would lie on his little bed in the living room and watch something on the television, like the Bionic Man or the Incredible Hulk. We spent the rest of the time outside, in those cold wintery days, walking, eating at fast-food restaurants, and sightseeing.

One afternoon, Kambiz, Aper, and I went to Rockefeller Center. Kambiz was thrilled to join the other kids on the ice-skating rink. Aper went with him while I watched from the freezing sidelines of the arena. They were doing great, gliding along with the other skaters in a steady circular motion, their faces lit with excitement and concentration. I wouldn't have lasted a second, and the last thing I needed was a broken bone. A part of me was happy to see my child smiling and playing just like the other kids. But another part of me felt like I was standing on the edge of a precipice, looking down, knowing that any moment I was going to fall. I tried to push those feelings away, but they were always there, like vultures, following a wounded animal.

Kambiz really wanted to see the newly released *Superman*, starring Marlon Brando, Gene Hackman, and Christopher Reeve. So one night we went to watch it in the theater with Aper. For more than two hours, we were transported into a fantastical world where an alien orphan, sent from a dying planet to Earth, discovers his superpowers, and uses them for good helping others. I watched the large screen with the same big eyes as Kambiz. We soared through the sky with Superman, leaving behind all our worries. I also enjoyed seeing Marlon Brando play Superman's biological father, Jor-El—what a phenomenal actor! The little girl in me watched in awe as Christopher Reeve's iconic character flew across the sky, tirelessly battling villains. *If only someone could rescue me*, I thought. We left the theater that night with a sense of excitement, something I hadn't felt in a long time.

When our two weeks together came to an end, I tried to hand Kambiz over to the air hostess at his flight's gate. But he held my hand tightly as tears streamed down from his innocent eyes.

"Mama, please don't send me back!" he said, sobbing in between words. "I wanna stay with you! Please, Mama!"

I could barely breathe with the huge lump in my throat. He couldn't stay with us in that suite, in that hell. And I couldn't afford to move to Switzerland with him.

"Kambiz jân," I said, kissing his forehead, "you've got to go back to school. I promise, it'll go by so fast. We'll be back together in Tehran in no time!"

But I had no idea when I would be returning to Tehran. Everything was hanging, frozen in the air. The pain in his eyes broke my heart. When we finally got him to follow the air hostess, I felt a sharp pain, as though a piece of my flesh was being torn away. I went back to our suite that afternoon and smoked for the first time in a while with Homayoun.

New York City, late April 1979

Homayoun finally collapsed on the couch in the hotel suite's living room with the glass pipe nearby. *He hasn't slept in two days*, I thought as I stared out of the window, my eyes fixed on Seventh Avenue, twenty floors below.

Jump.

I remembered my first trip to NYC and falling immediately for its charm, with its unique hustle and bustle as well as its unapologetic passion for art and music. But I couldn't see any of this anymore. I couldn't see past this messy dark room with empty take-out boxes piled by the door, past the frighteningly thin and pale figure covered in bruises, with dark circles around lifeless eyes staring blankly at me in the window's reflection. *Jump*.

Months had gone by since we had checked into the Sheraton Hotel, and God only knew when we would check out. A lot had changed in the meantime. The Shah and the Shahbânu had left Iran on January 16, 1979. I remembered getting up that day, sometime around noon, and hearing the news on BBC Persian radio.

Officially, the royal couple had gone on vacation. The reporter added that millions were seen cheering in the streets of Tehran, celebrating the Shah's departure while calling for the return of Ayatollah Khomeini. Khomeini had been living in exile in France, where he had been granted refuge after being expelled from Iraq, his first place of exile. *The Shah and Shahbânu left Iran*, I said to myself as a wave of unease washed over me. My stomach churned, and although I couldn't fully explain why, deep down I felt that what was coming wasn't going to be good for people like me. They left and never returned. Ayatollah Khomeini did, however, on February 11, 1979.

Soon after, the Shah's regime, led by Prime Minister Shapour Bakhtiar, collapsed. Days later we learned through the newspaper *Kayhan*, newly confiscated by the revolutionaries, that some members of the former regime had been executed, including Imperial Army generals. The paper published horrifying pictures taken at the morgue, exhibiting the mutilated, naked, and lifeless bodies of these once powerful men. By April 1, Iran had become the Islamic Republic of Iran. And Googoosh was persona non grata, with rumors circulating that I was a SAVAK agent.

I was devastated on April 7, when I heard the radio broadcaster reporting the chilling details of the execution of Prime Minister Hoveyda by the revolutionary government. I couldn't believe it. After the Imperial Army declared neutrality under Prime Minister Bakhtiar, Hoveyda had the opportunity to flee. He was being held in a secure SAVAK safe house when his guards eventually abandoned their posts. Before leaving, they handed him his car keys and a pistol for self-protection, and left the doors unlocked—giving him every chance to escape. But, instead, he decided to present himself to the Islamic Revolutionary Court, believing that since he had done nothing wrong and since it was an Islamic court, he would be fairly tried and released. He was sentenced to death in a mock trial, not long after a disgusting pseudo-interview conducted in his cell by the Belgian-born journalist Christine Ockrent. My heart ached when I thought of him alone in his cell, waiting for the firing squad. This was the man who had called to check on me at Mehr Hospital, the man who had helped me at one of my most vulnerable moments. He had even sent me flowers after I had given birth to Kambiz in 1968. He didn't deserve this fate. Cold beads of sweat trickled down my neck as I looked below.

Large clouds loomed over Manhattan. Rain poured down with no end in sight. I could barely breathe because of my bruised rib cage, let alone lift my arm to grab the window handle. Everything hurt. As I painfully turned the lock, my eyes caught the fresh scar at the base of my left hand, just above my wrist—a reminder of that deep cut from the night I almost collapsed onstage at Cabaret Colbeh in Los Angeles. I took a deep breath. I opened the large window. Raindrops splattered over me and the carpet, while shocks of pain reverberated throughout my body, shocks that I felt even in my teeth. Homayoun couldn't remember what he had done to me less than forty-eight hours before. How could he, being possessed like that?

I had just returned to the suite from doing my closing act at Darvish. Homayoun was shouting nonsense in the bedroom. I shuddered. He smoked with me, alone, and with others, morning and night, as much as his body would let him before shutting down. I had never seen him like this. I knew he loved to party. But at least back home he worked, he had responsibilities running Hafez, the insurance agency franchise that he co-owned, and he was held accountable by his family. His snobby mother once told me that she regretted her son hadn't married the girl she had introduced him to, the one from a "similarly" noble family. Instead, her son had picked Googoosh.

I took off my coat and my shoes by the main door when I came home that night, and quietly picked up the trash—he still wouldn't let the housekeepers in; he was now convinced that they had been hired to kill him. It was around midnight. *If only he could see this*, I had thought, remembering the Homayoun I had lived with just six months ago, the Homayoun who would wipe down any seat as soon as its occupier got up.

I was running out of bags, having already filled up three. As I looked around the living room, sure there was one lying around somewhere, Homayoun flung the bedroom door wide open and charged through. His eyes were filled with murderous rage.

I had never seen him like this, and before I knew it, he lunged right at me. He punched and kicked me with all his might. He had a brown belt in karate.

"It's me! Googoosh!" I tried to shout.

He wouldn't stop. My body couldn't take the pounding. I fell to the ground. He paused mid-motion, his gaze turning blank. He then turned around, with his back toward me, and started shouting nonsense again. I crept to my feet. All I could see was an unopened can of tuna within arm's reach on the coffee table. I grabbed it right as he was turning to face me. Just as he was about to pounce on me again, I whacked him across the head. The sound of the tin can hitting his skull resonated across the room.

He backed off, with no sign of blood. Then he sat quietly on the couch with a blank look on his face. Not a move.

I grabbed my coat and my shoes and ran for my life. The next thing I knew, I was sitting on a bench in Central Park, in the dark. I was freezing and I couldn't move. The slightest effort felt as though he were kicking and punching me all over again. I wasn't even angry with Homayoun. Despite everything, I knew that he was risking a lot to be with me, now that Googoosh had become a public enemy back home. He was clearly here for me, not for Googoosh, not for the fame. I knew he loved me, even though the drugs had brought out his inner demons, demons found within every single one of us. I hated myself. I despised that person sitting on the bench, that skeletal figure huddled in a ball. She was weak, pitiful. She wasn't a mother, a lover, a friend, or an artist. She wasn't me. She wasn't Googoosh. She had given in to her inner demons, demons that I had to get rid of once and for all. *Fucking jump!*

As I now gazed down twenty floors to the bustling chaos of Seventh Avenue, the rain splattering against my face through the wide-open window, I felt as if my body were already plunging into the abyss below. I felt the rush, the relief. Then, I saw Kambiz's face.

I remembered his amazement at the blaring yellow taxis and towering skyscrapers. I remembered the sparkle in my boy's eyes as we strolled into the city's iconic toy store or as he skated around the world-famous ice rink with Aper. I remembered how we watched *Superman* and how we both felt like we soared through the sky, leaving all of our worries behind. I remembered how we would go to the suite at night and watch TV, pretending that everything was normal on that twentieth floor, as well as back home. I remembered those innocent eyes that had been filled with tears at JFK airport at the end of his visit, how he wouldn't let go of my hand and cried, "I wanna stay with you! Please, Mama!"

Looking down at Seventh Avenue, I remembered feeling that sharp pain when I had finally got him to follow the flight attendant. What would they tell him if I went through with this? That I'd abandoned him? That I'd selfishly killed myself after becoming a junkie, a junkie that sleeps in Central Park?

I wasn't the mother he may have wished for, the one who would always stay by his side, the one who would choose him over her career, or the one who would always choose him over her demons. But he was my son. I loved him with all my heart, and I couldn't do that to him. He needed to grow

In Papa's arms, when I was about two or three.

Papa and Uncle Nader in their dance outfits, early 1950s.

One of my earliest performances with Papa, sometime in late 1952 or early 1953.

My mother, Nasrin, in her twenties.

In Esfahan, at age six or seven, posing at one of Papa's friends' homes, dressed in his friend's wife's oversize dress, clutching her purse and already showing off my early love for head wraps.

Papa and me performing the comedic and romantic operetta *Arshin Mal-Alan* in Azeri Turkish when I was about five years old.

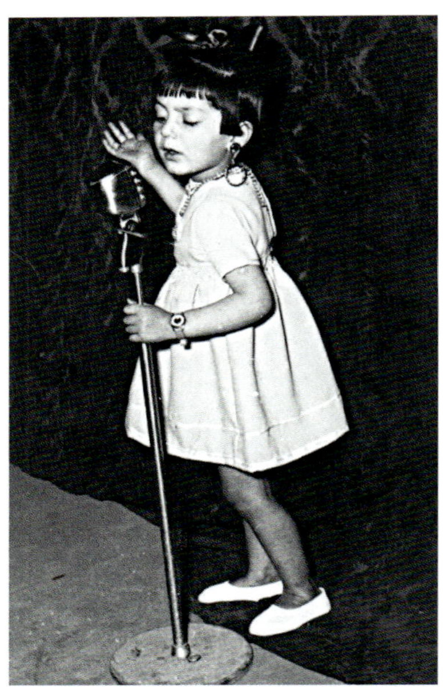

Singing in a theater in Esfahan, around 1954 or 1955.

In Esfahan, circa 1955 or 1956, with our troupe, proudly holding the certificates for our silver cup prize in recognition of our performances. Papa stands behind me in his light-colored suit jacket.

From left to right: Mehrdad and Fariborz at Fariborz's seventh birthday party. For years they believed they were just good friends.

Mama and me when she first came back into my life, 1955.

Dancing the Azeri Ghafghâzi at Parvin Ghaffari's birthday in 1956 or 1957—she is in the floral black dress.

Posing with Mouness and Papa when I was six or seven years old. They were likely engaged at the time, though I didn't know since Papa took many photos with beautiful women.

With my dearest Mahboubeh—Bahbah—for my uncle Farhang's wedding, sometime around 1958 or 1959. That's Fery's head peeking over my shoulder.

At twelve years old, dressed in a boy's red tuxedo, singing at the luxurious Darband Hotel perched above Tehran.

I was sixteen here, performing at Couchinie around Christmas 1966, singing in English and Italian with Beppe Flavi.

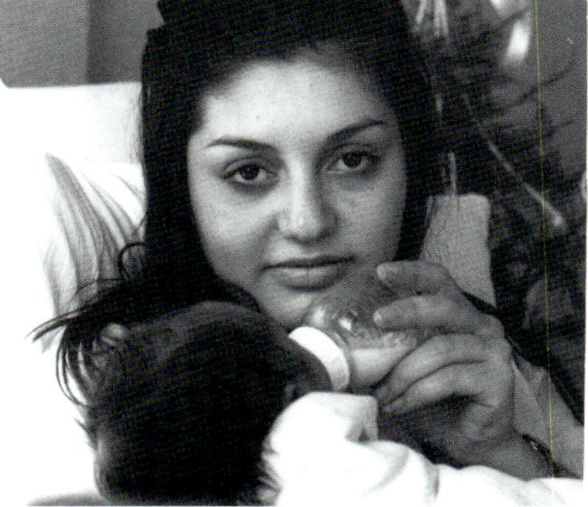

Shortly after Kambiz's birth, November 13, 1968—his first bottle, my full heart.

In Paris in 1969 or 1970, before my record deal with Eddie Barclay, when I was performing with my band on the first floor of the Eiffel Tower.

Posing at a photographer's atelier in Tehran, likely in 1969.

With Eddie Barclay at his home in Paris, 1970.

Meeting the legendary French singer Charles Aznavour in Tehran during his visit in 1969.

In Paris, recording a French song for Barclay's record label, 1970.

Comforting Kambiz outside Notre-Dame de Paris, 1970.

Performing at Tehran's Cabaret Baccara n 1970 with three French backup singers I had recently worked with at the MIDEM festival in Cannes.

In Las Vegas in 1972, shortly before the end of my U.S. tour and the start of my RCA recording session in Rome. From left to right: Iranian singer Martik, me, Mahmoud, and musician Andranik Madadian.

Kambiz and me in front of the Trevi Fountain in 1972.

Fery and me in 1973, exploring Capri and Naples shortly after my divorce from Mahmoud.

Receiving the Sepâs award for my lead role in *Bita* in 1973, shortly after my return from my one-month stay in Paris.

Meeting Federico Fellini at the recording studio in Rome in 1972, during my time working with RCA Italiana.

Performing at Cabaret Miami in 1972, following my divorce from Mahmoud. I'm wearing a beautiful woolen burnous I had bought on my first trip to Tunis.

One of the two nights I performed in Dhofar (Zaffār) in 1973 or 1974, for our Iranian soldiers sent by the Shah to support the Sultanate of Oman against a separatist Marxist group.

Playful photoshoots from 1972 to 1974.

Papa lovingly embraces Kambiz at Cabaret Miami, in what was likely 1973.

Photoshoot with my brother Fery. Tehran, 1974.

Performing in 1974 at a special event at the Tehran Royal Hotel.

Filming of *Shab-e Gharibân* (Nostalgic Night) in Tehran, 1974.

Backstage at Cabaret Baccara, around the time we were filming *Mamal Amricayi* (1975).

At the presidential palace in Tunisia in 1975, for President Habib Bourguiba's birthday bash.

Behrouz and me watching Ray Charles perform at the International Festival of Carthage in Tunisia, 1975.

At Cabaret Vanak with Behrouz after my performance.

During the filming of *Nazanin* in 1975.

Performing at a fashion show at one of Tehran's international hotels, 1975.

Performing alongside Martik at Cabaret Vanak in 1975.

At Fery's *aghd* (marriage ceremony) in 1975. From left to right: Mama, me, Monir (the bride), Fery, and Papa.

Performing in Cannes at the famous Palm Beach Casino in the summer of 1978, before my world was turned upside down.

Performing at a wedding in Tehran sometime in 1976.

At a dinner party in Tehran, summer of 1979, with Homayoun to my right and actor Akbar Abdi to my left. Television director Masoud Forootan is in front of lighting director Ebi Pâsdâr in the lower right corner.

This picture was taken shortly before my unofficial arrest at Mr. Mesbahzadeh's home in September 1980.

At a friend's home in the months following my release from the unofficial prison on Vozarâ Street.

Kambiz and me in Velenjak, late 1979.

Kambiz and me in Velenjak eighteen months later—most likely on one of my darker days.

At Daryâ Kenâr with Homayoun in the early 1980s.

Sitting in the upstairs TV room of my home in Velenjak in 1986.

Kambiz with Mama in Tehran, early 1980s. She's watched him grow through the years, always with that same quiet love.

Winter of 1988 at Iran's Dizin Ski Resort during my stay with Maryam and Hossein.

Sharing a quiet moment with my dear brother Mehrdad in my rental apartment sometime in the early 1990s.

Masoud Kimiai and me in Europe in 2000 during my comeback world tour.

Masoud and me in Cuba during a one-month break in my comeback tour imposed by the promoters due to the optics of performing during Ramadan; he used the time to scout film locations.

A memorable moment in London in 2011—performing live on TV for the first time in more than thirty years on Manoto TV's *Googoosh Music Academy*, broadcast into Iranian homes via satellite. The talented contestants from that season are standing around me. *Photo by Sina Tehrani for Manoto*

Seeing the Shahbânu in Paris, 2016.

Dining with my siblings Joseph and Roya at a restaurant in LA, summer

A night out with Kambiz and my grandchildren, Daara and Mya, in LA, summer 2017.

In Toronto, reunited with my two brothers: Fariborz to my left, and Adel to my right.

May 12, 2018. An unforgettable night at the iconic Hollywood Bowl. *Photo by Payam Arzani*

up in a world where his mother faced her fears, even if it meant standing before a firing squad.

I stepped back from the window and then collapsed on the wet floor. The next day I asked Jaleh for help. She drove me to her sister Marzieh's place in Long Island, where I spent two weeks sobering up. When I came back to Manhattan, I told Homayoun that I had to go back home, that I would rather die in my homeland at the hands of zealous revolutionaries than dying little by little, day after day, in exile.

Within a week, we left NYC and landed in London with Homayoun's brother-in-law, Moussa, a flight engineer for Iran Air. Initially the plan had been for us to stay in the UK while the dust settled back home, but I couldn't wait any longer. Moussa promised Homayoun that he would help get me through the airport, while Homayoun stayed behind. There was no point in putting him in danger for Googoosh. If all went well he would get on the next flight.

I wore my favorite checkered pantsuit and got on a flight to Tehran less than twenty-four hours later. My heart raced at takeoff. None of the passengers would look at each other. The silence was heavy, filled with the unspoken tension of returning to a changed, uncertain world. My stomach sank when the captain informed us of our descent. I closed my eyes, and for an instant, I felt as though I were falling off my seat at forty thousand feet. I felt the cold air and gravity pushing and pulling me down toward the ground. I opened my eyes and took a deep breath.

As we landed, I prayed to God to give me the strength to face my fate with courage and grace. I then waited in my seat for Moussa, who was still in the cockpit, as the last passengers slowly disembarked the plane. I imagined finding the Revolutionary Guards waiting for me with their rifles on the tarmac. I could barely breathe.

"Follow me," Moussa said.

I made out the shapes of the last few passengers on the tarmac, lagging behind with their suitcases. *They must be waiting for me inside*, I thought. We walked swiftly toward the entrance of Mehrabad Airport, the same one I had left from all those months ago. Inside, we avoided all eye contact with others until we reached Passport Control. A man sat behind the counter, wearing a camouflage uniform with a gun strapped to his waist. He was a Revolutionary Guard. I took another deep breath and then handed him my passport as calmly as I could. He glanced at the page with my picture and then at me. His gaze lingered.

"Look what we have here," he uttered with a sinister grin. "A dead woman walking!"

I felt my heart in my throat. *This is it*, I thought. I had been preparing myself for this moment. Moussa stepped in.

"Bahram jân," he said to the Revolutionary Guard, "listen, she's under my supervision. I've been asked to personally escort her directly home."

"Wait here," the guard said to me, seemingly indifferent to Moussa.

He then left with my passport. Moussa looked at me nervously and tried to reassure me with a wink. I imagined a group of Revolutionary Guards stomping in with their large Kalashnikovs. I wondered how my mother would find out. I thought of Kambiz and how I had promised him that we would see each other soon.

The same Revolutionary Guard returned minutes later.

He handed me my passport, open on the page with the official entrance stamp.

"*Khâhar* [Sister], you're free to go," he said in a surprisingly kind tone.

I couldn't believe it. He pointed to my luggage and asked someone to help load the taxi outside.

"You should've worn a headscarf or covered your face with a fake mustache or a beard or something," he added.

"But I don't have a fake mustache," I said.

He looked at my neck.

"Put that scarf around your head and hide your face. You know, people are in a revolutionary mood, too much excitement in the air, if someone recognizes you, who knows what they'll do . . ."

Moussa took me straight to my mother's, where I learned the next day that it was Bahram's superior, Masoud Fardmanesh, who had given the clearance for me to walk out of the airport. The same Masoud Fardmanesh who had written the beautiful lyrics of my song "*Ma Be Ham Nemiresim*" (We Will Never Be Together). He had become the representative of the attorney general of Mehrabad Airport and the commander of the Revolutionary Guards located at the airport. I knew it was God's doing, sending an angel like him to help me that day, for without him, surely I would have been a dead woman walking.

Had I known I would be sitting in this basement, a little more than a year later, would I have still gotten on that flight to Tehran?

Chapter 10

Nahid

From the little window, I could see the wind was gusting over the cherry tree, bending its branches with its green and yellow leaves every which way on this late afternoon. Marjan was resting beside me as I watched the invisible waves knocking the reddish-brown branches back and forth, up and down. The leaves shuddered in submission. They didn't fight back. They accepted their plight, all the physical torment they were subjected to. Perhaps they already knew it wouldn't last forever. Or perhaps they had simply given up.

Two days passed, and neither Marjan nor I had been taken upstairs. Neither one of us knew what they really wanted from us. I had answered all their questions, I had given them everything they wanted, my passport, the deed to my house, my career, and my voice. I had surrendered. I had nothing. They had everything. What more did they want?

As the wind slowly dwindled, the branches and their leaves swayed peacefully once more.

Abolfazl appeared not long after, pulling on the curtain on the other side of our steel-barred door. I never thought I would be relieved by his presence. He cleared his throat as he turned the key in the lock and then recited the same instructions from yesterday, reminding us that he wouldn't be too far. He then entered the cell, where he stood still, glancing hesitantly at us, always careful not to look directly into our eyes. He seemed to be waiting for something, a response perhaps. I wanted to know if I could call Mama to check on her and Kambiz. I hadn't been allowed to use the phone since I had arrived, nor had Marjan. Neither of us had had any contact with the outside world—for all we knew Saddam Hussein's tanks were less than a hundred miles away from Tehran. But I didn't ask him that. Instead, just as he turned around to leave, I blurted out, "We're all going to get sick from that bathroom." I had nothing to lose. "So will the guards," I quickly added.

He stood quietly as I spoke of the health hazards of the filth and the flies. All I could hear was Marjan clasping her hands on her lap. I couldn't tell if he was thinking or whether he was getting ready to burst out in anger. He then timidly glanced over at Marjan before exiting the cell.

Marjan and I rushed to the bathroom despite everything. My bladder was filling up so quickly these last two days, and as I learned, we only had access four times a day (the fourth time was right after the dinner trays were collected).

Our trip was fast—you could hardly breathe in that stench—and the rest of the basement's inmates were not long behind. Soon enough, Zari, Fahimeh, Niloufar, and some of the others joined us in our cell. They were wearing the same clothes as yesterday, just like Marjan and I, and they were just as desperate for some distractions as we were.

Zari with the polka-dot headscarf sat in the same spot as yesterday, below the window, and Mojgan with her bright-colored headscarf next to her. The others sat or stood wherever they could. Niloufar quietly leaned against the wall to the side. Zari handed me a cigarette.

"Can I have one?" one of her cellmates whispered.

"Me too!"

Zari counted her cigarettes. There were more than yesterday. I wondered where she was getting them.

"You're each only getting one more today," she said to them before passing around the pack.

"Have you been upstairs with Afshoun?" one of the women asked Marjan and me with a thick Shirazi accent.

"Haven't you paid any attention?" Zari asked. "Always asleep, these Shirazis," she added with a half smile and a raised brow. "Too lazy to get up."

Tehran was a big melting pot with people moving in from different regions across the country. It was customary in our culture to make playful jokes about regional stereotypes—these playful exchanges played a part in bringing people together across provincial lines, creating some national unity. For example, Azeri Turks are sometimes called stubborn or strong-willed, while those from Shiraz in the south are often depicted as laid-back and fond of poetry and relaxation. Tehranis, on the other hand, might be teased for being cosmopolitan and pretentious. Of course, it required careful balance to ensure the jokes didn't become mean-spirited. I knew most of the unflattering jokes on Azeri Turks, and Mouness liked to repeat their punch lines, and only the punch lines, whenever she felt like belittling Papa.

The Shirazi woman laughed.

"What am I supposed to do? I'm always stuck in that corner, I can barely move," she said.

There were many women in their cell. They couldn't turn in their sleep unless they all turned at the same time.

"And," she continued, "I can't hear anything with all the howling next door!"

These cries of agony had never ceased since I first stepped into the basement, ringing out night and day. It sounded like a handful of people, men and women, though the female cries were closer. I wondered if these women had any idea who they were and what they had gone through. You could drown out the yelling momentarily in the day with chatter, the comings and goings of the guards, the walks to and from the bathroom, or Nahid shouting in the corridor. But they were still there. Everyone could hear them.

Zari's half smile disappeared.

"You'd be howlin', too, if you'd been in Aghdas's shoes," she fired back in her thick Tehrani accent before flicking the ashes into the cup of her palm. "Thrown in like that into that hellhole of a cell, after first sayin' they were gonna kill her?!"

The room hushed. Who were they talking about? Who was Aghdas? Just then, I remembered my first night in this cell, waking up to the guard shouting at someone in the corridor.

"Don't stop! Walk faster, you piece of shit! You think you're tough, huh? I'll get you to spit it out soon enough, you kessâfat*!"*

There were three cells in our wing, the girls explained. There was the cell that Marjan and I were in, located at the entrance of our corridor, right next to the bathroom, then there was the one Zari and the girls were in, and a third one at the end of the corridor, where all of the drug addicts were locked up in (mostly heroin and opium addicts). They had all been subjected to forced withdrawal without any medical care or unlimited access to the bathroom.

"It's hell in there!" Mojgan whispered.

They explained that the cries were coming from there.

"It's pitch-black, all day long—the guards never open the curtains," Fahimeh said quietly. "They've got no air, and the girls are forced to lay in their filth, since no one comes to clean up."

I felt sick to my stomach. Fahimeh's eyes were reddened with rage, while Niloufar's tears symbolized our collective horror.

Just then Nahid, with her adolescent frame, delicate features, and long curly hair barely covered by a ruby headscarf, fumed into the cell.

"He thinks he can scare me with his threats? He thinks I care what my father says? They can both go to hell!" she shouted.

"What happened, Nahid?" the girls asked in a hushed voice, hoping she would lower hers.

"What did Afshoun say?" Zari asked.

"He said that my dumb, good-for-nothing father wants me dead," Nahid said.

"He's lying!" one of the girls said.

"No, he's not. Not about this," Nahid answered as she jerked the silk scarf off her head. "I watched my father with my own eyes begging the

Komiteh to kill me. He always wanted me dead. He always said God had cursed him with a daughter instead of a son. Why else would he wanna marry me off to a disgusting old man?"

She briefly looked over at Marjan and me. I could see why the guards fell for her. She had a doe-eyed prettiness about her that made her look vulnerable, like a beautiful damsel in distress, but also a magnetic gaze that pulled in everyone's attention.

"Afshoun said that if I'd beg for my father's forgiveness and obey his wishes, then he'd consider letting me go."

"What did you say?" they asked her.

"I told him I'd rather die here," she replied, loud enough for the guards to hear. She was the only one who didn't control her voice—even Zari, the tough one, mostly kept her voice down. Nahid paused as she looked down at her thin headscarf, now crumpled between her fingers. She then turned her captivating hazel eyes toward us and said, "Saddam will probably beat 'em to it and bomb Tehran!"

Nahid was a teenage girl, perhaps only an inch or so taller than me, with long lashes and pink cheeks, but she didn't sound like one. She sounded more like a *gardan koloft*, literally translating to "thick neck," meaning a thug ringleader, but one who protects the weak. She had the same *på'in-e shahr* accent, with the same intonations and expressions of the many *gardan kolofts* I had seen as a child when living at Dâyi's. Perhaps she had grown up around these alpha-male types—although her father seemed to be a religious conservative—or perhaps she had spent years imitating them from films. Perhaps a part of her was desperate for her father's love, a father who had always wanted a son, and so she acted like one through her boisterousness.

"Is that Marjan?" she asked, glancing at her.

"Yes," her cellmates answered.

"And Googoosh?" she asked, our eyes locking.

"Yes," they answered again.

Her face softened. She then introduced herself as she sat down in the only spot available, facing Marjan and me. She couldn't wait to tell us her story. She had been arrested by the Komiteh a week ago with her boyfriend after she had run away from the religious wedding ceremony her father had arranged with an old, wealthier man. I admired her courage. The Komiteh didn't know what to do with her, or her father, so they had sent her here to the Monkarât.

Nahid explained to us how much she and her boyfriend loved each other. He was about the same age as her. He wrote her poems like they did in films, she said. She explained that she was willing to die rather than marry anyone else. Her eyes glistened as she spoke, her delicate features looking even more childlike. She was a child, brave and outspoken, but a child nonetheless, who had no business being in this basement.

"We're like Leyli and Majnun, or Romeo and Juliet," she said, unfolding the delicate ruby silk she had kept in her hands.

I, too, had been a hopeless romantic at her age, until I married Mahmoud. I had believed wholeheartedly in the tragedy of love while devouring films like Elia Kazan's *Splendor in the Grass* (1961). Tears filled my adolescent eyes when fate gleefully separated soulmates. It never crossed my mind that our own actions could also be responsible for failed loves. Perhaps this was the only thing my adolescent self and Nahid had in common. I never dared to stand up to authority figures the way she bravely did, except for that one time I stopped Mouness from slapping me when I was fifteen.

"We're like Atefeh and Ali in *Hamsafar*!" Nahid said before loosely wrapping the scarf around her head. "We even escaped on a motorcycle!"

I smiled and nodded, even though their story was nothing like that of the characters Behrouz and I had played in Masoud Asadollahi's 1975 film. Nahid's actions took more courage than anything the fictional character Atefeh had done. Atefeh was a spoiled young woman helplessly pursuing a successful, manipulative, and married older man she thought she loved, to the point of her own destruction, until she met Ali (played by Behrouz), a struggling working-class man, hired by her father to track her and bring her back home. While Atefeh and Ali set out to conquer the social barriers for their love, Nahid was fighting for her right to have a say in her future within an Islamic Republic. She was paying a high price for her bravery, here in this basement, a price that Atefeh would never have had to pay in her fictional life in pre-revolution Iran.

I worried for Nahid, but I couldn't help but envy her fearlessness, her unapologetic defense of who she was and what she wanted out of life. Even as an adult, I often found myself trying first to please everyone else, whether it was devoting all my free time to my partner's interests or acting in an improvised scene that I had repeatedly told a director had made me uncomfortable. The only place I ever felt such fearlessness and the utter freedom to do as I pleased was onstage. Only music would give me that power. Only music could allow me to express my true self, everything I had buried deep inside.

"I love the scene of you and Behrouz on the bike!" the woman with the movie posters blurted out. "He's such a hunk!"

"It was so romantic!" Mojgan added.

Nahid's eyes sparkled.

They were talking about the scene in which Ali brings Atefeh back to Tehran on his motorcycle along the narrow, winding stretch of the Châlus road, carved into the jagged cliffs of the Alborz mountains, with terrifying drop-offs plunging into the void below.

"We nearly died there," I said to them.

Behrouz was driving the motorcycle, making me laugh with his usual jokes and wit as I held tightly onto his strapping chest. We were no longer acting, even though the cameras were rolling. We had been together for two and a half years by then, and this was the happiest I had ever been after weeks of filming together without fighting once, so much so that I had wished that the drive would never end. Just as Behrouz leaned into one of those tight turns with zero visibility, an oncoming bus swerved right in front of us. *This is it*, I thought, knowing that there was little room for maneuver with the edge of the cliff so close to us. Then Behrouz veered to the right, miraculously avoiding both disasters. One of the two cameras on our convoy caught the moment on tape, a moment barely noticeable on-screen. I had always been thankful to God, to the universe, that we didn't drive off the cliff that day.

"I loved the song in that scene!" someone else said.

"Can you please sing it for us?"

"What about '*Man Amadeh-am*' [I Have Come to You]? I love that one," the woman with all the posters said.

"Marjan, please sing '*Kavir-e Del*'!" said the woman with the Shirazi accent.

"I love that song!"

"And '*Sekeh Khorshid*' [Sun Coin]!"

"Googoosh, I love '*Pishkesh*' [Gift]!"

A deluge of song requests filled our cell. Marjan and I argued that the guards and Zahrâ were nearby.

"You don't have to sing loud," Mojgan added.

"What if you whispered?" another person suggested.

But I couldn't. I remembered the document I signed in Evin Prison, less than seven months ago.

"I, Faegheh Atashin, also known as Googoosh, declare that from this day onward, will not sing or engage in any artistic endeavors, will not attend or participate in any social or political gatherings, and will be forever loyal to the principles of the great Islamic Revolution."

"The guards won't do a damn thing," Nahid declared. "We've seen them stealing a bunch of cassettes from the closet."

"There's a closet upstairs, by the foyer," Mojgan explained before briefly pausing to listen for the guards, "where they stuff everything they confiscate."

"Alcohol, cassettes, books—"

"Drugs! I even saw a *manghal* in there!" someone whispered, referring to the small portable charcoal grill also used to smoke opium.

"One of them took my Hayedeh cassettes! You saw them, didn't you?" the woman with the posters asked Nahid.

Nahid nodded while Zari gave her cellmate a dirty glance as though she had heard one too many times about her stolen Hayedeh cassettes.

"Please!" several girls insisted while Zari took another long drag from her cigarette and Niloufar bit her lower lip.

"Maybe another time," we said.

"Please, just one song!"

"Just one!" others repeated.

I couldn't help but notice the sparkle in Nahid's eyes as well as excitement on Niloufar's face.

"Just one," Marjan and I finally agreed.

"One each," they playfully insisted.

We left it up to them to choose the song. After some debating, they asked me to sing my hit upbeat love song "*Man Amadeh-am.*" The song was kindly gifted to me by Afghanistan's renowned composer, poet, and singer, *Ostâd* (Maestro) Jalil Zoland, in 1976, during his visit to my home with his son, Farid Zoland, whom I had already made hit records with.

I looked over at Marjan, still unsure. She looked happy. There was no backing out. It was nice to see her smile again.

I knew every note, every word of this song. Trouble was, I didn't know how to sing covertly. I had never had to. I couldn't hum it; humming could also be too loud. I had to find a way to sing it as softly as possible without being heard beyond these four walls. I couldn't recite it because that wasn't what they had asked for. And most importantly, I couldn't let myself get carried away. I always sang with emotion. I had to. I always knew there was nothing special about my voice. It was a good voice, but not exceptional. So, from very early on, I learned that singing with emotion made up for my technical limitations. I learned that whenever I felt the lyrics, the story, and the rhythm in my very core, then I could get the audience to also feel it deep within themselves. After all, I had never thought of myself as a singer, but rather a performer, who had to become one with the song, the music, and the audience.

The room went silent. All eyes were on me. I imagined carrying baby Kambiz in my arms and lulling him to sleep with a soft voice, a soft melody. It was worth trying.

As I whisper-sang those words of love and yearning from one heart to another, I suddenly felt a flow of happiness, warmth, longing, desire, and hope rush through and around me. I could see it on the women's faces, faces that looked somewhat different with expressions I hadn't yet seen in this basement. I could almost see Nahid staring lovingly into her boyfriend's eyes, or the first time Fahimeh felt butterflies for her husband. I could almost feel a younger Zari's heart beating faster as she exchanged a smile with a young man who lived down the same road.

The same thing happened when Marjan sang the famous song "*Zendooni*" (Prisoner) that I urged her to sing. Gone were the dirty carpet, the little window, and the four walls. However hushed, her delicate, warm voice carried us away to another place, into another time. That was the wonder of music, like a magic carpet that whisks you away thousands of miles across land and sea, into the atmosphere and across galaxies, where you lose yourself and feel whatever that was once sealed, buried, and forgotten deep within you burst free, making you feel all that much lighter.

Our guests asked us for more. Even I wanted Marjan to sing another song. But just as a new round of negotiations started, I noticed whispering by the entrance. Slowly the whispers reached Marjan and me. It was about Dâdâsh Abolfazl. He had been seen standing by the entrance of our corridor this whole time.

Chapter 11

Evin Prison

Late March 1980

Not many people would have predicted, during the anti-Shah riots in the fall of 1978, that Iran would soon become an Islamic Republic. When the Shah's regime was toppled in February 1979, few imagined what would come next. Ayatollah Khomeini swiftly called for a national referendum on the creation of a free and democratic Islamic Republic, guided by the principles of Shia Islam. It was a closed vote, boycotted by major political factions (the Tudeh Party, MEK, the Freedom Movement, and the National Front), and reportedly approved by 98 percent of the eligible voting population.

Not many could have predicted this outcome, especially since the revolutionaries were not all Islamists. Members of the communist Tudeh Party, as well as young secular college students and liberal elites, joined forces with the Khomeinists to overthrow the Shah. Khomeini had led many to believe that once Iran was rid of the Shah, the oil wealth would be redistributed among the people and he would withdraw from politics and return to the holy city of Qom, where he would continue his Islamic teachings. The twenty-four months that followed the referendum were a bitter shock. Universities were shut down to purge secular and leftist influences, Islamize the curriculum, and suppress dissent; women were forced to cover their hair. On July 23, 1979, Khomeini issued a fatwa banning music, declaring it a tool of the devil, "no different from opium."

But I wasn't shocked. I had seen the writing on the wall as soon as the Shah's regime fell. The cabarets, theaters, and cinemas on Lâlehzâr Street were some of the first casualties. They were torched, along with bars and discotheques. By the late 1960s and '70s, Lâlehzâr had already lost much of its original glamour and artistic flair, becoming increasingly commercialized. But for me, it remained sacred ground. It was where I found my voice, where I first experimented with different vocal ranges, where I experienced the intoxicating thrill of performing—losing myself in the music, in the song, in the waves of emotion from the audience. Now it was all reduced to broken glass, rubble, and charred remnants of a past that was slipping away faster every day. My home, my sanctuary, was gone, buried under the ashes of another era. What had once been a haven for music, art, and expression was now a place where they were condemned.

There were also other signs, like the story of an attack on a grand piano in a hotel in Kish, an Iranian resort island in the Persian Gulf. The revolutionaries had reportedly torn off its keys, one by one, before destroying its whole body with hammers, batons, rocks, or whatever they got their hands on. They said it was a symbol of Western imperialism that needed to be destroyed.

So I wasn't surprised when, in late March 1980, Ali Tehrani confiscated all of my music cassettes and recordings during my last day of interrogation in Evin Prison. All of them, gone. Then again, nothing surprised me after those first words that came out of Ali Tehrani's mouth.

I would never forget our first session together, only days after I had been summoned to Evin Prison's makeshift courtroom run by the nasty mullah. There were four of us that day, Maziar, Jaleh Olov, Ali Tabesh, and me, and we were blindfolded as soon we entered the prison walls. I was sure they were going to take us before the firing squad this time as they tied a dirty rag over my eyes. Instead, they walked us through some corridors, with a few turns before going down one story, and into a room where a man who presented himself as Ali Tehrani was waiting for us. I immediately recognized his long Humphrey Bogart–like face as soon as my blindfolds were removed. I saw him on March 8, 1980, my first time inside Evin Prison. He sat quietly in the corner of the courtroom, interrogating the singer Firouzeh, while the rest of us faced the bitter mullah. He made her cry more than once that day.

Tehrani's tone was different from the mullah; it was almost warm and docile. He began questioning my peers, and when it was my turn, he did something completely unexpected. He switched from Persian to *motrebi*, a made-up pseudo-Persian language, once spoken in the artistic milieu, where the first and last letters of every single word are switched around, making it incomprehensible to unfamiliar ears. *Motrebi* was likely created in an attempt by entertainers to share their secrets from employers.

"How're you doing?" he asked in the secret language.

His *motrebi* was impeccable, leaving me confused and speechless. *Maybe he's one of us*, I thought. He seemed charming and confident—I could have easily pictured him onstage, without the thick beard, in some *ruhowzi*, that form of popular theater similar to the Italian commedia dell'arte, performing a rendition of "*Sultan o Shaban*" (The Sultan and the Shepard) somewhere on Lâlehzâr Street. All types of entertainers both drank and went to Friday prayers at the local mosque.

But why was he speaking *motrebi* to me? What was he trying to tell me?

He gently smiled in response to the bewilderment on my face.

"I'm okay, thank you," I responded, also in *motrebi*.

"How about Saber?" he asked, still smiling.

"He's good, thank you," I answered more confidently.

Truth was I hadn't spoken much to Papa. Last I heard, he was running an underground taxi service and telling customers that he needed the money to help his "poor little Googoosh."

"He still drinking?" Ali Tehrani asked with the side of his lips still curled upward.

My heart sank. Alcohol was banned and the bars had been burned to the ground. I couldn't tell him the truth, not after what had happened to the nation's beloved radio news anchor and game show host, Taghi Rouhani.

When Taghi Rouhani had been detained in Tehran in September of 1979 for questioning about his news coverage during the Shah's reign, the Revolutionary Guards smelled alcohol on his breath. He confessed he had had something to drink that night. He was later sentenced to five years in prison in the city of Khash for "obstructing the people's revolution," as well as eighty lashes for drinking alcohol. As he was being escorted onto the plane to Khash, he was kidnapped by unknown individuals and taken near the Behesht-e Zahrâ cemetery (located in the south of Tehran), where he was severely beaten and left for dead. The butt of a rifle crushed part of his skull, but miraculously he survived, though he was paralyzed and mute for the remainder of his life.

"No," I replied in Persian.

"Good," he said in *motrebi* with a smug look on his long face before switching to Persian. "How often did you see the Shah?"

I was allowed to go back home later that evening with instructions to return fifteen days later. At my second interrogation session with Ali Tehrani, it was just Nasrin—a famous singer—and me, sitting side by side like two young pupils before their teacher. He went back and forth between the two of us with his questions fit for gossip columns. He kept asking me whether I had seen so-and-so at royal events and parties—clearly fishing for damning information—and I kept telling him I couldn't remember, since there had been so many events, so many parties ever since I was a child, and that I had always been too focused on my performance to notice particular individuals. I wasn't entirely lying. Ever since I was little, I had learned that singing was a job like any other, one that required hard work and focus.

"What about before your performances?" he asked with that soft voice, like a friend kindly asking you to share details of your long day at work.

"I was getting ready backstage," I explained.

I could have also told him that the time I had before my performances was sacred to me, being the only time and space just for me, to meditate and to call upon the muses of music, but I doubt he would have been interested in those details.

After several long hours, Ali Tehrani dismissed Nasrin, but not before having her sign a document, just like Pouri, Nasser, and the others had signed on the first day, and Maziar, Jaleh, and Ali on the second. I could hear my heart thumping in my chest as Nasrin shut the door behind her. Here we were now, Ali Tehrani and me, sitting alone in some office, somewhere underground in Evin. I had to appear as calm as a rock.

He took his time shuffling through my file, licking the tip of his finger before turning every page.

"Tell me," he said with a smile, "who did you sing '*Âghâ Khoobeh*' [Good Sir] for?"

I knew this was going to come up. Many speculated that I had sung this rhythmic love ballad, officially titled "*Hazrat-e Eshgh*" (Saint of Love), to declare my devotion to Khomeini, while others said I was singing it for the Shah. I couldn't blame them, since the record was released without my knowledge, while I was away playing with fire in the U.S.—I was shocked when I first learned about its release, seeing as we hadn't finished recording it. The lyrics were actually written by Mohammad Saleh Ala, who imagined his mother expressing her love and adoration for her husband, his father. And back in 1977, even before I had started recording the track, I had dedicated it to Bijan Saffari, an artist, a painter, a true visionary, and a dear friend, who I greatly admired and missed since he had fled the country shortly after the revolution. But people believe what they want to believe.

"No one in particular," I replied.

He looked puzzled. Perhaps he was expecting me to eagerly reply, "Khomeini," after which he would have maybe handed me the document to sign and let me go.

As Ali Tehrani flipped through the pages again, I wondered what sort of plays he had acted in on Lâlehzâr Street. I wondered whether he had a singing voice and whether he had experimented with his vocal range. I wondered whether he was ever able to command the stage with the same quiet authority as Humphrey Bogart, whose similarly unconventional looks—deeply etched lines on his face and slightly crooked teeth—were central to his lasting appeal, setting him apart from the polished Hollywood leading men of his era. But Mr. Tehrani didn't strike me as having even an ounce of Bogart's magnetic presence, of his authenticity that radiated experience and resilience, and that drew in and mesmerized the audience.

"Who did you sing '*Darigh*' [Loss] for?" he asked, again with a gentle smile.

Everyone assumed I sang it for Behrouz, as it was a song about painful heartbreak. But that wasn't the case. My connection to those lyrics was deeper, more absolute. The pain expressed wasn't tied to one person; it was universal. Besides, I sang "*Mashough*" (Lover) for Behrouz, not long after our divorce, with lyrics like: "One day you are the pain itself and one day you are a cure."

"No one in particular," I replied.

Mr. Tehrani's smile faded, and his eyes dropped, clearly disappointed by my answer.

"I just loved the words, the poetry, and thought the public would, too," I continued. "Besides, the lyricist writes the song, while I, the singer, only perform it."

I could have said more. I could have said that I always used my emotions when picking songs, that I needed to feel some connection with the story, with the words. I needed to believe the story, I needed to feel it along with the words, as though they were my own—listeners can tell when you fake it. I could sing one happy, upbeat song with pure joy rushing through my body and then immediately after sing a melancholic song about loss with a tight chest and genuine tears running down my cheeks. Music helped me cry my pain and yell my joy.

Mr. Tehrani looked directly at me, fixedly, with a severe wide-eyed gaze I hadn't seen on him before.

"Why did you sing at all?" he finally asked with a deep frown. "Didn't you know that singing is *harâm* [sinful]?"

I felt my face heating up.

"Didn't you know that a woman singing for men is sinful?" he continued with a look of disgust.

I felt my blood boiling. I clenched my shaking fists on my lap.

"Sir, no one ever told me not to sing, or that singing is sinful," I said while trying hard to control my voice from cracking. "No one ever said anything like that at school, at home, not even my conservative relatives. Ever since I was a kid, people paid to hear me sing, whether in cafés or in cabarets, then they bought my records. They showed nothing but love and support."

He threw me a pitiful look. I looked away. There was nothing I hated more than being pitied.

After a long pause of silence, his eyes narrowed onto another written question. He asked why I had done the nude scene in *Dar Emtedâd-e Shab*. My stomach twisted—just like it had weeks earlier, upstairs in the courtroom, when the angry mullah had demanded the same explanation. How many times was I going to have to answer this?

Parviz Sayyad's film was a romantic drama, tragic like Arthur Hiller's *Love Story* (1970), about a young man named Babak, suffering from leukemia, who sets out to win over the heart of the woman he loves most, Parvaneh, a famous singer and actress who knows nothing of his existence.

"Didn't you know that's sinful, too?" he insisted with an exaggerated look of concern. "That it's unlawful in Islam for a woman to expose her body like that?"

What could I say? That the scene wasn't added to the script until the last minute and that I had refused to do it at first? That I had argued back and forth with Parviz Sayyad over this? That I had to convince myself that doing the scene would let me grow as an artist by pushing me to perform outside of my comfort zone? That I'd been promised that my breasts wouldn't appear in the shot, that they'd be hidden by flames in the two-sided fireplace? That this was an artistic endeavor, not pornography? That it was the character Parvaneh he saw on-screen, not me? Or that there was nothing sinful about our human bodies created by God?

"Mr. Tehrani," I said, clearing my throat, "it was a big mistake. I thought I was doing something artistic, but now I realize I was wrong."

He smiled to himself.

After a few minutes of silence, interspersed with the sound of shuffling pages, he looked at me and said, "You can go now. But"—he paused briefly—"come back tomorrow with all your records and audio cassettes and you'll be free."

From what I could tell, I was the only one ordered to return—while my peers were released after signing a document I was never allowed to see. But this upcoming fourth session would be my last, Mr. Tehrani promised.

As soon as I got back home that day, I rushed to gather all my records, cassettes, and original reel-to-reel tapes, including demos recorded in the studio. There was a lot. By then, I had released more than forty singles, with many of my songs specifically recorded for several of the twenty-nine films I had acted in. I bagged everything, whether they were my songs or not, Iranian and foreign. Everything had to go. I didn't want to leave anything for the Komiteh to find during one of their many random raids of my home. I just wanted peace.

The next day I handed Mr. Tehrani several large bags, and in exchange, he gave me the document to sign—where I had no choice but to sign away my voice.

He called my home later that night.

"Ms. Atashin," he said—I still wasn't used to being called that. "I didn't find your song '*Sâhel o Daryâ*.'"

"But I brought you everything I had," I replied anxiously.

The line went quiet.

"Shame," he then dolefully answered. "My wife really likes that song."

Ali Tehrani was killed, shot in the head while he slept, months after that phone call. No one knew why—perhaps it was a settling of scores. Maybe it was just another example of how the revolution devours its own children. After I heard the news, I couldn't stop picturing him, a younger him with the same long face, waiting behind the curtains, waiting for his cue to get onstage.

Chapter 12

Upstairs

Day 5

There was no mirror on the mold-ridden wall above the stained sink in the bathroom, but still I felt the weight of the dirt on my skin and clothes as well as the grease in my hair, covered under a dark headscarf that equally needed washing. I felt like a sponge, absorbing all the filth around me. I hadn't showered nor brushed my teeth in five days. Five days had gone by since I had first stepped into this former home, five days since I had been locked in this basement.

I quickly rinsed my face, impatient to get away from the stench. It was still nauseating, even though Abolfazl had gotten someone to fix the flush and clean up most of the filth. Not long after I mentioned the bathroom to him, I asked him if they could bring us real sanitary pads, showing him the dirty slabs of cotton fibers, which I had done my best to clean. I told him of the dangers of infection while he stood quietly by the door, his head nearly touching the frame. The next day, Zahrâ marched in and removed the slabs with a resentful look on her face—she still hadn't said a single word to either of us—before shoving store-bought sanitary pads into a cupboard in the bathroom. I told Marjan how I intended to ask Dâdâsh Abolfazl to have my family bring me a Gobelin stitching kit to pass the time. I couldn't ask for a deck of cards to play my favorite mind-numbing game, solitaire. Card games were now illegal.

"Don't push your luck," Marjan warned me with a smile.

As I rushed out of the bathroom, I found a couple of new faces standing by our door, while our familiar neighbors had taken their usual seats for our "hour of freedom." They had gloomier faces than the previous days. Niloufar wasn't there. I didn't dare ask why, remembering the fear in her gentle eyes.

"It's Googoosh!" one of the new faces whispered.

"He said you'd be here—we didn't believe him!" the other one said.

"Who?" Marjan asked them.

"They're new," Zari said to us in an almost apologetic tone.

The two newcomers had just been arrested.

"The interrogator! This morning! He said—"

"We call him Afshoun," Zari retorted with a sly smile.

"Afshoun," the woman repeated to Zari before turning back to us. "He said to us, 'Your chief, your madame, Googoosh, she's waiting for you downstairs'!"

My stomach churned.

"We thought he was just being a prick!" the other one added. "Googoosh, I love your songs, I love '*Choob Mizani*' (You Strike with a Stick)!"

"Afshoun!" Zari scoffed, ignoring her new cellmates. She then paused to look down at the half-smoked cigarette clutched between her calloused fingers. "Mr. Virtuous!" she added before taking another drag of her cigarette. The room went still as she expelled the thick smoke toward the ceiling. "That son of a bitch thinks he can fool us with a shitty suit and those fake glasses? Talkin' down to us like he's a somebody now? Actin' tough like a sheriff he'd seen in those cowboy flicks!" she continued. "He isn't foolin' nobody! The girls remember that dirty face of his, standin' on that same corner, day after day, no suit, no glasses, sellin' *jettons* the men needed to get through to us!"

She was talking about tokens that men had to purchase in order to sleep with the prostitutes.

"Zari," the women whispered, "they're listening!"

"Let 'em listen, let 'em learn—their boss was a whore, like us!" She paused for another drag of her dying cigarette. "He was a pimp. He wouldn't have made a damn penny if it weren't for us!"

"He'd sell his own mother if he could!" one of her cellmates interjected.

Nahid's voice rang out in the corridor, yelling her usual insults at the guards and Khomeini. "That kid," Zari said. "The only virtuous one here—speakin' truth!"

"She's going to get killed," Fahimeh said with a worried look in her eyes. "Nothing terrifies those cowards more than a strong woman's voice."

The room hushed again. Even the new faces kept quiet.

It was early evening when Dâdâsh Abolfazl pulled open the curtain once more and unlocked our door.

"Follow me," he said, looking timidly my way.

My heart raced. Marjan gently grabbed my hand and pressed it in hers, as if to wish me good luck.

I followed Abolfazl through the dimly lit narrow corridor filled with chatter and intermittent shrieks of pain. I quickly looked back, silently bidding farewell to the women trapped behind the dark curtains, wishing them luck and a swift release.

More chatter and shrieks echoed outside our wing, this time coming from the opposite corridor, from the men's side of the basement. Abolfazl stopped and directed me to go up the staircase, to my left, the same one that had led me here five days earlier. It felt like weeks ago. He followed me upstairs, always three steps behind.

I could already see dirty boots and khaki hems stationed in the grand foyer. I remembered how I had been shocked that very first day, seeing armed Revolutionary Guards in Mr. Mesbahzadeh's home. It was even more shocking now to think that this place had ever been a home.

The light in the foyer felt too intense, almost blinding, clashing with the darkness we were perpetually subjected to downstairs. As my eyes struggled to adjust, I recognized the profile of the young guard. I hadn't seen him in a few days. I quickly looked away, even though he was busy talking to someone else. I followed Abolfazl's directions to the former ballroom, into the makeshift interrogation room, where five days ago, I had sat next to my uncle and Kambiz in front of Afshoun.

As soon as I walked in, Mama, Homayoun, and Uncle Farhang jumped from their seats.

"Thank God!" Mama said with tears in her eyes. "You're here!" She took me in her arms. She was shaking, as was I.

"Did they hurt you?" Homayoun whispered as he placed his hand on my shoulder—the only gesture allowed, even as my husband.

I couldn't believe Mama was here—just like when I was a girl and first saw her standing outside my school. I couldn't believe Homayoun was here. I could tell by the dark circles around his eyes that he had barely slept in days, and not because of freebase cocaine—he couldn't easily find cocaine these days. And Uncle Farhang looked as frightened as the day he brought me here.

"No, I'm fine," I said.

I didn't look fine. I could feel the weight of the dirt clinging to my skin, the fabric of my clothes stiff with sweat and grime. My hair, once soft and clean, now felt heavy and matted. My mouth was also sour, and my lips were rough and cracked. I wondered if I smelled as bad as the basement, with its pungent, rancid odor of the toilet mixed with the stench of sweat and moldy air.

Abolfazl insisted we take our seats before he went and sat down behind Afshoun's unoccupied desk at the other end of the large room.

I'm not being released, I thought when I saw the bag of my stuff by Mama's feet.

"They called me the day after your arrest," she said, her voice nearly choked up. She rarely showed her emotions like this. "They said to me they were going to execute you in less than twenty-four hours!"

My heart sank to the bottom of my stomach.

She then turned toward Abolfazl and said in a loud and furious tone, "What kind of sick person calls a mother to scare her like that?"

Uncle Farhang tried to calm her. He looked as pale as that first day. But Mama wouldn't have any of it.

"And they call themselves the *monkarât*?!" Mama continued in her fury. She wasn't afraid. She didn't care that they were armed or that they had the power to arrest her without a court order, just as they had arrested me. She could have said all of this to me in Azeri, but she purposely spoke in Persian so that he would understand.

"How's Kambiz?" I asked her, doing my best to control the pitch of my voice. I couldn't let them see my fear. Not Mama, not Homayoun, not Uncle Farhang, and especially not Abolfazl.

"He's fine," Homayoun replied.

Mama wiped her tears and answered in a calmer tone. "He misses you. He's worried. He asks me every day when you're coming back. 'Soon,' I tell him."

Kambiz had been living with me for more than a year, ever since I withdrew him from Le Rosey at the end of the school term in 1979—without the possibility of working, I couldn't even afford a single week of its astronomical tuition.

"Tell him I'll see him soon."

"Are they—what is—what—what are they giving—have you eaten?" Homayoun asked. I had never seen him like that before, so uncertain, so disarmed, stumbling over his words like that.

"Yes," I replied. I then forced a smile and added, "One of the girls is convinced that they're feeding us leftovers from Evin. By the time the *adas polo* gets to us, there's no trace of chicken and barely any lentils left—just the plain rice."

Homayoun smiled, perhaps to make me happy, but Mama was in no mood to fake a smile. I imagined her leaping up without warning and attacking Abolfazl. She wasn't a violent person, but then I remembered that story involving her ex-husband's car. One day, her second (and last) husband packed all his things and left her and their young children for his mistress. The story goes that the next day, she drove to the mistress's apartment, got out of her car, and carefully poured gasoline over his parked Mercedes-Benz. Then she lit a match.

I wanted to tell them about the bathroom, about Zari, Niloufar, and the others, about the shadows, the lashings and the screams. I wanted to tell them that some of the girls had seen Afshoun sell jettons in Shahr-e No. I wanted to tell them everything, but I couldn't, not with Abolfazl sitting a few steps away.

"I spoke to your brother Fariborz," Homayoun said. "He's worried sick about you. I'll tell him I saw you."

Homayoun then glanced over at Abolfazl and saw the guard buried in files. He turned back to me and whispered very quietly, "Fereydoun's been calling every day, asking about you."

He was talking about Fereydoun Farrokhzad, the beloved and occasionally controversial entertainer who was also the brother of one of the most influential modern Iranian poets, Forugh Farrokhzad.

"Tell him I'm okay," I said.

"They're after him, too," Mama added.

Mama explained that the Committee of Vice and Virtue had officially published a long list of "wanted" entertainers, including me, Fereydoun, Marjan, Sepideh, and Seyyed Karim—we knew Seyyed, the stand-up comedian, was here, as we had heard him ironically singing the *azân* (the Muslim call to prayer) all the way from the men's side of the basement.

Fereydoun had gone into hiding, fearing for his life. The Monkarât wouldn't simply punish him for his "sinful" profession. His homosexual relationships were a well-known secret, a secret that, under sharia, was considered a crime punishable by death.

Abolfazl started realigning the towering stack of files, tapping the bottom of each folder against the surface of the table, before moving on to the next one.

I would've been dead by now if that was what they wanted. They were after something else. What? I didn't know. I'd given them everything.

"I've kept an eye on Velenjak," Mama said, perpetually worried that the Revolutionary Guards would confiscate my house or take my things again.

I could have reminded her that they already had the deed to my house. The new Department of Treasury had placed a lien on it, claiming that I hadn't paid the entirety of my 1977 taxes, and that they couldn't find my official contestation of the erroneous claim that I had owed 3 million toman (more than 430,000 U.S. dollars at the time) to the former administration. Apparently the Islamic Republic was still interested in collecting debts owed to the Shah's regime without honoring due process.

Home. How I missed my home. I had lived there since I was twenty-two years old. I was finally free from my unhappy marriage to Mahmoud, madly in love with Behrouz, and in the prime of my career—the sky was my limit. Before moving in, I made a few changes, including creating the TV den and adding a small sauna (which my brothers ended up using more than I did). I had nine coniferous trees planted along the tall sidewalls for more privacy, just as the neighboring homes had done, as well as a cherry tree, a lemon tree, and the weeping willow Papa gifted me. Over the years, their roots grew deep, and the willow soared by 1977, needing frequent trimming to keep the light from being blocked. I grew roses in every color by the terrace that overlooked the garden. I loved watching them blossom.

My trees, my flowers—they were all my beautiful babies. *If only they'd let me go home, back to my plants, they'd never hear from me again, not a sound,* I thought.

Abolfazl stopped rearranging the stacked piles and stood up from behind Afshoun's cluttered desk.

"It's time to say your goodbyes," he said, his voice firm but gentle as always, as he stepped out from behind the desk and walked toward us.

Mama grabbed the bag that was resting by her feet and began calmly listing every single item she had packed, including clothing, toiletries, and cigarettes.

"Five packs of cigarettes should be more than enough until you get out," she finally said, her words deliberate, her attempt to push back against Abolfazl's order. But I could tell from her eyes that she was frightened. After all, she had witnessed her father's execution, and her mother had died in prison.

I hugged Mama as tight as I could, while Homayoun placed his hand on my shoulder.

"I'll take care of Kambiz," my uncle said as he handed me the bag. I knew he was also speaking about Mama.

I thanked him and turned around before any of them could see the tears welling in my eyes and followed Abolfazl out of the former ballroom, my bag in hand, without looking back.

Back in my cell my head pounded as I told Marjan about the list of entertainers they were after and the call Mama had received. She listened quietly as her brown eyes filled with fear, anger, and confusion, just like that first night. She barely uttered a word, even after I was done. I couldn't blame her. We avoided everything and anything that had to do with this basement. We only spoke of the past, tiptoeing around the elephant in this tiny room, for fear that it would crush us.

"Googoosh," Marjan cried out abruptly, "what more do they want from us? I don't get it. They won! We lost! What do they want? They've taken everything! And what about my kids?" she uttered furiously—she didn't care if they could hear her. "Why did they terrorize my stepson like that? Storming into our home, dragging me away like that in front of him? He's just a kid!"

I remembered Kambiz sitting quietly upstairs, waiting for hours for that man in the brown suit with that stern face to release his mother and then his tears as he and my uncle were forcefully taken outside.

"They've taken everything!" Marjan continued in a choked voice. "Everything! But they act as if we've just broken into their home and committed some crime. What crime? For God's sake!" Her hands quivered as she readjusted her headscarf. "It's our home, our country, too!"

I rummaged through the bag, hoping Mama had packed my migraine pills. I was out of luck. I looked for a cigarette instead, hoping the nicotine would ease the pain, or at least distract me from it. As soon as I found a pack, I tore off the seal and lit a cigarette with the matchbox my mother had included. I filled my lungs as much as I could, as though the smoke could magically save me from my migraine and from this place. It didn't.

I kept thinking of my loving grandmother Bahbah. I loved her so much. She died when I was about fifteen years old. It wasn't until much later that my uncle Farhang told me about the depth of her hardships. She lived through the Bolshevik Revolution in her youth. She and her family fled Russia—I never learned from which part—and found refuge in the newly established Azerbaijân Democratic Republic, a secular, democratic nation that was later absorbed into the USSR and renamed Soviet Azerbaijân. Years later, in a twist of fate, after all her family had endured under communist hands, she fell in love with and married my grandfather, one of many communist sympathizers in Iranian Azerbaijân. Despite her own experiences, she followed my grandfather and his political dreams. I understood Bahbah, in that neither of us were driven by politics. Like her, I was only captivated by love, swept up in the allure of following the heart.

After her husband's execution and her banishment from Miandoâb, my grandmother rebuilt a life for herself and her children, in exile, in Tehran. She made the best of her situation, finding work at the Soviet Hospital thanks to her background in dentistry, and provided for her children without ever complaining about the cards she had been dealt. Back then, I was too young to realize that behind her radiant smile was the deep ache of longing, the kind only those living in exile truly understand.

In 1964 or 1965, my aunt Fakhri and her husband decided to move to Soviet Azerbaijân, chasing what they imagined was the Soviet dream. Bahbah, who was in her late sixties, made the bold decision to join them. Fully aware of the dangers of being caught trying to pass through the Iron Curtain, she followed them anyway, driven by the promise of going back to her childhood home one last time. She bid farewell to my mother and Uncle Farhang, perhaps knowing that the journey carried great risks, but feeling the pull of her homeland too strong to resist. I understood that pull all too well. It was something physical. Even in my darkest hours in that room on the twentieth floor in New York, I kept thinking of the majestic Alborz mountains that loomed over Tehran. How I had longed to see them one more time, those gentle giants protecting the city like a mother holding her infant against her bosom. That pull is relentless, stronger than fear or reason, even as your homeland is caught in the throes of political turmoil, even if it means facing a firing squad. It's that unshakable connection to your motherland, even when it changes, even when it betrays you, that keeps pulling you back.

The three of them somehow managed to miraculously sneak their way across the border. But they were arrested by Soviet Azerbaijâni forces and locked away in prison as potential anti-Soviet spies. Aunt Fakhri and her husband were released months later and stayed a few more years, but the experience left them deeply disillusioned. The harsh realities of extreme poverty, hunger, and daily struggles had shattered their idealistic hopes. Like many at the time, my aunt and uncle hadn't yet learned about the catastrophic famines and the millions of deaths under Stalin in the Soviet Union and Mao in China. But their own suffering was enough to break their resolve. Unable to bear the crushing weight of the system any longer, they decided to return to Iran a few years later, realizing the dream they had once chased was nothing more than a mirage. But Bahbah would never make it out of that first prison. Tragically, she died in those early months from a medical complication, alone, behind bars.

I sometimes pictured her last moments, sitting in that prison cell with her beautiful long white hair, waiting for someone to save her. I wondered what was going through her mind. Was she angry? Filled with regrets? Or had she still been hopeful, despite everything? I wondered whether she had thought it had all been worth it, just to have touched the soil and breathed in the air of her beloved homeland, even for just a brief moment. I wondered if she could see me now, sitting in this basement.

Chapter 13

The Sharia Judge

Day 7

Hajj Agha Ansari, the clerical judge, entered our cell, late on the morning of the seventh day since my arrest. Our cell neighbors had warned us about him. Their description was fair. He was a middle-aged man with a long gray beard, a slightly hunched back, and terrible breath—a mixture of onion and rotting teeth. His small head sat atop a round face, giving him an oddly childlike appearance that clashed with the deep wrinkles etched into his skin. His dark, beady eyes, narrow and unfeeling, glistened with a self-satisfied detachment, as if nothing beyond his own concerns truly existed. He was much thinner than the heavyset mullah in Evin, but just like him, his brown clerical robe reeked of perspiration with a tinge of rose water—that mild perfume preferred by the men of the cloth. And just like him, he was the only judge around here. He was responsible for the slashes and bruises on Fahimeh's back, as well as the terror in Niloufar's eyes.

"Get up!" the young guard ordered us as he escorted in the judge.

Marjan and I obeyed while making sure our hair was properly covered. Once the mullah sat down on the floor, he carefully ran his fingers along the sides of his white *amâmeh*, his turban, checking to see that it was still sitting perfectly on top of his small head. He pushed back his large-framed glasses from the tip of his nose before dismissing the young guard with a single hand gesture—similar to the way he signaled for us to sit on the floor.

"*Bismillah ir-Rahman ir-Rahim*"—in the name of God, most Gracious, most Merciful—he said in a surprisingly high-pitched voice. "I don't have to ask either of you why you're here," he continued without looking directly at us. "You both know why. And most importantly, *Khodâ*—God—the Almighty, knows why."

His eyes darted between us. His thick-lensed glasses slowly slid down his small oily nose as he sought to catch an admission of guilt or perhaps some sign of protest. But Marjan and I knew better; we stayed as calm as we could. There was no arguing with the judge. Not in this basement.

He pushed up his spectacles with his bony index finger before pointing at us.

"Only *Khodâ*, the Almighty, will decide on Judgment Day whether to send you to hell for all of your sins," he said, his finger waving in the air as his putrid breath hovered over us.

He paused again, waiting for a reaction, while shrieks of pain filled in the silence.

"You should start begging for forgiveness," he finally said, stroking his beard with complete indifference to the cries coming in from the corridor.

Neither of us moved. Not a blink. I could feel Marjan fighting the urge to answer him, just as much as I was.

"Who knows, the Almighty may take pity on a bunch of brainwashed women," he continued in a self-righteous tone. "After all, the Shah—that corrupt and vile piece of trash! He knew exactly how to control your feeble minds, steering you away from the Quran and onto the stage in miniskirts!" He stopped to catch his breath.

I felt Marjan clenching her teeth, the rage boiling in us both.

"Lucky for you," he said as the corners of his mouth slowly curled up, "I'm here to undo his evil, to cure his disease."

The shrieks grew louder as he fiddled with his turban.

"You," he said, pointing at me, before pushing up his glasses again. "Have you heard of the *Usul-e Din*, the principles of Shia Islam?"

I nodded.

"What are they?"

"*Tawhid*, oneness of God; *nubuwwat*, the prophets; *adl*, justice of God; *emâmat*, authority of the imams; *ma'âd*, day of resurrection," I replied.

"How many times a day must one pray?"

"Five times."

"Where must one pray toward?" he asked.

"*Ka'bah*, *Makkeh*, Mecca."

He paused again and cleared his throat. He then asked with a sly smile, "Tell me, how many mandatory *rak'ats*, the single unit of prayer, are there in the *Asr*, the afternoon prayer?"

"Four," I replied.

He looked at me with a puzzled frown.

"What about *Zohr*, the noon prayer?" he blurted out.

"Four."

"*Maghreb*, or sunset?"

"Three."

"*Sobh*, the morning prayer?"

"Two."

"And what about *Isha*, the nighttime prayer?" he asked distrustfully.

"Four."

Hajj Agha Ansari cleared his throat once more. After a brief pause, his sly smile returned.

"Which can be shortened if you're traveling?"

"You can shorten the *Zohr*, *Asr*, and *Isha* by two *rak'ats* each," I answered.

His jaw nearly dropped.

Not many people knew that I was a believer, that I observed Ramadan, or that I had been to Mecca twice, where each time I performed the *Umrah*—a non-mandatory pilgrimage for Muslims that can be performed at any moment of the year. I had always been private about my faith. I never liked to talk about it. It was no one's business. What mattered to me was my connection to God, a connection that grew from the moment I had learned to pray as a child at Dâyi's home on Molavi Street.

"What is the *Namâz-e Mayyet*?" he asked after another long pause, while his wrinkly forehead creased further in confusion.

"The prayer for the deceased," I replied without hesitation.

His eyes lingered over me for a minute or two, still in disbelief, while I looked down at my hands, purposely avoiding his gaze. He then ran his fingers along his *amâmeh* once more. As soon as he was reassured by its position, he turned over his attention to Marjan, watching me every so often from the corner of his eye.

I was about seven years old when I first really thought about religion and God. It was around the time Papa had married Mouness and left Fery and me with his maternal uncle, Dâyi. Dâyi lived on Molavi Street, one of the oldest streets of the capital, just south of Tehran's Grand Bazaar. It was a conservative working-class neighborhood nicknamed the Haft Katchaloon, or "Seven Baldies," after the seven tough bald brothers, renowned *gardan kolofts*, who ran the neighborhood.

Like most of their neighbors, Dâyi and his wife, Khadijeh *Khânoum* ("Lady"), as we called her with love and reverence, lived with their three children and grandchildren. They all resided in a traditional old home, a remnant of the bygone Qajar era, with tall mudbrick walls covered in plaster that enclosed a central courtyard adorned with a small garden and a *howz* (a little fountain). The main living quarters opened onto the courtyard and was accessed only through the courtyard. The towering walls acted as a shield from the harsh climate as well as from prying eyes of neighbors and passersby. There were no street-facing windows, and even the main entrance was designed to block direct views into the private spaces when the door was opened.

I loved that home—it was humble, cold in the winter, and smelled of dust in the summer, but it was filled with love. During that time, I still saw Mama regularly, as our families stayed close even after her and Papa's divorce. It was the best year of my childhood. They enrolled me in school for the first time—Papa hadn't gotten around to do it the year before, even though I was old enough—and when school was finished I would just come home and play with Fery and their granddaughter,

Simin, who was about Fery's age. I only worked two afternoons a week. And I loved being around Khadijeh Khânoum. She was so loving to me, just like my grandmother Bahbah. Every night, Simin, Fery, and I would sleep in the main living area on mattresses rolled out side by side with Khadijeh Khânoum and Simin's mother, Bahieh. I always made sure I got to sleep beside Khadijeh Khânoum, so that I could gently hold on to her soft and wrinkly neck (like I used to do with Bahbah) and smell her wonderful jasmine perfume as I fell asleep. It was Khadijeh Khânoum who led me toward faith.

She and Dâyi were pious Shia Muslims, unlike Papa, who never spoke of God let alone prayed, or Mama and her family, who were staunch atheists. Khadijeh Khânoum, who was a devout, uneducated traditional housewife, had one of the biggest hearts I had known. She always wore a light-colored printed chador, the full-body-length cloak worn over clothing, outside of her home, while the dark chador was reserved for periods of mourning like Ashura, the tenth day of Muharram—the first month of the Islamic year. I couldn't help but notice how she always seemed to be at peace, even though she had to deal with her husband's constant crabbiness. She must have loved him, as she was as caring and thoughtful to him as she was to the rest of us. Dâyi, however, had no patience for children, noise, or laughter; he was a cranky old man who was either busy with his five daily prayers or fiddling with the broken timepieces in his clock-repair shop. But nothing seemed to get to Khadijeh Khânoum—she barely raised an eyebrow that time Simin and I goofed around, like kids do, at the local *tekyeh* (Shiite holy shrine) near the Grand Bazaar during Ashura. She prayed five times a day, every day. She always made sure she was home at those five specific times of the day. Men usually went to the mosque, or prayed inside their stores, away from the public gaze, if they couldn't make it.

It was odd and yet mesmerizing, watching Khadijeh Khânoum get down on her knees, where she paused for a moment before resting her forehead on the floor, only to get up and repeat the whole process again, all while whispering to herself. It seemed like a carefully choreographed dance. So one day, I started praying with her, copying her every move and gesture, trying to learn the Arabic words, even though I had no idea what they meant. It calmed me. It gave me peace. It made me think about God, about this higher power that somehow started feeling to me like a beloved family member.

The prayers I learned in those twelve months helped me a lot in the years that followed, during those darkest days with Mouness. I didn't pray five times a day like Khadijeh Khânoum, but I prayed often, when I needed it most. I never would have experienced such a connection to God had I only followed the Quran classes at school, where you were made to learn to recite *âyât*, or verses, of the Quran in Arabic without really understanding the meaning of those foreign, tongue-twisting words that felt heavy on the throat. I needed to feel them with my body, with my heart, the same way I had to feel every lyric and every beat before connecting with a song.

Over the years, my connection grew stronger as I learned how to pray in my own words, in Persian. I felt I could share anything with God, anything without feeling shame or fear. My faith was solidified when I was twenty-one or twenty-two on my first trip to Mecca. I remember asking God for help, asking for a way out of my marriage with Mahmoud. Mahmoud was refusing any talk of divorce, and I already knew the tremendous backlash I would face if he were to magically agree—it was still very much a man's world despite all the progress that had been made for women's rights. My divorce came less than a year later.

My second trip to Mecca in 1977, at the age of twenty-seven, was even more powerful. I had lost everything: Fery, my marriage to Behrouz, my sense of purpose. All I wanted was to be alone with God. During my trip, I performed the Sa'i ritual, retracing the steps of Hagar, the wife of Abraham, who desperately ran between the hills of Safa and Marwa seven times in search of water for her infant son, Ishmael, until she miraculously found the Well of Zamzam beside him. As I walked back and forth between the two hills of Safa and Marwa—the path now enclosed indoors in a big hall for the huge number of pilgrims to walk on—dressed in the ihram, the traditional white cloth, I kept repeating in Persian, "My contentment is

Your contentment, whatever Your will may be, it shall be." I remembered then feeling this rush of love flowing through my entire body. Pure bliss. I kept on walking with that feeling, the feeling of being alone with God, with my dearest and oldest friend. I felt at peace.

Just like music, prayer brought me peace. But I couldn't pray here in this basement. I couldn't, not even secretly in my own words. I wouldn't. I didn't want the guards, Hajj Agha Ansari, or even Marjan and the others to think that I was trying to curry favor or that I was looking for pity and forgiveness. I had done nothing wrong, and God was my witness.

Chapter 14
Afshoun

Day 12

I sat by the open door, trying to catch the soft early-afternoon light for my Gobelin stitching kit—Mama had brought it to Abolfazl, and true to his promise, he had a guard deliver it to me. I was stitching as much as I could over the last two days with whatever light came in from the little window or from the corridor when the curtains were pulled aside. Pushing and pulling the needle through the canvas hushed the thoughts that had rushed through my head for the twelve days since entering this basement. It also allowed me to be more present for Marjan, who needed my attention more than ever with what the sharia judge, Hajj Agha Ansari, was putting her through.

Hajj Agha Ansari had been visiting our cell every day for the past five days, a pit stop on his self-proclaimed "disease curing" rounds in the basement. He left me alone, despite that same quizzical glance he threw at me every now and then. He was on a clear mission: to lecture Marjan on the Quran while grilling her about her property on the coast of the Caspian Sea, as well as her romantic status. He must have heard the rumors that she was living with actor and director Fereydoun Jourak outside of marriage, a serious offense.

"What am I going to do?" she whispered to me as one of the guards was busy unlocking the rest of the cells in the corridor. "I'm not getting alone in a car with him and the Revolutionary Guards! And for four hours?!"

Hajj Agha Ansari insisted that she show him her property.

"And what if Fereydoun's there?" she worried.

"You answered him perfectly," I replied.

Marjan had followed my advice and told him yesterday that she could only go if her male relatives were present.

"But what if he keeps insisting that I go alone with him?" she worried.

I reached out and held her hand, trying my best to comfort her. But we both knew we were at the judge's mercy. Just then, footsteps approached us. Someone must have overheard us, we both thought. But it was just our neighbors lining up to use the bathroom right outside our door. I wondered if Niloufar was there. No one had seen her since she received thirty-four lashes five days ago. No one knew if she was immediately released or transferred to another facility, or even another unknown basement. The guards wouldn't say, and the only one who would, *Dâdâsh* Abolfazl, was lately too busy upstairs to make his rounds.

As my finger felt the canvas for the next stitch, I heard heavy footsteps approaching the door frame. It was a large woman. The top of her face was loosely covered by her headscarf, the ends of which dangled down her shoulders, over her long and unruly charcoal black hair. All I could see were her plump cheeks, covered by faint traces of mascara. Marjan and I politely said hello as she limped into our cell, groaning every step of the way. She slowly leaned against the wall, right below the window, the lower part of her face contorted with pain. As soon as she regained her strength, she pulled back her headscarf and looked directly at me with her bloodshot eyes. She was older, perhaps in her late forties early fifties, with a deep frown line running across her forehead, deep dark bags beneath her brown eyes, and her gray roots peering out from under her headscarf. She introduced herself as Aghdas.

"Khânoum-e Googoosh, you see what they did to me?" she said in my mother tongue, Azeri, turning around and pulling up her shirt. From the top of her shoulders and all the way down to her waist her skin had turned as dark as an eggplant.

I shuddered.

"Oh my God! What happened to you?" I asked her in Azeri.

"Goes down all the way to the backs of my knees," she said with a hint of pride.

"What happened?" I asked again, putting down the stitching kit.

"They took me up one day, 'bout two weeks ago, covering my eyes . . ." She paused. Her eyes closed, and her mouth contorted as she let out a loud and painful sigh, similar in tone to the shrieks that had woken me up that first night and that I had heard day and night since my arrest.

"They threw me in a ditch or a large hole," she finally managed to say moments later, her eyes open again. "Then I heard loud clangs—a rifle being loaded." She leaned toward us. "Then silence. I was sure they were gonna shoot me! Finally they screamed at me, 'Where's your gold? Where'd you hide it, you fuckin' whore? Tell us or we'll shoot you in the head!'"

"What did you say? Did you tell them?"

"Nothin'," Aghdas said. "I said nothin'. Three days they threw me in the hole, loaded their weapons, and I said nothin'. Then they done this to me." She pulled up her top again and pointed to the purple bruised skin stretched across her body.

My entire body shuddered once more.

"Why didn't you tell them? They could've killed you!"

She took one step forward and then painfully squatted in front of me.

"Khânoum-e Googoosh, for years I'd cook and eat *âbgoosht*, a poor man's meal," she said, taking her time enunciating each word. "I'd eat leftovers from the stew for days, then move on to scraps." She paused once more, this time to look down between her legs. "You see, for years I'd let 'em have this for money," she said while slapping her crotch. "Money I'd save and then buy me some gold," she added with a smile, revealing a gold tooth in the back of her mouth. "And now what? I'm supposed to give 'em everythin'? All my hard-earned gold?" She chuckled.

"Can't you just give them something? Why are you putting yourself through so much pain?"

Her smile vanished.

"Khânoum-e Googoosh, why would I do that?!" she asked with a dumbfounded look. "I told 'em," she continued with a raised voice, "if being a whore is *harâm*, then why do you want my gold? If it's *halâl* [permissible], then why are you punishin' me for it?!"

"But don't you think that if you'd just give them something, anything, then you'd be free? Live your life in peace?"

She stood back up and smiled.

"They can whip me all they want and lock me up in that dark room," Aghdas said with that same fierce look in her dark brown eyes, "but they're gettin' nothin' from me! Never!"

It must have been 10 or 11 p.m., hours since I met Aghdas. I had just managed to fall asleep and forget about her bruised body when the ground gently shook beneath me. Had Tehran been hit? But there were no loud sounds, other than the usual cries from our neighboring cells. Just as I was slipping once more into the sweet oblivion of sleep, the curtain was yanked to the side and a key unlocked the iron-barred door, pulling me back to this nightmarish reality.

"You!" the young guard said, snapping his finger at me.

My heart raced, while Marjan jolted in panic from her sleep.

"Get up!" he shouted with his hand hovering over the Colt revolver hooked to his belt.

I stumbled to my feet and followed him into the corridor.

Upstairs, he led me past the Revolutionary Guard with a Kalashnikov and straight into the former ballroom, where I had seen Mama, Homayoun, and Uncle Farhang three times now. There was Afshoun, sitting behind his large desk with his permanent frown, wearing that same loose brown suit from the first day I saw him. The young guard swiftly exited the room.

"Sit," he said, addressing me in the familiar *tô* instead of the formal *shômâ*—they all did, it was another way to belittle you. After all, to him I was a "madame," a whore.

I sat quietly, now fully awake, as he examined the dozen handwritten pages spread across his desk. I couldn't tell what he was reading as he randomly underlined some words and circled others. Minutes went by like this. My mind raced between their call to Mama, the list of entertainers, the sharia judge, and the grease on Afshoun's hair and face, shining ever more brightly under the lamplight. I realized I still didn't know his real name.

He cleared his throat, like an amateur actor would right before delivering a pivotal monologue.

"Why were you in the U.S.?" he asked with a projected voice, his pen touching the paper. "What was your purpose?"

I gave Afshoun the same answer I had given Mr. Tehrani back in Evin, the true answer, that I had no money left after my manager had wiped my account clean and that I had been offered to perform at the opening of Cabaret Colbeh in Los Angeles.

"Who'd you meet there? Outside the cabaret?" he asked while his eyes scrutinized every inch of my face. "Don't bother lying, I'll know," he added, his words slicing through the air. He was as sharp-tongued as the mullah in Evin, not interested in earning my trust like the soft-spoken Mr. Tehrani.

"No one," I replied.

"No Americans?" he asked, rubbing his thick black stubble.

"No."

"No Americans contacted you?"

"None, except for the Sheraton Hotel staff with their bills."

His eyes darted at me with irritation.

"Then where'd you get that thing they found in your house up in Velenjak?" he asked.

My mind scrambled as he cleared his throat again.

"Don't play stupid with me!" he suddenly roared, just like my stepmother used to before one of her beatings.

My heart started racing as I remembered those young men in civilian clothes, their patchy beards and rifles strapped across their shoulders, going through the rooms of my house in Velenjak. It was just days after I had returned from the U.S. in late April 1979. I had never seen Komiteh agents before, but there they were, inspecting my personal belongings before returning my keys, as ordered by the revolutionary prosecutor. My house had been illegally occupied earlier that spring by my cook, who thought I would never return. When he refused to leave, I got it back, thanks to Masoud Fardmanesh—the same man who had cleared my name at the airport upon my return—after I followed his advice and wrote to the revolutionary prosecutor, explaining that I hadn't intended to flee Iran or abandon my house for those seven or eight months (starting in late September 1978); I had simply been stuck in America the entire time. As the Komiteh agents inspected my things that day, I couldn't help but wonder if these were the same men who had initially gone through my house months earlier—the ones Mama had called me frantically about while I was in New York City, worried that they were marking it for confiscation as new university housing. I tried to guess which of them had taken my stage outfits, and whether they had given them to their wives, girlfriends, or sisters, telling them their new dresses had once belonged to Googoosh.

Afshoun was talking about my speakerphone that had puzzled the young men—one of them had held it away from his body as though it were an explosive. It was similar to the device seen on the American hit series *Charlie's Angels*—the one Charlie uses to communicate with the Angels about their new mission. They had taken it back to the Komiteh station and couldn't get it to work. They thought SAVAK had given it to me, or that it was some spying device "from those Americans." They weren't fully convinced when I explained to them what a speakerphone was. They quickly moved on to asking me where I had hidden the golden doorknobs that I had supposedly cleverly replaced with metal ones.

Now Afshoun barely blinked, waiting for an answer.

"Sir, I bought that phone myself," I finally replied. "I've always loved gadgets."

But just like the young scruffy-haired Komiteh members had quickly moved on to the matter of my supposed hidden golden doorknobs, Afshoun quickly moved on through the rest of the scribbled pages.

"How often did you see the Shah?" he asked after another long pause.

How many times did I have to answer this? I had performed regularly for Mohammad Reza Shah and the royal family ever since I was very little.

I must have been four or five years old the first time. It was at the *Kâkh-e Marmar* (Marble Palace) with its huge dome covered in arabesque tiles, towering high ceilings, and enchanting carved doors. I didn't know what "Shah" meant at the time, but I figured he was very important, given Papa's excitement.

I met the royal couple right after my performance, under Papa's delighted yet watchful eye. The Shah was married to Soraya Esfandiary-Bakhtiari then. I was mesmerized by Soraya's beauty, with her large blue-green almond-shaped eyes, her natural full lips, and even more so by her gown. It was so dreamy, white and puffy, that to Papa's horror I had turned my back to the Shah while tracing the majestic white waves with my fingers, without looking up when the royal couple asked me questions, the kind one asks a child of that age. I imagined Papa, standing by the entrance across the huge hall, nervously waiting for me to look up, just like he did when I got sidetracked by the grasshoppers that hopped onstage during my outdoor performance—sidetracked, but never off beat. Princess Shams (the Shah's older sister) and Princess Shahnaz (his daughter) were also there. They were also warm and friendly to me; Princess Shahnaz took off her pair of shimmering earrings and gave them to me to take home.

I must have been nine years old the second time I visited the Shah. This time, he was remarried, to Farah Diba. I had learned by then who they were, but I still knew nothing about protocol. As soon as I got onstage, I ran toward them in full character—I automatically switched into entertainer mode the moment my foot touched the stage—and eagerly reached out for a handshake while greeting them with "*Salâm!*" When I finished my bit, the person in charge of the entertainment was furious.

"Who told you to go shake their hands like that?" he scolded me.

But the Shah and the Shahbânu didn't seem to care.

For more than two decades, I performed for the royal family at different events, birthdays, weddings, sometimes several times a year—I watched their four children grow up before my very own eyes. And when I desperately needed help, I turned to them, especially the Shahbânu.

I always had a soft spot for the Shahbânu. She was a true patron of the arts, a defender of avant-garde movements, and a staunch believer in society's vital need for artistic expression. She always made a point to first greet the artists and performers before other guests. She had elegance and grace, as well as warmth, charm, humor, and humility.

My relationship with the Shah was different. It was much more formal and distant, that of a king and his subject. I was intimidated by him, by his trademark serious composure, but I never felt belittled by him, like I had by some members of the royal court, who looked at me with their noses pointed upward. I was nervous around him. I remembered a time, in the early 1970s, when I was performing at a private event held at the home of former Prime Minister Amir Asadollah Alam, and I was looking to get four of my band members temporary leave from their active military service—I needed them to accompany me to Paris for a unique opportunity to perform for thirty nights on the first floor of the Eiffel Tower. The Shah's cousin, Sohrab Mahvi, insisted that I bring the matter up directly with the Shah. As soon as we came face-to-face, my voice became shaky.

"Mr. Shah—I mean, Your Majesty the King—Mr. Shah—Your Majesty—Your Highness!" My face turned red as I rambled on. The Shah smiled—he was probably used to these kinds of reactions—and quietly listened to my case before granting me the permission.

For years, the Shah and the Shahbânu encouraged me in my artistic endeavors. They invited me to perform for world leaders, to share with their esteemed guests the wonders of our Persian poetry wrapped in mid-tempo, pulsating rhythms with majestically orchestrated strings. I always felt their support, their encouragement, in spite of the few times when the Shah's secret police, SAVAK, censored certain abstract lyrics in my songs (including in "*Pol*" [Bridge], "*Ye Nafar ye Rouz Miâd*" [Someone Will Arrive One Day], and "*Katibeh*" [Inscription]) that could have been interpreted with anti-regime undertones—if one insisted on finding them.

I didn't care for censorship. I continued to sing the censored lyrics in my live performances, including in front of the royal family, without ever getting in trouble. And the one time a SAVAK agent told me that I had to change my outfit—specifically a pair of trendy hand-patched jeans—before performing at the wedding of Parviz Sabeti, a leading figure of SAVAK, I left the wedding. I wore the same outfit days later when singing for the royal family at a private gathering.

I never cared about the politics, I never cared about finding political references hidden behind metaphors. All I cared about was poetry, the emotions and the sensations that allowed me to release whatever I had pent up, and doing so in jeans, a miniskirt, or a kaftan was my right, my decision.

"When was the last time you saw him?" Afshoun asked, sweat trickling down his temples.

Again I gave him the same answer Mr. Tehrani had written down somewhere in that file. I had last seen the Shah sometime in June of 1978, at the *Kâkh-e Sa'dâbâd*, his royal palace. Hayedeh and I had been asked to perform for their guests, King Juan Carlos and Queen Sofia of Spain.

"He say anything to you?" Afshoun added.

"I can't remember," I replied. But I was lying.

I remembered that night so vividly. The stage had been set up in the palace gardens on that warm summer evening. I performed first, singing the Shah's and the Shahbânu's favorites, "*Kooh*" and "*Harf*" (A Word) respectively, as well as Spanish songs. The orchestra was flawless, the sound system was working perfectly, and I hit all of the notes I wanted to. And when it was Hayedeh's turn, I sat on the sideline of the stage and listened to her divine voice singing her *pop-sonati*, or popular traditional songs, beloved by millions. In addition to her contralto voice that commanded so much power and grace, Hayedeh had the gift of poetic delivery that would give you goose bumps, much like the revered Delkash before her.

Toward the end of Hayedeh's emotional and stunning performance, an official helicopter parked on the palace grounds prepared for takeoff—it was going to transport the royal couples to their next destination. As the rotor blades spun faster and faster, the orchestra's musical notes went flying into the air, along with Hayedeh's skirt. When the Shah walked past me, he turned to me and said with his timid smile, "You're lucky you sang first." Those were the last words he said to me, the last words he would ever say to me. He died in exile in Egypt on July 27, 1980.

"Why'd you work for them?" Afshoun asked with a piercing stare, the same reptilic stare as the young guard.

"I've never been political," I replied. "Ever since I was a child, I was taught, '*Khoda, Shah, Mihan*' [God, King, Homeland]. '*Khoda, Shah, Mihan.*' That's all I've known. I've never—"

"Have you no shame?!" he burst out, hitting the table with the palm of his left hand.

I froze.

"Didn't you see what they were doing to us—the greatest Shia power in the world?" he continued in a raised voice, with the vein in his forehead pulsing with every syllable. "Corrupting our people with Western music, alcohol, pornography? In exchange for what?" He paused to catch his breath. "A little pat on the head from *Amrika*—those filthy dogs?" he blurted in a thick *på'in-e shahr* accent.

He paused again to catch his breath.

"But you didn't give a shit about anything—besides your fame and fortune! *Did you?*" he blasted, spit flying out of his mouth, nearly hitting me across the table.

"You didn't give a shit—exposing yourself like that on camera! For young boys and men to see—to pay to see! To get excited to! Like a whore!" He stopped to catch his breath again, while more sweat trickled down his flushed temples.

All at once, I felt utterly naked in front of him.

"Those days are finished!" he roared, with his chest puffed up. "What've you got to say for yourself?!"

"Sir, I made a mistake," I replied as calm as I could, keeping my voice as steady as I could. "I made a big mistake."

"A big mistake!" he repeated.

His lips then slowly curled with satisfaction, just like my stepmother's would sometimes after unloading her fury onto us. *Remember his face*, I thought as my heart pounded, *in case there ever comes a time when I need to identify him.*

Chapter 15

The Lady Doctor

Day 18

I was pushing and pulling the needle through the last row, nearly finished with the orchid flower design, when the guards finally escorted the female doctor into our cell. Marjan and I had pleaded several times to Dâdâsh Abolfazl to transfer the khânoum doctor, or lady doctor, as everyone called her, into our cell. For twenty-four hours she was locked up with the addicts in their overcrowded cell, in that filth and perpetual darkness. We had room and *dâdâsh* knew it. Luckily, he listened. But you never knew what was going to happen. Some weeks ago, they brought Sepideh into our cell, the actress who was also mentioned in the list of wanted entertainers, and then released her less than twenty-four hours later. As much as Marjan and I were relieved for her, we couldn't understand why. Why did she go free, while we were rotting away down here for the past eighteen days? The three of us had worked in the same industries. There were also the last-minute, unannounced releases, first with Niloufar, then Nahid, followed by Fahimeh. We never got to say goodbye to any of them.

The doctor sat down in the corner, where she could stretch her long legs out in front of her, something she said she hadn't done in twenty-four hours. She was a relatively tall woman. And stunning. There had been much talk about her beauty, with her light-colored, almond-shaped eyes, high cheekbones, and naturally pouting lips, much like the Shah's second wife, Soraya. She must have been in her late thirties or early forties. Zari and the girls next door said they had never seen *dâdâsh* blushing like this before. *Dâdâsh* had even personally escorted the khânoum doctor into our cell this morning—he was rarely seen downstairs before the afternoon.

"I never thought I'd ever go to prison, let alone in the same cell as Googoosh and Marjan," the khânoum doctor said with a smile, though the slight quiver in her voice, her pale complexion, and the way her fingers nervously twisted the edge of her sleeve betrayed her fear.

She had led a serious life, she said, a life she shared with her husband, who was also a physician. Growing up she studied and worked hard to become a doctor, which would have been inconceivable, probably scandalous, earlier in the twentieth century. There was no room for a mistake, no room for fun for a young female medical student, she said. Her family had been supportive, but she knew from the very start that she would have to work twice as hard as any man to move ahead in her field, a disadvantage her brother never had to deal with while climbing up the military ranks. Her voice cracked every time she mentioned him.

"He knew what the mullahs were doing to the country, the country he loved so deeply," she whispered as tears welled in her reddened eyes. "He just couldn't sit back and—" Her voice choked up again.

Her brother, Lieutenant Colonel Kouros Azartash, was arrested on July 11, 1980, along with more than a hundred other military officials stationed at the Nojeh Air Base near the northeastern city of Hamedan, following the discovery of a planned coup to overthrow the newly established Islamic Republic and its government. After her brother's execution, the khânoum doctor cooked batches of sweet *halvâ* in his honor and distributed them in the neighborhood, as done in our tradition. But when her nasty neighbor told on her to the local Komiteh station, Revolutionary Guards stormed her home. *How dare you honor a traitor like him*, they had roared at her. Trouble was, they couldn't arrest her for handing out *halvâ*. So they searched every inch of her house, until they found a set of miniature liquor bottles, gifted to her and her husband on her wedding day nearly two decades prior by a Swiss physician. She explained that she and her husband weren't much drinkers, so they had used the gift as a decorative object in their living room, a decorative object that would cost her forty painful lashes.

"I tried to explain all of this to the sharia judge," she said, her eyes filled with the same horror I had seen in Niloufar. "I even told him that my husband's in Sweden right now, on their behalf, working hard to import medicine, medicine that will become even more valuable in the ongoing war with Iraq." She paused to catch her breath. "And they called my brother a traitor! He knew what they were capable of . . ."

Marjan and I just listened, trying to absorb it all. It was hard to make sense of our new world. Shortly after, we were joined by Zari, Mojgan, and the woman who boasted about all the celebrity posters she owned (including the one of me and Behrouz), while new frightened faces lingered by the doorway.

"You'll never believe what we just heard!" Mojgan whispered as she pulled on the knot of her bright-colored scarf out of excitement. She looked to Zari for confirmation.

Zari nodded as she lit a cigarette.

"Tell 'em!" the woman with the posters said to Zari with childlike enthusiasm.

Zari took a long drag of her cigarette and then loosened her polka-dot headscarf, purposely taking her time, all with a raised eyebrow, revealing her own delight in the news she was about to share.

"Turns out the kid wasn't released," she finally uttered in her deep smoky voice as she flicked the ash off her cigarette.

She was talking about Nahid. She was taken upstairs one day and never came back, just like Niloufar.

"She was shipped off to Passal's mansion," Zari continued.

Sabet Passal, whose real name was Habibollah Passal, was a prominent Bahá'i entrepreneur who introduced television to Iran in 1958. As religious minorities, the Bahá'i were enemies of the new regime. Passal's assets were confiscated by the Revolutionary Tribunal, and his palace-like home was used as an unofficial detention center, much like Mostafa Mesbahzadeh's.

"And that's not it! You'll never guess what happened next!" the woman with the posters interjected with a large grin. "Tell 'em, Zari!"

Zari glared at her enthusiastic cellmate before continuing. "They say the kid broke out, got away with the boy on his motorcycle."

I remembered the sparkle in Nahid's eyes when she had compared herself to Atefeh in *Hamsafar*. Inside I rejoiced like the woman with the posters, who could barely contain herself, clapping before her cellmates hushed her, warning that the guards were close by. I imagined Nahid holding tightly to her love as they drove away on his motorcycle toward freedom. I felt goose bumps thinking of her courage. At fifteen, she had no intention of standing down or of giving up her freedom.

"I wonder how he's going to take it," Mojgan said with a smile.

Those of us who had been here long enough knew she was talking about the young guard.

"I hope she doesn't get caught," Marjan said.

"Nah, she's tough!" Zari said as she shifted in her seat, trying to hide the tears that had welled in the corner of her eyes. She cleared her throat and changed the subject. "Those new girls standing by the door know you've been singing for us—"

"A few times even!" the woman with the posters interrupted.

"'Cause someone couldn't keep it to herself," Zari said as she threw another irritated glance at her eager cellmate. "And now that's all they talk about, how they wanna hear you sing," she added with her typical mischievous smile.

"Please!" one of the new faces interjected, her worried look replaced by a sudden burst of enthusiasm. "I love '*Man Amadeh-am*'!"

"Marjan, please sing '*Kavir-e Del*'!"

"Googoosh, I love '*Gahvâreh*' [Cradle]!"

I could see the smile even returning to the khânoum doctor's face.

"I loved all your films!" another new face exclaimed to me. "I spent all my time after school making photo albums of you from magazines and newspaper clips, so much so that my mom hated you. She even tore up one of your posters off my wall—but that never stopped me!"

Marjan and I were once more inundated with song requests under Zari's amused, watchful eye. I hadn't sung in a few days, maybe even a week. For days, I felt like a jackhammer was trying to bash in every corner of my skull. I had similar terrible migraines after Fery's death, sometimes up to three to four times a week, the kind that required Novalgin injections—a nurse would come from the Vanak clinic to Cabaret Vanak to administer the injections of painkiller to me before my shows. Now, without the injections, I was at the mercy of the pain that squeezed me tighter in its grip, tighter with every shriek that echoed incessantly all the way to our cell every hour of every day and night. It was relentless, ever since I saw that rage in Afshoun's eyes. Nothing helped, not even the countless aspirins they brought me from upstairs. I couldn't move, eat, talk, or sleep. I couldn't even lie still. Marjan was so worried, she had pleaded to Dâdâsh Abolfazl to do something.

The guards finally took me to the hospital. The young guard taunted me relentlessly the entire drive, his words dripping with sarcasm and contempt.

"Does the poor little diva have a headache?" he sneered, mocking my discomfort.

He didn't stop there, jabbing at my suffering in the basement, comparing it to my "golden mansion." His voice oozed with bitterness as he continued, grinning. "Must get lonely down there with just Marjan. Nothing like those Pahlavi orgies, huh?"

He was referring to the wildest rumors of debauchery within the royal court. His final insult was a jab about someone he knew who had died from a similar headache. But I wasn't too bothered by his attitude toward me; it was expected from a young guard who used his newfound power to mask his insecurities. What came next, however, was the most painful moment of the last few weeks.

The whole time in the car, I kept imagining how I was going to tell the doctor about my unofficial arrest, the basement, and the squalid conditions. I would ask him or her if they could call someone, to get the word out.

The doctor was a man in his forties, with salt-and-pepper hair and a clean-shaven face—a daring sign of defiance against the new order's bearded look—who stood next to a desk adorned with pictures of his children. He looked just like the men who used to bring their families to Motel Ghoo, or the cabarets, the same men whose weddings I performed at. He looked like someone who might help me.

My heart raced when the guards left us alone in the office and our eyes met, hoping he recognized me. He did—a flicker of recognition crossed his face, a brief hesitation—but he quickly looked away. He continued with the medical exam, addressing me the entire time with the formal *shômâ*, in stark contrast to the guards, all while ignoring the elephant in the room.

"I've been told aspirin isn't helping with your pain," he said in a monotonous voice.

I nodded.

"Have you had migraines before?" he asked.

I told him about the Novalgin shots as he quietly examined my pupils.

The doctor then pressed on my sinuses, followed by my temples, provoking more waves of agonizing jackhammers to pound against my head. I could barely breathe as he then felt my lymph nodes in my neck.

Say something, this is your last chance, I thought as he quietly took my blood pressure.

"This should help," he finally said as he gently injected the Novalgin into my arm muscle.

I fought back my tears as I was escorted out of his office, seeing that, like so many others, this doctor had turned his back on Googoosh. I had always believed doctors acted in their patients' best interests, but here he was, indifferent to my plight. For all he knew, I was being tortured in some basement. And yet he said nothing.

It helped enormously knowing that these women, here in this basement, hadn't turned their backs on me. The khânoum doctor also looked hopeful, her eyes bright with anticipation as the song requests continued pouring in. Even Marjan chimed in. She needed the distraction from the endless questioning by the sharia judge. And so Marjan and I took turns, whisper-singing like before, and momentarily transporting everyone beyond the four walls of our basement holding cell.

Day 22

Zahrâ entered our cell with a slight bounce in her step. Her face looked different. Her permanent air of disgust—she looked as though she were always in the presence of smelly cheese—was gone and replaced instead with a large toothy grin. No one had seen her smile before. No one had seen her surprisingly straight, pearly white teeth—her best feature. She even looked five years younger.

She was here to carry out the lashings on the khânoum doctor. She had come in earlier this morning with the grim news that today was the day. We told the khânoum doctor about the trick other inmates had learned—wearing extra layers under the chador for the lashings, as required by their beloved sharia rules, to lessen the pain. But even as her body trembled, she insisted she would be fine.

As she ordered the khânoum doctor to get up, Zahrâ's taunting smile grew bigger upon seeing the terror in her eyes. And it was no secret why—Zahrâ's crush on Dâdâsh Abolfazl was painfully obvious, and she couldn't bear how his face would light up around the beautiful doctor, while he barely spared her a glance. Now her romantic rival faced physical punishment. And Zahrâ would be the one to administer it.

The doctor followed her orders, as gracefully as she could, without her knees buckling beneath her. I felt sick to my stomach. Marjan turned as pale as a ghost.

"Put this on!" Zahrâ ordered as she tossed her the black chador.

Meanwhile, Abolfazl carried a garden hose and placed it by Zahrâ's feet, close to the doorway.

"Get down on your stomach, toward the middle, with your head facing that wall!"

The khânoum doctor froze momentarily.

"Get down now!" Zahrâ roared to the doctor like a sadistic circus trainer to a helpless animal.

She did as she was told, while Zahrâ reached down and grabbed the hose. As soon as the doctor lay down, I noticed the dried brownish stains covering the chador.

"You two, hold her down!" Zahrâ ordered as she untangled and unfolded the hose with some difficulty—it looked heavy.

We froze.

"I can't have her arms flapping in the air," she said in a softer voice. "You don't want her to get hit all over, do you?"

Marjan and I sat by the khânoum doctor. I put her head on my lap, without Zahrâ saying a word about it—she was too busy stretching out the thick rubber hose on the ground along the doctor's body. We figured this was part of their sick psychological torture, but we each grabbed one of the doctor's hands, squeezing tightly to let her know we were here for her as she was being subjected to this barbaric act. Then I began secretly praying for a miracle. I imagined Marjan was doing the same.

Zahrâ was finally ready, towering above us, tightly gripping the garden hose a little less than five feet away from the tip with both hands. She stood still for a minute or so. Then, as if she had been given the green light by some invisible force, she lifted her arms as high as she could reach above her head, while the rest of the hose dangled behind her. Before we knew it, the hose came smashing down against the khânoum doctor's back. Her body jolted violently, with her arms and legs jerking up toward the sky despite our grasp. The doctor screamed from the top of her lungs. Without a moment to waste, Zahrâ's arms went back in the air.

Second lashing.

Third lashing.

Fourth lashing.

Zahrâ stopped to catch her breath, having put all her strength and all the weight of her medium-built body into each swing. Sweat beads dripped down from her forehead, over her bushy brows, and onto her flushed temples.

Fifth lashing.
Sixth lashing.
Seventh lashing.

Eighth lashing.

Ninth lashing.

Tenth lashing.

Eleventh lashing.

Twelfth lashing.

Zahrâ stopped again, visibly exhausted by her efforts. She hadn't been raising her arms as high as before for the past five lashings, which she wasn't ever supposed to do from the start. According to the dictates of sharia, she was supposed to be holding the Quran under her arm, both symbolically, to uphold its sacred guidance, and for safety reasons, to prevent the arm from going any higher, thus minimizing the swing. Zahrâ was breaking the rules.

Marjan and I quickly checked on the khânoum doctor, who had stopped making any noises, worried that she was either unconscious or, worse, dead. But she began moaning aloud again.

Zahrâ couldn't go on—there were twenty-eight lashings left. She turned to Abolfazl, who had remained still by the doorway, and then handed the hose over to him without a word.

Just as I was about to cry from relief, believing it was miraculously over, Abolfazl lifted his arm, much higher than Zahrâ had ever reached. And with a blank stare, he yanked the hose, which came smashing down against the doctor's back.

"*Dâdâsh*, why you?!" the khânoum doctor yelled in confusion, having turned her head to look him dead in the eyes. "Why are you doing this to me?!" Tears rolled down her cheeks.

Down came the hose again, pounding on her back. The doctor sobbed.

Zahrâ had broken another one of their own rules—having a man carry out the punishment. I kept praying that Abolfazl would stop, realizing the pain he was inflicting on the poor doctor—the same doctor he was so fond of—but he continued, almost mechanically, devoid of any emotion or reaction to the khânoum doctor's cries and pleas. Only after the eighteenth lash did he begin to show signs of fatigue. Yet, he didn't falter. Taking his role seriously, he methodically carried out the full sentence, lash after lash, until he reached the fortieth.

Finally, it was over. The khânoum doctor shrieked as she lay on the ground. The stained chador now also bore streaks of the doctor's blood.

Day 26

I was struggling to fall asleep. My mind wouldn't stop. I couldn't talk to Marjan. She had finally dozed off, taking long and gentle breaths. It was late, maybe 10 p.m. or midnight—it was hard to tell time here in the basement. The room was colder and strangely smaller now that it was just the two of us again. Of course, we were happy to see the khânoum doctor leave this hellhole, even though we avoided looking over at her empty corner. She had spent her last day with us in absolute agony, lying on the dirty carpet, unable to move, sobbing and moaning from pain.

The chador, with just her long-sleeve top underneath, had not protected her. The fabric stuck to the fresh cuts, and each time the hose came smashing down, the fabric moved and pulled on the open wounds.

"As though the crushing blows weren't enough, I felt like I was being stung all the way down to my bones," she said as soon as she was able to talk.

But just like Fahimeh and the others, the throbbing, bruised skin on her back was nothing compared to her feeling of shame.

"But they're the ones who should feel ashamed," we protested. "Not you!"

"They're the ones acting like savages," Marjan added, loud enough for anyone in the corridor to overhear.

I wondered if Abolfazl was plagued by guilt. We hadn't seen him around here since.

"But I don't regret anything," the doctor said to us in a choked voice, not long before her release. "I don't regret what I did for my brother. Never. I'd cook *halvâ* all over again if I had to, even after all this."

Now it had been twenty-four hours since the khânoum doctor was freed, twenty-four hours since Marjan and I stopped talking about that dreadful day. We pretended that none of it had happened, even though the sound of that very first lash echoed in our heads, along with her screams that would be forever lodged somewhere in those hollow caves of our memory—you can never unhear those sounds. We pretended that we were okay, just as we had every day for the last twenty-six days. We shared stories from the past, I continued stitching, we had our daily meals, our three interspersed visits to the bathroom, the hour-long visit from our neighbors—I even saw Mama and Homayoun again, who brought me a change of clothes, more cigarettes, and reassured me that Kambiz was doing all right.

Just when I had dozed off, the rattling sound of keys woke me. Even in that muddled state I knew what I was in for. It was the third time they had done this to me, the third time they had awakened me like this to take me upstairs. It was part of the punishment; everything to exhaust you, to make you more confused and defenseless, everything to get you to feel less like yourself, less human.

For the third time in fifteen days I was escorted to Afshoun's large desk, where he was seated with that smug look on his greasy face, pretending not to see me standing before him. I couldn't tell who was more arrogant, him or the sharia judge. Hajj Aâghâ Ansari was certainly enamored with himself and his *amâmeh* that he readjusted every three seconds, and understandably so, as the revolution bestowed him with the power to "cure" society. But there was something uneasy about Afshoun, about the way he carried himself. Everything about him, his frown, his brusque hand gestures, his severe tone, and the words that came out of his mouth all felt exaggerated, just like his oversize suit.

"Sit!" he finally snapped as he continued to shuffle through the pages without looking up.

He wasn't wearing his glasses I noticed as I took my seat. I had never seen him without those smudged lenses always falling from his nose. He didn't seem to have a problem reading the documents without them. *He must be nearsighted.* Then I remembered Zari saying something about his glasses being fake. Perhaps he was just trying to keep the girls from Shahr-e No from recognizing him.

The desk seemed more chaotic than the other times, with files and loose pages covering its entire surface. It looked like Abolfazl hadn't been around to reorganize. For a second, I questioned whether he had even been to work since that dreadful day. But I didn't dwell on it too much. Besides, I had to say something to Afshoun about what Zahrå had done. Now was the time.

"Mr. Afshoun," I said after gently clearing my throat.

His dark beady eyes darted right at me from across the wide desk. They widened as he listened to my account of the missing Quran, and a man carrying out the khânoum doctor's sentence (I didn't name Abolfazl). His pen was frozen in the air, long after I had finished, as though he were still processing all of this new information.

"Don't worry," he said in a surprisingly soft tone, a tone that reminded me of Mr. Tehrani.

His lips curled upward.

"You'll soon get a taste of it yourself," he hissed.

My heart pounded against my rib cage.

"Now, Miss Atashin," he said, "answer these questions . . ."

Hours went by of the same gossip questions: Who did you sing "*Do Mahi*" (Two Fish) for? "*Vaghtesheh*" (It's Time)? "*Âghâ Khoobeh*"? Did you see this actress with that general at that party? That actress with the Shah? What about that singer? See her around the Shah? Who did you see hanging around that filthy Ashraf? Where did Farmanara get the money to make that filthy movie (*Dar Emtedâd-e Shab*)? Who was so-and-so with at Shiraz (Festival of Arts)? Who else did Egyptian president Anwar Sadat meet with during his visit?

Then, suddenly, he smashed his pen against his desk for no apparent reason.

"Who the hell do you think you are?!" he shouted, his eyes slightly bulging from his skull, just like the mullah's eyes bulged in Evin Prison.

"Sitting on top of that hill like you owned the goddamn city!" Afshoun continued.

My cheeks burned from rage.

"Singing and dancing like that in public?!" he screamed as he pounded his fists against his desk. "Corrupting the minds of our innocent youth with your filth?! With your sinful voice?!"

My entire body shook with fury as he rose to his feet.

"Who the hell do you think you are?!"

He was out of breath.

I wanted to fire back. I wanted to scream that I had never wished to become Googoosh. That I was brought unwillingly onto the stage at the age of three and kept there by my father when he realized my talent could make him money. I wanted to tell him that as I got older, it was the audience's applause, encouragement, and love that kept me going. That my fans came from all walks of life, from every corner of our country and beyond, welcoming me into their cities, towns, villages, and homes for years. I wanted to tell him that even his own guards snuck out music cassettes containing sinful voices, my sinful voice, and that even Abolfazl would quietly linger in the corridor just to hear Marjan and I sing. I wanted to tell him that there was nothing filthy about music, that music was what allowed me to feel peace in my core, the same peace described in the divine books. I wanted to tell him that it was music that had protected me all these years, that kept me sane, that healed my wounds from a broken head to a shattered heart! Not money! Not fame! Not power! Not drugs! But *music*!

Instead, I swallowed the lump in my throat and said, "You're right, I'm nothing. I made terrible mistakes. I'm nothing . . ."

He cleared his throat, as though he were getting to launch another tirade, but sat back down instead.

"Name every property you own, every source of income," he said with his pen in hand, seemingly regaining his composure.

"I don't have an income, I'm not allowed to work," I replied.

After everything he had accused me of, every insult he hurled at me, at Googoosh, he was still interested in the income generated by my "sinful voice." The irony was laughable, if I weren't trembling inside with fury.

Day 28

"You're free to go," Afshoun said in an irritated tone, two days since his outburst, twenty-eight days since I'd been locked up.

Only minutes earlier I had imagined being taken before the firing squad. Why else would they come for me before sunset?

"But, sir, I don't understand," I blurted. "I don't understand why I was arrested in the first place without any official conviction! And now, you're letting me go?"

As soon as he noticed the immediate regret in my eyes, his lips curled upward.

"Maybe you'd rather stay here with your girls?" he asked with that disgusting smile.

He took one last look at my folder before dismissing me and said, "You're just going to have to pay the *khums mâl* [Islamic tax of one-fifth of income]."

I tried to remind him that I didn't have an income, but it fell on deaf ears.

I was allowed to go back down to retrieve my things. I didn't care about my Gobelin stitching kit, the cigarettes, or my clothes. I wanted to say goodbye to Marjan.

"They're letting me go," I said, crouching down beside her.

Her eyes welled, just as they had when the doctor was taken upstairs.

"What did they say?" she asked.

"Nothing."

It never made any sense.

"But they must've finally realized how broke I am," I said with a forced smile, "and probably thought, 'If we keep her any longer, we'll have to line her pockets with cash just to get her out the door.'"

We both chuckled. But we both knew how devastatingly empty this tiny cell was going to feel. I never would have made it without Marjan's soft voice, without our long talks, our laughter, and even our whispered singing. And now she would have to carry on alone.

"Call me as soon as you're out," I whispered into her ear as we hugged tightly, fighting back tears.

I turned around, bag in hand, and left without the heart to look back.

Marjan was the only one I said goodbye to. I didn't get to say goodbye to Zari, Mojgan, and the woman with the posters, or the women locked in the dark cell, just as I hadn't gotten to say goodbye to Niloufar, Fahimeh, and Nahid. I never found out what happened to them, or to the men we heard across the basement. Marjan was released not long after.

One day, months after my release, I read somewhere that the Committee of Vice and Virtues' unofficial prison on Vozarȃ Street had been shut down. Then I remembered the time when Azam Taleghani, a newly elected member of Parliament and daughter of none other than Ayatollah Taleghani—the same ayatollah whom Hayedeh and I were once rumored to have tortured—stepped into our cell. She had come in person to inquire about the living conditions in the basement. Although she purposely ignored Marjan and me the entire time, barely an hour after she left, her assistant called for me. I was escorted by one of the guards to the telephone at the bottom of the staircase. She invited me to speak about my experience in front of the Parliament. I turned down the offer. I couldn't trust her. Besides, I thought, the Parliament of the Islamic Republic doesn't care what Googoosh has to say.

Aghdas, with her golden tooth, had stayed true to her word. She gave Azam Taleghani an extensive testimony of what she had been put through, including photographs of the cuts and bruises she had suffered, as well as a detailed account of that hellish cell, the filthy toilet, the flies, and all the other sordid conditions we had been forced to endure.

"They're gettin' nothin' from me! Never!" she had declared.

And she gave them nothing. She stood her ground until they shut down the basement in Mr. Mesbahzadeh's home, a basement that would forever echo with gut-wrenching shrieks. A prostitute had made this happen when no one else could. I admired her. I didn't have her courage—not even an ounce. As soon as I had gotten into the car with Homayoun after my release, I began sobbing uncontrollably, just as I had after losing Fery. I couldn't stop. Unlike Aghdas, I had given them everything—my career, my honor, my voice. I had given them Googoosh.

Part II

Chapter 16

Papa

January 25, 1987

The phone rang, but neither of us moved. Not an inch. Homayoun and I had only just gotten to bed. We had stayed up all night watching Tony Scott's *Top Gun* (1986), followed by Oliver Stone's *Platoon* (1986). We did this nearly every night for years, watching whatever new bootlegged foreign film hit the black market when we weren't out socializing with friends. Most foreign films were banned, and most domestic ones never made it past the Ministry of Culture's scrutiny. Then, just as the early birds started chirping, we would climb into bed, where I would lie awake until the sleeping pills kicked in. I couldn't sleep without them, not ever since I was released from the unofficial prison seven years ago.

We needed the distraction, especially these last nine days, as missile attacks and aircraft bombings shook the city—the latest in a series of Iraqi air raids on Tehran that began in the spring of 1985. Unlike most, Homayoun and I didn't hide in a basement during the siren's wail—we didn't have one. Instead, we'd lie on the floor away from the windows during the blackouts, holding our breath, waiting to see whether we would survive.

The phone rang again. I looked over to the electronic clock on my nightstand. It was 9 a.m. This time, the ringing seemed to grow louder, one ring after another. I knew in that foggy state that it would continue to ring until one of us picked up the receiver. It had to be me, since Homayoun lay dead asleep beside me.

"*Allô?*" I said in a provincial accent—a trick I had learned to filter out calls from a female stalker or bored Komiteh agents—and in an unintentional raspy voice.

"Googi?"

I didn't recognize the voice.

"*Allô?*" I repeated with the same thick accent.

"Googi, it's Uncle Nader," he said in Azeri. Just like Papa, my paternal uncle always spoke to me in Azeri. "*Azizam*," he continued in a shaky voice.

"What's wrong?" I asked.

"It's about Saber," he replied, his voice choked.

What about him? I thought as he paused. *Did he have another heart attack?* Papa had two of them in the last ten years. *This time, I won't be able to visit him at the hospital*, I realized anxiously. Papa was all the way in Istanbul, where he had been permitted to travel less than a month ago.

"He—" He stopped again, his voice trembling.

He couldn't bring himself to say it.

"He died?" I asked, my heart sinking.

"He left us last night," he finally uttered before breaking into uncontrollable sobs.

Once he regained his breath, Uncle Nader explained that Papa had died from a heart attack on Saturday, January 24, 1987. My half brother, Adel, who was with him at the time, was going to help repatriate his body to Iran.

I was wide awake now, the effects of the sleeping pills finally worn off, as I raced down the snaking road toward Uncle Nader's in Gisha. I was alone. I didn't bother to wake Homayoun. He never met Papa, and besides, he never really cared much about any of my relatives with the exceptions of Fariborz and Mehrdad. I replayed my uncle's words in my mind as the ice-cold winter air rushed in through the cracked open window of my cobalt-blue 1974 Toyota Celica—I had gotten rid of my treasured brown Jeep Renegade from before the revolution, since the Komiteh agents and

Revolutionary Guards recognized it from miles away and frequently stopped me without any pretext.

He left us last night.

I couldn't believe it. I thought about that last lunch we'd had together as I sped down Parkway—no one ever called it by its new name. It was less than a month ago, right before he left for Turkey. I remembered forcing myself to go see him that day, also coincidentally at Uncle Nader's. Generally I avoided Papa as much as I could.

Our relationship never recovered from those years with Mouness and only got worse after my divorce from Mahmoud. One night, when I was twenty-two or twenty-three, Papa showed up at Cabaret Miami, where I had just finished my nightly closing act—Mahmoud offered me the gig, despite our divorce, since Googoosh was always going to be very lucrative for his family business. Having changed out of my performance outfit, I stepped out from backstage to join the friends I had invited to the show and spotted Papa across the cabaret floor, at the bottom of the stairs to the main exit. He was swaying slightly, his eyes glazed and unfocused, and most likely reeking of vodka. Seeing him like that, I thought, *Oh God, what now? How much does he need this time?* Ever since Mouness had left him, his unchecked drinking continued to drive a wedge between us, deepening a rift that had been growing for years. He was already a heavy drinker when she was around, but afterward, there was no one left to hold him back. Papa only came to me when he needed something. I had just bought him a new car a month earlier, but I knew he must've sold it and spent all the money, just like with all the previous gifts. He burned through whatever money I gave him as quickly as he knocked back his drinks.

"Where you going?" he said to me in Azeri, his words slurred, as I got closer.

"I've got guests, Papa," I said to him, pointing to my friends, who started climbing the crowded stairs behind the rest of the audience, trying politely to make him understand this was not the place or the time.

Just as I was about to explain that we were heading off to my friend's home, Papa shouted, "Why did you talk bad about me in the *Zan-e Rouz* magazine?"

"I didn't talk about you, I talked about my life, my childhood, and Mouness," I replied, trying to contain my anger.

He suddenly slapped me across the face. He was a big guy, and the force of his slap knocked me to the ground. I was shocked. He had never hit me before. One of my friends rushed over to help me up before they escorted Papa and me through the stunned crowd into Mahmoud's office.

"I know where you go off to smoke up!" he said before he broke down sobbing.

He meant Pouran's house. This was not long after my nervous breakdown and the mediatized chaos that followed. Papa believed everything he heard, including the rumors that I had overdosed on opium. I also suspected Mahmoud had wound him up—they had become buddies over the years, despite Papa's initial dislike for him, and continued to see each other after our divorce, nearly weekly, since Papa had a strong attachment to Kambiz.

"My dearest Googi, I don't want anything from you!" he articulated with difficulty as tears ran down his cheeks. "I'm just—just—looking out for you—want you to be safe!"

My body shook with anger. I started crying.

"Papa, all those years you never cared about what I was going through!" I shouted in between sobs. "Right under your own roof!"

I had never raised my voice at Papa before.

"But now, now that I'm a divorced woman with a young child in my arms, now you want to protect me?!"

But Papa was too drunk to hear me, or maybe he just didn't want to hear any of it.

"I'm here to protect you!" he shouted back.

It was too late, I told him. The truth was that in my heart, I blamed Papa for everything. A small part of me had even wished for his death a few times. He was the one who brought Mouness into our lives. Maybe Fery would still be alive if it hadn't been for all the endless strain Mouness forced on his fragile body—the cold floors, the freezing water—day after day. Papa was the one who was supposed to protect us. Why didn't he? Were we not worthy enough? Feelings of worthlessness from those dark days of my childhood haunted me even after I became the biggest pop star in Iran, feelings that played an important part in the breakdown of my marriage to Behrouz, feelings that lingered all the way to now, living here as a persona non grata in my own country.

I tried to avoid Papa as much as possible after that night. I continued to give him money, to buy him cars and whatever else he needed, but I stayed away as much as I could. I maybe saw him a handful of times a year, always briefly, while he saw Kambiz regularly through Mahmoud.

He loved Kambiz so much, his first grandchild—you could tell by the way he looked at him—and remained a constant loving figure in my son's life, regardless of our own strained relationship. But even Kambiz became a sore subject between us.

"I miss Kambiz," Papa said to me at our last lunch.

I missed him, too. I hadn't seen my son in two years.

By 1985, Kambiz was a typical sixteen-year-old who loved to dress like the punk rock idols of the time, flirt with his crush, and spend his afternoons breakdancing. But he couldn't do any of it openly, living in Iran, where all of that was illegal. One morning while he was at my house, we got into one of our usual arguments, either about Homayoun or his latest run-ins with the Komiteh agents—he had recently received forty-five lashings for attending an underground party with girls and boys his age and passed out from the pain after the tenth. Kambiz couldn't stand Homayoun, especially after seeing him hallucinate on LSD or freebase cocaine in my home in Velenjak a few years after the revolution—drugs occasionally given to him by friends who managed to find some. And Homayoun made no secret of thinking my son was spoiled. This permanent tension meant Kambiz lived with us on and off, staying a few months before returning to his father's or my father's home. That day, he stormed off in the middle of our argument, and later, Papa called to reassure me that Kambiz was with him.

A few days later, Fariborz called. He explained that some twenty-four hours earlier, Mahmoud (who was in hiding from the regime due to the nature of his family business) had picked Kambiz up from Papa's and headed with him to the Turkish border with the help of human smugglers. My heart felt like it would stop. I could barely breathe for weeks until Kambiz called me to say that he finally made it to Istanbul, and that he was sorry and wanted to come back home. I told him to stay put and listen to his father. It was all I could do, being completely helpless without a passport—I still wasn't allowed to apply for a new one.

Ultimately, it was the right decision. Kambiz was two years away from being drafted into military service during a bloody war that had already claimed hundreds of thousands of lives; had he not been an only child, he could have been drafted as young as thirteen. Now that he was eighteen, he couldn't come back or else he'd be immediately shipped off to the front line. Still, I was furious with Mahmoud for not discussing his plans with me and upset with Papa for not bothering to call as it was happening. If I had known, I would have dropped my tough-love act that morning and hugged Kambiz tightly one more time. God only knew when, or if, I'd see my boy again.

As Papa went on about Kambiz during what turned out to be our final lunch together, I tried to push my anger aside. He then told Uncle Nader and me about Mahmoud's offer to join them in Istanbul. Not only would he get to see his grandchildren, Kambiz and Kimia (Adel's daughter) but he would also perform at the opening of Mahmoud's new cabaret. By then, a large population of Iranian refugees had settled in the Turkish capital. He couldn't refuse the offer, and he was still free to travel—they hadn't taken away his documents.

"For nine years I've done nothing but stay home, nine years away from the stage," Papa had said to Uncle Nader and me at that lunch with tears in his eyes.

In the years leading up to revolution, I would get Papa some odd jobs, mostly appearing in the films I was playing in, trying to boost his acting career. Unfortunately, he spent most of his time performing in small, dingy venues where alcohol was always plentiful—places that were not worthy of his natural talent.

"Can you believe it's been nine years?" Papa asked us.

I could. I had spent more than eight years confined in my home.

"It's going to be great, Papa," I said to him.

His eyes glimmered.

"I'm getting old, Googi. It's now or never."

Papa did make it back onstage, in Istanbul. And now, less than a month later, he was gone, I thought as I parked outside Uncle Nader's home.

Everyone was sitting in the living room, including Mama. She arrived sometime after Khadije Khânoum, Simin, and Bahieh—Dâyi had passed away some years earlier. Mama didn't say much as she discreetly wiped the new tears that formed in the corners of her eyes. Perhaps she never stopped loving him, I thought. Seeing their tears, including Mama's, triggered my own. But hearing Uncle Nader weep was something else. It broke my heart. He and Papa were close, as close as two siblings could ever be, just like Fery and me.

Long before I was born, Papa had introduced Uncle Nader to the world of dance and acrobatics. They still danced onstage together when I was very small. They would perform different folkloric dances, including traditional Azerbaijâni ones that Papa and I would later perform together, like the Lezgi and the Ghafghâzi—dances I found most challenging as a kid, since they required so much energy and strength for the repeated fast leg movements that lasted entire songs. The two of them had great rhythm and made it look effortless, even though it was the result of years of tireless practice. Then one day, in 1954 or '55, Uncle Nader was given the opportunity to join the dance troupe of the Ministry of Culture and Art. It was an opportunity of a lifetime that he couldn't refuse. While he and his troupe traveled across Iran, Papa chose to manage my budding career, and as time went by, he did so gradually more from backstage. But even after they had gone their separate ways, the two brothers always had each other's backs. I remembered the year we went to live at Uncle Nader's, with him, his wife, and their five kids; it must have been around the time Papa met Mouness, in between tours when he, Fery, and I had nowhere else to stay.

Tears welled in my eyes each time mournful relatives showed up at Uncle Nader's door, each time they expressed how sorry they were for

Papa's sudden disappearance—he was only sixty years old. They shared old memories of Papa, funny shenanigans only he would get into. I could see the Saber they knew and cared for, that fun, generous, and jovial man who made them chuckle, who showed them a good time no matter what. He was incredibly funny, someone they could always count on for pure entertainment. There would never be another Saber Atashin, they said. Yet, beneath their memories, I sensed a deeper despair. It wasn't just for the loss of a loved one. Their eyes expressed a profound sadness for the life that slipped away with every arrest, execution, bombing, civilian casualty, and senseless death at the front, including of children as young as twelve ordered to walk over minefields to clear paths for the army tanks.

Tehran, like the rest of the country, was suffering under the harsh realities of war—though it was our Western cities that were being physically devastated, bearing most of the brunt of the conflict. Inflation soared, making everyday goods increasingly expensive and difficult to afford for millions. War coupons became essential for securing necessities like food and fuel through rationing, but even with them, shortages were rampant—a stark contrast to nine years ago, before the war, when shops were full and life was far less restricted. We waited in long lines for essentials, and if you had the bad luck of being a little late, you often found empty shelves by the time it was your turn, especially for what were now considered luxury goods, like chocolate and sanitary pads.

For the last seven years, the city was in a constant state of anxiety, with wailing sirens and blackouts. There was a relentless, sometimes paralyzing fear of not knowing when or where the next attack would be. Families mourned the loss of countless loved ones, young men were sent to the front lines with little chance of return. The air in Uncle Nader's living room felt heavier, almost suffocating.

"Googoosh Khânoum, Saber loved you so much," Papa's friend interjected out of nowhere. "He was so proud of you, always showing us your pictures," he continued with a smile.

I remembered those pictures. I remembered those last years before the revolution, how he would sometimes show up backstage at the trendy

Cabaret Baccara, where I was performing as the closing act, and ask to take a picture with me. Then, almost systematically, he would pull out another picture of the two of us from his wallet and ask for my autograph.

"Why?" I would always ask him. "Why do you want an autograph when I'm your daughter, your Googi? I'm yours!"

"My dearest Googi, I just like to keep it in my wallet," he often replied with a smile.

Sometimes I wondered if those pictures were just another way for him to manipulate me into getting him what he wanted. Or if they were another gimmick he would later use to pick up women, like all those times I had caught him giving away "Googoosh's things," including my clothes and jewelry. Growing up, I often wondered what went on in his mind. Aside from the jokes and all the whimsical stories, Papa was a man of few words. He never spoke of feelings, the past, hardships, or dreams.

I forced a smile and then politely excused myself, explaining to Papa's friend that I needed to go speak to my cousin Simin.

As I navigated my way among the sorrowful faces, I couldn't help but remember seeing Papa asleep on his hospital bed after his second heart attack in 1985. I remembered how I had found his gray stubble most disturbing. He hated beards and was always clean-shaven. I remembered how it had suddenly hit me, like a ton of bricks, how much Papa had aged, how he was no longer that young athletic man who used to balance two chairs on his chin with me sitting on the very top. He was no longer that young man who enchanted women with his strong build and contagious smile, but a heavyset middle-aged man whose body was turning against him. I remembered how he opened his eyes and looked at me and how I thought he was still a handsome man, despite everything. I remembered wondering what was going on in his mind as we looked at each other in silence. Then I remembered wondering whether this was it for him, and that deep down he knew it as he stared out the window. I remembered how all my sympathy disappeared when he said in his typical self-pitying tone, "Googi, look at what happened to your poor old papa . . ."

He wanted something. I was convinced, as he gave me that self-pitying look he always wore whenever he asked for a material favor. But what could he have wanted at that point? I had nothing left to give.

"Stop it, Papa, don't say these things," I replied, trying to shake off the anger. "You need to rest, and you must listen to what the doctors tell you."

"I do listen, Googi," he said. "But this is different! Your papa's heart is in so much pain . . ."

The more he tried to get my pity, the angrier I got, though I never showed it. But as soon as I left his room that day, I felt terrible seeing the man who was once my rock, lying there, crushed and alone in his hospital bed. I felt terrible for all the times I had wished him dead, and terrible that I still couldn't forgive him.

I kept going over the to-do list as I drove to Papa's, south of what was still known as Farah Street (originally named after the Shahbânu), by Takht-e Tâvous Street, one of Tehran's central boulevards. It had become our new headquarters over the last five days, where more people would gather as news of his passing got around town. His house was never empty, filled with acquaintances, friends, relatives. Even his three ex-wives sat in the same living room with his latest wife, although Mouness, in typical Mouness fashion, continuously scanned the room for the faintest sign of slight toward her with her not-so-discreet side glances.

There had been so much to do. It took me days to organize the repatriation, days to find an administrative clerk among the different ministry departments who was willing to call the Iranian embassy in Istanbul and to coordinate the transfer from the Turkish morgue. It also took me days to find the necessary funds, with the help of friends and relatives, to pay for everything. After all, Homayoun and I were barely scraping by on the meager interest from the proceeds of his sold insurance business—less than a couple hundred U.S. dollars a month. The war coupons provided us with essential goods like food, fuel, and household items. Selling my house wasn't an option, since the government still refused to remove the lien, despite my repeated reminders that I had officially contested the 3 million tomans in unpaid taxes to the Shah's regime with all of the necessary documentation. Somehow my appeals magically disappeared overnight after the revolution.

Financially, things were tight. We couldn't afford new clothes, not even socks. Most of our cash went to cigarettes and opium. I would join him for a smoke once a day, while he spent hours hunched over his small, silver portable charcoal grill, heating the opium. Some days, I couldn't get out of bed without a puff from his beloved *vafoor* (Persian opium pipe)—it eased my sciatica and gave me a bit of energy to do the cleaning.

The final issue concerned Papa's burial plot, since Mama refused to let him be buried in the one I had originally bought for myself next to Fery in Behesht-e Zahrâ cemetery all those years ago.

"But Fery's my child!" she screamed, her voice piercing the air. "I gave birth to him! I have to be buried next to him!"

As soon as she started, I was thrown back to the day of Fery's death, when I had lost control and screamed at her. She had become hysterical, wailing and hitting herself—a common display in our grieving tradition—until I snapped, accusing her of not being there when he needed her most, telling her there was no point in making a scene now.

"Stop it or leave my house at once!" I shouted at her that devastating day, almost eleven years ago. It was a cruel thing to say to a grieving mother, but all of that bottled up rage had finally exploded. This time I was more understanding with her. Luckily Papa's friend stepped up and generously bought him a new plot in the same cemetery.

I had also managed to secure a permit to hold the *khatm*, the memorial ceremony that comes after the burial, at the Safi Ali Shah *Khânehghâh* (which literally translates to House of Present Time, originally a Sufism school), near Baharestan Square. It was another grueling process, just like for the repatriation, being sent left and right across town to different offices, to different condescending faces. Then, just as I was handed the permit, the stout clerk said there was one condition: I was not to have my father's obituary published in any of the papers, including any details regarding when and where the ceremony was going to be held.

"You see, we can't have Googoosh starting a commotion at a time like this," he said in that typically arrogant tone the regime agents spoke in. "Not when we're so close to glorious victory against those filthy Iraqis!"

I could feel the heat gathering in my cheeks.

What commotion? People didn't care about Googoosh! If people ever mentioned her it was to repeat rumors, like the one where I had married a rich mullah and was living lavishly in some secret mansion adorned in gold. They didn't know any better—after all, the media was forbidden to report on Googoosh and other pre-revolution icons, in a deliberate effort by the regime to erase us from the public eye. And what glorious victory was he talking about? With hundreds of thousands of people dead, including innocent women and children on both sides of the border, with bombs bringing down entire buildings in our neighborhoods? What glorious victory when neither Khomeini nor Saddam were ready for peace?

"Understood?" he snapped.

I nodded and assured him that the ceremony would take place the day after the burial with great discretion.

Everything was ready, I finally concluded, as I parked the car in front of Papa's, now five days since his passing. All that was missing was his body, which Adel was accompanying all the way from Istanbul to the morgue here in Tehran.

His body. Papa's body. It still felt unreal.

When Adel finally arrived from the Tehran morgue he was swarmed by friends and relatives who hadn't seen him since he moved to Turkey two years ago. Everyone loved Adel, seeing right past his serious demeanor, straight to his sweet nature. He was about five or six years younger than me. We didn't grow up together, as he went to live with his mother after Papa and she split less than a year after his birth, but we grew closer over the years. He was the other most reliable member of the Atashin clan, someone you could always count on, taking after his mother when it came to family values and responsibility. Even after all these years, she remained a graceful and gentle lady, showing up alone at Uncle Nader's home upon hearing about her ex-husband's passing, even with her son still in Istanbul.

As soon as the commotion around Adel dwindled, he and I sat down in a corner, just the two of us, where he began sharing details of what happened unexpectedly to Papa that fateful night.

"It was the strangest thing, Googi," he said with dark bags under his eyes. "Papa seemed fine, his usual self.

"He had some rich *kaleh pâcheh*, sheep's head and hooves soup, which he washed down with vodka before getting onstage," Adel went on in his more typical serious tone. "He was doing that funny drunk character, you know the one," he said with a tired smile.

He was referring to a routine inspired by Charlie Chaplin's "The Tramp" character—Papa loved Chaplin. The character stumbles into a bar at the end of the night, just before the owner is about to close the door. Sitting on a barstool with a newly poured drink, he asks the bartender to sing him a song and then as the bartender goes on singing, he laughs so hard that he falls off his stool. Papa always got the audience roaring with laughter.

"You should've seen his face, Googi! Both nights! He was so happy. I hadn't seen him like that in years," Adel said as he choked up.

I, too, felt a huge lump in my throat.

"He did everything just like the previous night, stumbling and mumbling, filling the room with the crowd's infectious laughter. But this time, after he fell down, he never got back up."

Adel paused and wiped his tears.

"Everyone laughed, so did I, just like on the previous night," he went on with a smile as tears streamed down his cheeks. "But I—I knew something was wrong when I saw his tongue." He paused. "He died right there on that stage."

Hearing this, I was overwhelmed with awe and moved to tears by the thought that he had passed away on the one place on earth he loved the most—the stage. His final moment was so fitting for the life he had lived.

"You know what's incredible, Googi?" Adel asked as he wiped his cheeks with the sleeve of his shirt. "Even with his death, Papa made people laugh."

Even with his death, Papa made people laugh.

Forty-eight hours later, I parked a block away from Safi Ali Shah *Khâneh-ghâh*. I wanted to make sure there were enough seats being set up for the memorial ceremony. If the memorial was going to be anything like the burial, I had nothing to worry about. We were less than thirty people at

Behesht-e Zahrâ cemetery just a day earlier. The only surprise had been Pouri Banayi. She and I had been through so much together—Pouri had been my shoulder to cry on during my tumultuous relationship with Mahmoud, and later, in an unexpected twist, I ended up falling in love with her ex, Behrouz, long after they had parted ways. Despite everything, we always found our way back to each other in difficult moments, even as we became targets of the new regime. And here she was again, by my side.

I was numb before seeing her, numb at the sight of the large hole dug into the ground, and numb to the outpouring of grief around me. It felt like something inside was blocking me from feeling anything at all, and I couldn't understand why. This was my papa's funeral, after all—the man who had shaped so much of my life, for better or worse—and yet I felt strangely detached. *What's wrong with me?* I wondered. Then, as soon as Pouri embraced me, tears rolled down my cheeks. As Papa's body, wrapped in the white cotton kafan, was lowered into the earth, I found myself thinking more about Pouri's loyalty. Her presence, her deference to him as a fellow artist, moved me more for his legacy than for the finality of his burial.

I reflected on all of these moments from yesterday as I walked closer to the entrance of the *Khânehghâh*, where I saw signs posted across the gate from the Department of Endowments and Charity. Large bold letters in black ink said: "TODAY'S CEREMONY HAS BEEN CANCELED."

I stopped mid-stride and stared dumbfounded at the sign. The regime officials were canceling Papa's memorial. A wave of anger surged through me as I stared at the sign, my disbelief quickly turning into rage. My last chance to honor Papa, to say goodbye, was snatched away just like that. They couldn't let me have this; they just couldn't let Googoosh mourn her father in peace! They were never going to let me be.

I went over to my half sister Roya's house—Mama's daughter from her second husband. I tried to warn those I could think of over the phone, but many went to the *Khânehghâh* as planned, only to be turned away by armed Revolutionary Guards stationed around the entire block. I didn't stay long at my sister's, my head was pounding, and my sciatica was at it again. I told Roya and Mama that I needed some rest and rushed home.

Despite my pain and exhaustion, I started rummaging through a box of dusty cassettes in my upstairs den. I couldn't explain why, but I felt like I had to find this one particular song right then, even with all of the pain rushing through my lower back. I emptied the box on the floor, barely leaving myself enough room to move around the mixtapes sent to me by friends from abroad, tapes containing new releases from all over the world, including Iranian singers in exile. I knew it was here. I had taken it over to a friend's not so long ago for a listen, like I did with all of the cassettes I received; I had stopped listening to music in my own home ever since I handed over the cassettes to Mr. Tehrani in Evin Prison. I had also stopped singing and humming alone—occasionally I sang in a whispered voice for friends at secret dinner parties, at their behest, or along with my fellow banned singer Soli and his harmonium. Homayoun couldn't understand why I went as far as selling my prized piano. I had to remind him of the revolutionaries smashing the piano keys with the butts of their rifles in the main grand hotel of Kish Island. I didn't want to take any risks, not with those random Komiteh visits, or with some neighbor reporting me for un-Islamic behavior. But I didn't care if anyone would come banging at the gate tonight. I needed to hear that song.

I flipped over the cassettes, one by one, looking for Turkish writing. Twice I read through all of the titles until I finally saw it. I inserted it into the dusty old cassette deck and pressed play. I shoved the pile of cassettes to the side and sat on the floor with my legs crossed like I did as a kid waiting for a particular song on the radio. Soon enough, the melancholic cries of the violin and the piano flooded out of the speakers. My heart started to race. My throat tightened. As soon as the high-pitched tenor voice of the famous Turkish singer İbrahim Tatlıses reached my ears, I felt warm tears running down my cheeks.

Ever since Adel told me about the night Papa died, I kept thinking of this Turkish song "*Yalnizim*" (I'm Lonely) that Tatlıses sang in the film *Ayşem* (1984). The song, which is about a person's overwhelming feelings of regret and loneliness, is heard in a moving scene where Tatlıses's character dies while singing onstage. As the lamenting melody made its way into my body, into my bones, I could see Papa sitting on that barstool. I could see Papa smiling as the adrenaline rushed throughout his body. I could feel his happiness.

Even with his death, Papa made people laugh.

I remembered that time when I was four or five years old when we traveled with a troupe across the northern provinces of Mâzandarân, Gilân, and Iranian Azerbaijân. On one of our days off in eastern Azerbaijân, Papa went about, as usual, exploring the town on his own, leaving me with a member of the troupe. But this time, he didn't come back for days. No one was able to calm me down. Eventually someone told me that Saber was fine, but that he had gone hunting and had accidentally shot himself. I cried from joy and anger when he finally came back a few days later. I learned much later that Papa didn't hunt. He would never say what had happened (perhaps it was a bar brawl over a woman), but he got back onstage just weeks later and performed the strenuous Azerbaijâni folk dances by my side. He seemed undefeatable, swiftly moving his long legs and strong upper body to the rhythm despite the newly removed stitches and bloodstained gauze hidden under his garment. Performing had been his life. Without the stage he was alone. Without the stage he suffered.

I began sobbing uncontrollably as I let Tatlıses's words wash over me. I couldn't stop. It had finally hit me. My papa was gone. The one who had been my rock was gone. The one who led me to music, who discovered my talents, who created Googoosh was gone. The one I had wished dead so many times was gone. He would never be able to tell me he was sorry, and I would never be able wrap my arms around his neck and tell him I forgive him. Years of tears and pain rushed out of me.

Papa had been my everything, my partner onstage, my buddy, and then he'd gone and married Mouness. If only he had seen what she was doing to us. If only he hadn't been blinded by love. Perhaps we would have been like all of those families I carefully watched when I was twelve from backstage in Cinema Royal, in between my Friday morning performances. Perhaps like them, we would have sat close together and laughed at Norman Wisdom or Jackie Gleason on the big screen. Perhaps he would have been proud of me for finishing school and going off to college. Perhaps I would have made better decisions in my relationships. Perhaps I would have been a better mother to Kambiz. Perhaps we wouldn't have lost Fery so early. Perhaps we would have had a chance at healing.

I wish I had forgiven Papa all those years ago. It was even easier for me to forgive Mouness. She was sick after all, and so she was the first to suffer under her own hands. In some ways, I was thankful to her. She made me a stronger person. Her moods helped me seek refuge in music. Her kicks and blows pushed me to release my pain through singing, urging me to channel my anguish through my voice. Her anger fueled my constant desire to become a better performer. She indirectly prepared me for all the challenges that were going to come my way. Maybe it was destiny that brought her into our lives. Maybe without her, there would have never been Googoosh.

As the song came to an end, I took a few deep breaths before playing it once more. I lay down on the floor and closed my eyes, and I started to remember the good days that I'd locked away somewhere deep within me. I remembered that first time I sat on top of the two chairs resting on his strong chin and thought how powerful my papa was. I remembered how he caught me midair as I was plunging toward the ground. I remembered that night we performed the Azerbaijâni comic and romantic operetta *Arshin Mal-Alan*, side by side, when his foot fell through the makeshift wooden stage and how I desperately tried to control my laughter. I remembered that one time while touring in Shiraz when he decided to take me on one of his adventures and drove us about an hour north to the majestic site of Persepolis, where he made me laugh with his made-up stories of the olden days. I remembered the sixteenth birthday bash he threw me, and how he had looked at me with so much pride. I remembered how the macho man I knew smiled with tears in his eyes when he first held Kambiz and said to him, "My dearest boy." I remembered his thick Azeri accent and how he always pronounced the number sixty-six in Persian "*sashto-seesh*" (instead of *shasto-sheesh*). I remembered how happy he got when I found him small roles in my films, like in *Hamsafar*. I remembered that lunch he had invited me to in his home, sometime after he was released from the clinic, where it was just the two of us and how he had cooked *dolmeh*, the delicious stuffed grape leaves, because he said he knew it was one of my favorites. I remembered how during that same lunch he had mentioned how much he missed the stage. I remembered how I shared his pain, but how I couldn't admit it. I remembered how he had bribed me to get me onstage as a toddler, and by doing so, how he had given me the greatest gift of my life: music.

I was going to miss him. Everyone was right. There would never be another Saber Atashin. The only comfort I had was knowing that, even in his final moments, he had the audience erupting with laughter. I knew there was nowhere else he wanted to be, nowhere else he loved more than that stage. I knew because he passed on that passion to me. And while I might not get to live out my passion ever again, I would forever be grateful to him for all those moments I was blessed to sing into the microphone.

My tears finally subsided, and I slowly drifted off into sleep as the cassette continued to play on.

The next day, to commemorate the seventh day of Papa's passing, I bought enough sweet confectionaries like *halvâ* and prepared tea for thirty guests (the same guests who had attended the burial) when, one by one, former beloved elites of our entertainment industries showed up at my door. Renowned actors, singers, music composers, radio personalities, and film producers, among whom were Pouri, Fardin, Marzieh, Jebeli, Ali Tabesh, Shahrokh Naderi, Ali Abbasi, Mehdi Soheili, Delkash, Manouchehr Nozari, and Mehdi Mosayyebi, all came to my home spontaneously to pay tribute to Saber Atashin. They came despite the risks of being arrested just to honor one of their own. I knew that somewhere above, Papa was watching all these people he admired, with those same sparkling eyes of his and that youthful smile.

Until we meet again, my dearest Papa, may you always perform in peace.

Chapter 17

Nowruz

March 21, 1988

The steaming green rice placed on the round silver *sini* was calling me. I hadn't had *sabzi polo ba mahi* in the longest time, not since before Papa's passing. The overwhelming aroma of dill, coriander, and garlic cooked in with the fluffy long-grained rice, along with the fried saffron-seasoned *māhi sefid*, a white fish from the Caspian Sea, drove my palate crazy in anticipation—I could almost taste it. I was happy that Maryam had prepared this customary meal reserved for our Persian New Year, Nowruz, despite the unspoken understanding across the country that the upcoming new year celebrations were canceled. I was happy to be away from my mother-in-law's, where Homayoun and I had been staying for the last few months, since his father passed away.

Hossein and Maryam Kharrazi called last night to make sure we were still joining their late lunch. A few others had canceled last minute, they said, having decided to leave the city with their children just like nearly a third of Tehran's population. No one could blame them. Even driving over today, the streets were eerily quiet—unusual for this time of year, even in the last eight years of this bloody war. The city usually buzzed with preparations for the ancient Zoroastrian festivities despite the government's disapproval of any pre-Islamic rituals. But not this year. There wouldn't be any jumping over fire on Châhârshanbe Suri to burn off the bad omens, no *haft-sin* displays for Nowruz, and no Sizdah Be-dar picnics to throw away the *sabzeh* thirteen days later.

Last year's bombings during the celebrations were still fresh in everyone's minds. The fear that Saddam's forces might strike again loomed over us, casting a shadow on any remaining sense of normalcy. After eight years, the war had become a relentless cycle of missile attacks and air raids, killing thousands—some say hundreds of thousands—and injuring twice as many. Everyone knew someone who had been maimed or killed.

I felt like death had walked past me twice. The first time was in February 1984, when Homayoun and I had just returned to my home in Velenjak after visiting friends and their newborn grandchild. Twenty minutes later, the walls and windows trembled as if there had been an earthquake. One of the first aircraft bombings struck near the home we had just left, shattering a window over the newborn's crib—thankfully, she only suffered minor injuries. The bomb crushed an apartment building right across from Ali Asghar Children's Hospital, the same building our friends Zohreh and Jamshid had just moved out of.

The second time was this February when I went skiing with Maryam and Hossein at Dizin. With the latest round of air raids, some friends suggested we escape the city for a day. I initially declined, hoping for a quiet day alone in Velenjak away from Homayoun and his mother, to clean, water the plants, and catch up on reading Louise Hay's latest book. But after much insistence, I gave in. For the first time in years, I felt alive as we swished down the slopes. My chronic sciatica didn't bother me that day, and I almost forgot about the war. Revolutionary Guards patrolled on snowmobiles, ensuring female skiers adhered to strict dress codes, but even that couldn't dampen my mood. Then we ran into a friend who casually mentioned that northern Tehran, including Velenjak, had been hit. When I returned that night, I was relieved to find my house still standing, though debris littered the garden, and the main entrance door had been blown outward. The impact was worse at the back, where all the windows had shattered and the tin roof of the courtyard behind the kitchen had collapsed.

I learned to become emotionally numb to it all, like so many around me—perhaps this was a survival mechanism when you're constantly walking a tightrope between life and death. Deep down, I felt like God was watching over me, sparing my life each time. But I couldn't understand why. Why was I spared when so many others weren't? What purpose did I serve, just staying at home for the last eight years? Maybe this was exactly what I was intended to experience. Perhaps this was my fate, to live in this constant limbo, or maybe it was only a matter of time before my lifeless body would be pulled from the rubble like so many others. We all knew our time could come at any moment, even now, seated at this table at the Kharrazi household with our hosts and three other guests, trying to celebrate Nowruz amid all the anxiety. Part of me had made peace with it. Though I was no longer religious, as I had been before the revolution, I still firmly believed in God, and in the divine will that guided each of our lives.

"This is exceptional!" I said to Maryam after my first bite—her cooking was phenomenal.

"Wow! This is seriously delicious," Ali-Reza, another guest, added. "I can go peacefully after this."

"He's right, Maryam," Ali-Reza's wife, Roshanak, said.

"I overcooked the fish," Maryam said with a regretful tone as she tucked her blond hair behind her ears.

"No way!" Ali-Reza exclaimed. "If today's *the* day, then at least we'll all go having had your amazing cooking one last time and having been in the best company."

Farifteh, another good friend of Maryam and Hossein, snapped, "Ali-Reza, why joke of catastrophe like that?!" while she nervously flipped the end of her glossy curly brown locks. It was unlike her happy-go-lucky attitude.

"Farifteh, don't listen to him," Roshanak said.

"I'm just saying that everything is great," Ali-Reza responded with a big grin. "Maryam jân has cooked us this amazing feast, we're listening to great music with great company—hell, we're sitting with Googoosh jân! So even if the worst were to happen, just imagine the headlines: 'An Iraqi Missile Has Killed Googoosh and Her Friends.' You hear that? 'Her friends!' That's us! We'll be famous martyrs!" he said, chuckling.

The state-controlled media proclaimed all civilian deaths as martyrs of the Islamic Revolution—their deaths hailed as noble sacrifices. The regime used such tragedies as propaganda, glorifying each senseless loss of life to foster nationalistic fervor and frame the ongoing war with Iraq as a sacred struggle. It may have worked in the beginning, but eight years later, these headlines were often met with anger and frustration, as we lost hope of a peaceful future with every latest blow. No one believed anymore in this war that continued to destroy so many lives, families, and homes. It was hard for any of us to see the relentless destruction as anything but a futile waste, a painful reminder of the regime's empty promises.

We all laughed. Even Farifteh's frown disappeared.

"Ali-Reza, you've gone mad!" I told him, still laughing.

But death had become such a part of our daily lives, it was easy to laugh about it.

"Hah!" Homayoun interjected with a sly smile. "Ali-Reza, don't hold your breath! Maybe they'll mention in small print that she became a martyr along with 'her husband.' It's the least I'm owed, right?"

"Come on, man, don't make us shed a tear for you!" Hossein said before anyone could nervously check on my reaction. "All these years spent beside Googoosh? Oh, you poor thing!"

They both chuckled.

I faked a smile as my sciatic pain started up again.

Hossein changed the subject. I tried to follow, but my mind drifted between the pain and my two inner voices arguing.

He's right. He stuck by my side all these years . . .

No one forced him to stay!

The two voices had grown louder ever since I left that basement nearly eight years ago. One voice was Faegheh, and the other Googoosh. I hadn't lost it. I knew they were both me. But there were times I felt like one of those cartoon characters, watching the cross fire between the tiny figures standing on top of each shoulder. Faegheh wanted to protect Googoosh and her reputation from the outer world, while Googoosh wanted Faegheh to stand up for herself. They were both right.

I knew it wasn't easy for him, living in the shadows of Googoosh. But living with Homayoun wasn't always easy for me, either. No one knew, before we moved in to my mother-in-law's, how he had experienced another violent episode under the influence of freebase cocaine. I can't remember what he was hallucinating when he started arguing and pushing his brother-in-law, Moussa. As I tried to intervene before it escalated into a fistfight, Homayoun knocked me down the staircase in the scuffle.

Sweet old Mansour Khân (the security guard who had been watching over our cul-de-sac since before the revolution) was the one to rush me to the hospital. I told everyone I had broken my ribs slipping down the stairs. I couldn't tell them the truth. I knew what they would say. But I wasn't ready to leave him. I wasn't ready to be alone.

After the meal, we moved to the living room for tea and cigarettes while music blared from the speakers. No one cared much about the Revolutionary Guards or morality police these days, not with the ongoing attacks on the city. When Maryam asked Hossein to change the song, he eagerly moved to his prized silver triple-decker stereo system, which he guarded closely—he had it smuggled in from Europe at great cost. As soon as Sade's "Smooth Operator" played, I started humming without thinking. Maryam and the other guests pleaded that I sing a song, while Homayoun brushed off the tiny traces of crumbs from his pants.

"Why don't you sing '*Zemestan*' [Winter]?" Homayoun suggested without looking up.

None of them had heard it before, except for him. I promised that I would at the end of this song, keeping Hossein on his toes by his sound system, his finger already positioned near the stop button for when the time came.

As I listened to Sade's beautiful voice emanating from the speakers, I thought back to all those nights spent in Soli and Giti's basement apartment during the early years of the war. Soli was also a pop singer and a musician, loved for the Afghan flair he brought to his music. He was the one who composed the song for my single "*Ma Be Ham Nemiresim*," the same song whose lyrics were written by Masoud Fardmanesh, the songwriter who became the Revolutionary Guard commander responsible for the airport. Just like me and the rest of our colleagues, Soli found himself banned from performing and out of work after the revolution.

Within those soundproof walls we listened to everything from *sonati* to Iranian and Western pop, rock, and soul—for five or six years—without risking resentful neighbors denouncing us to the Komiteh. When the cassettes stopped playing, we sang songs reminiscent of those warm sunny days spent on the gray shore of the Caspian Sea. We read and reread verses from the masters, like Rumi and Rudaki, as well as more recent works by contemporary greats, like Sohrab Sepehri and Mehdi Akhavan Saless. With their words, we expressed our pain, and we cried our tears.

It was during one of those nights that Soli started toying with a melody on his harmonium as one of us read out loud Mehdi Akhavan Saless's poem "*Zemestan*" (*Winter*) (1956) for the umpteenth time—it spoke to us with its portrayal of a cold and lonely world where "the road is dark and slippery" and where "Your greetings they'll ignore." Saless had beautifully captured feelings of despair and distrust, feelings that loomed in the air some thirty years later. I was hooked the very first time Soli played the finished melody, and I began singing along with his chords in a hushed voice—the same voice I used to sing with Marjan in Mr. Mesbahzadeh's basement. Singing it somehow always lifted my mood. Soon the song became our anthem, with Soli insisting every now and then that we would one day record it. I always smiled, knowing very well it would never happen. Not for Googoosh in any case, I thought. And we never did.

Up until 1984 or so, Soli and his wife had been the only ones remaining from my old circle of friends—I met Maryam through Homayoun. All my other friends, from the inner to the outermost circle, fled Iran within a year or two after the revolution and went to Europe or North America. They were all blacklisted by the regime from traveling abroad, like me, because of their ties to the entertainment industry, connections with the former regime, or because they were targeted for their successful businesses. Many companies and assets, like the abandoned houses, were seized in the name of "martyr funds," though many martyr families didn't see a dime. Many, rich or poor, escaped on foot across the Turkish border like Mahmoud and Kambiz, with just enough money to sustain their dangerous journey. A few were able to get through security and onto international flights with the help of their connections at the airport, including high-positioned employees of our national airline. Over time, I learned how so many had left the country with only the clothing on their backs, leaving behind their homes, prized possessions (including family photo albums), and even, with much sorrow, their pets. When Soli and his wife told me four years ago that they were leaving, I felt both happy and heartbroken—happy that they could pursue their hopes and dreams of a better life in a free country, but heartbroken to see them leave. I felt this way each time someone close to me left. It pained me to think that I would probably never see them again. The only way I could cope with their departures was to tell myself that they had died and I had to come to terms with it.

After Hossein pressed the stop button, I closed my eyes and sang "*Zemestan*" in that same hushed voice. It all came rushing back, every single word. I felt every single one of them with every atom of my body—that same feeling I used to get all those years ago when singing a song that I connected to for the first time. I ceased to be me, like some outer-body experience, and became the words themselves.

At the end of the song, Homayoun flicked the ash of his cigarette into the ashtray and said, "G.G."—his usual nickname for me—"just imagine the orchestra starts playing this and you enter the stage. Imagine how the crowd would react when you start singing these words . . ."

I didn't like to play this game. It was too painful. I would often say something like "Googoosh did what she had to do, she did her job, she sang her songs, and if anyone wants to hear my songs, they can listen to my old records." Just as I was about to respond, Farifteh jumped out of her seat.

"I need to get back home," she said as she threw on her headscarf. "My mother's alone!"

Farifteh lived on the upscale Farmânieh Street in northern Tehran with her elderly mother.

"Don't worry, they won't strike today," Ali-Reza said.

"How do you know?" Farifteh replied nervously.

"It's all psychological warfare," Ali-Reza responded. "They'll strike when we least expect it."

"How many more must die before they sign the goddamn thing?" Hossein muttered.

He was referring to the United Nations Security Council Resolution 598 from the previous year, July 20, 1987, which called for the immediate ceasefire by both Iran and Iraq and the return to prewar borders. God only knew how many more innocent lives were going to be sacrificed for this pointless war. Neither of the leaders seemed ready to sign the resolution.

"If only they'd get off their 'holy war' bullshit!" Homayoun said.

A heavy silence blanketed the room.

We left not long after Farifteh. Homayoun was also worried about his mother, whose health was deteriorating, and he went to check on her as soon as we arrived, while I went upstairs. I didn't mind living at my mother-in-law's home at first. We had separate apartments; she lived in the apartment below us. I tried to be helpful. I shopped for her groceries, I cooked and cleaned for her, and I even tried to make small talk with her. But it was useless. She wasn't interested in having a relationship with me, and to be fair to her, she had never hidden her feelings for me from the start. I learned to keep my distance. I left the groceries downstairs by her door, just like she wanted. The only interactions we had concerned Homayoun. She would sometimes call me from downstairs and hand me a plate of food without barely looking at me.

"I made this for Homayoun," she would say. "Tell him I want him to eat it."

I learned not to care. I did care, however, about her son's attitude. He was more irritable in this house. He criticized every little thing I did, especially if I made the slightest noise. "Don't walk with your shoes on, it bothers my mother," he would say. At night, he would tell me not to flush the toilet since "it'll scare her." I was walking on eggshells, whereas during all our years together I had given him permission to do as he pleased in my home, in our home.

It was one thing for me to be a tough mom to Kambiz and regretfully often quick-tempered, but it was another for Homayoun to talk down to my son when he was upset with him. I never said anything to him about it, just like I didn't complain to him that he made zero effort to make Kambiz feel welcome in his own home. Part of me resented Homayoun for this; I was reminded of it each time I spoke to Kambiz over the phone. It had been three years since I last saw him, and I missed him so much. He was now nineteen, and still in Istanbul with his father. He was working as a tour guide for all the Iranians escaping to Turkey trying to find a path to move to the U.S.

I never said anything to Homayoun all those years because I was afraid he was going to leave. I wasn't afraid of being lonely, but I felt reassured by his presence, especially when Komiteh agents showed up at my door. Deep down he must have also known that I was keeping him around for protection. We were both growing resentful.

Back in our private quarters in his parents' three-story apartment building, I was surprised to see Homayoun already heating up his small portable charcoal grill. I didn't hear him enter the bedroom because of the music playing in my headphones. I loved my Walkman for this. It allowed me to escape into my own world, far from this house, far from all the nonsense. My dear friend Mojdeh Rassekh (daughter of Mehry Rassekh, former head of the Department of Psychology and Education at the University of Tehran, and the first woman to be appointed head of any academic department in Iran), sent it to me as a gift from Switzerland. She had also sent me the ski jacket that I had worn skiing in Dizin, along with a new set of undergarments and socks that I otherwise would have not been able to afford. On top of that, Mojdeh and other friends sent me new clothes and mixtapes via friends or family traveling back to

Iran, as the postal service was out of the question, since the authorities confiscated censored books and music. The only way I could thank her was to knit her a couple of sweaters.

Those closest to me knew how bad our financial situation was. They also knew that I was prohibited from working, and that Homayoun wouldn't. For a time, I tried to enter the fashion business. For three seasons, I designed unique pieces for women with the help of famous Iranian designers and a team of seamstresses. I even held several private fashion shows with professional models. But I was never able to make a profit selling clothes; I barely broke even. The women who showed up were more interested in seeing what had happened to Googoosh than buying clothes.

While many knew Homayoun and I weren't working, most of them didn't know about our opium consumption. People who had fled the country didn't know that opium had become less taboo, so much so that even Homayoun's mother once remarked rather comically that before the revolution, smoking opium was done secretly, while dancing and singing were done publicly, and now it was the opposite.

Homayoun was already on his third or fourth puff of opium, while I worked on the latest puzzle included in the magazine—puzzles calmed me—when the siren began howling. My heart pounded as I crouched down on the floor beside Homayoun and his portable grill, away from the windows. He made sure to turn off the grill.

We didn't go to my mother-in-law's basement, as the government required. What was the point? The basement wasn't constructed to be used as a bomb shelter and so the entire building would inevitably crumble on top of our heads no matter what.

A minute or so later, the wailing siren was replaced by a deafening explosion. The entire room shook violently, and Homayoun instinctively wrapped his arms around me. My pulse raced, with each beat of my heart echoing in my ears, as fear surged through me. We waited in tense silence, bracing ourselves for another possible blast, every second stretching into an eternity. Once we thought the danger had passed, we rushed downstairs to check on my mother-in-law. Thankfully, she was unharmed, though visibly shaken. Without thinking, I grabbed the phone and dialed Farifteh's number. I usually called Mama after these attacks, but she had recently moved to L.A. to be with Roya and Joseph after her heart surgery—they had the means to take better care of her. I needed to hear Farifteh's voice, even though I wasn't particularly close to her.

"Are you okay?" I asked as soon as Farifteh picked up the phone.

"We've been hit!" she screamed hysterically. "We've been hit! We've been hit!" Then she hung up.

Homayoun and I dashed to the car and raced to their house on Farmânieh Street. We got there before the ambulances and the Revolutionary Guards. Smoke covered the entire block. All of the buildings around the block had been impacted one way or another. A crowd had gathered on the street, people from neighboring blocks, helplessly frozen in front of the wreckage, not knowing what to do, or where to begin, while bloodied survivors frantically yelled out names of their loved ones. Amid the chaos, Farifteh and her mother stood nearby on the curb, their faces pale and eyes wide, frozen in a state of shock and disbelief.

Farifteh was shaking, she could hardly get a word out. She managed to explain that when the siren went off, she and her mother found shelter in their hallway, away from the windows, which ended up shattering, and away from their living room, whose ceiling caved in. Thankfully they didn't suffer any physical injuries, unlike their next-door neighbors covered in blood. There were chunks of animal flesh nearly everywhere we looked; it seemed that there was a piece of land where sheep and chickens were being kept nearby where the missile had struck.

Information got around that the missile had struck a three-story single-family house located right behind Farifteh's family home, separated by an alleyway, killing all but one member of the family. The father of that household had rented a bus a week earlier, which he was going to use to get his wife, their kids, and his parents and in-laws out of Tehran and into safety. But for some reason they had decided to wait. No one knew why. So when the siren sounded across the capital, everyone in the family ran down to the basement—everyone but the eldest son, who was lying on his bed.

"I'm tired of this!" he had apparently said to his parents. "I'm tired of running up and down every day! I'm fed up! I'd rather die!"

When the missile struck, the eldest son was blasted out of his bedroom. He miraculously survived despite his injuries, but lost his entire family, his entire world.

We left Farifteh and her mother and drove by the three-story house, where we saw the teenage boy standing on top of the rubble, screaming from the top of his lungs while neighbors desperately tried to console him, "I wanted to die, not them! It was supposed to be me! Why God? Why them? Why not me?!"

Why them? Why not me?

Chapter 18

A Letter

April 1988

Dead leaves and insects twirled in a puddle at the deep end of the swimming pool, oblivious to the sweet scent of the blossoming roses, while I flipped through the translated copy of Louise Hay's bestselling self-help book *Heal Your Body*. I had recently moved on from binging history and philosophy books to anything that focused on the mind and spirit, whether it be an introduction to child psychology or Buddhism. I had already read this particular book, fascinated by the mind-body connection, by the idea that unhealthy thought patterns and stress could lead to physical illnesses. I had been hopeful that a positive attitude and affirmations would help reduce my lower back pain and migraines. And they had, a little, during my first read-through. But here I was now, sitting in my living room in Velenjak, on my chocolate-colored carpet, struggling to concentrate while that same old burning sensation ran up and down my left leg like it had in that basement eight years ago. Nothing seemed to calm my sciatica these last few weeks, not the affirmations, not the painkillers, not even the extra puffs I had taken from Homayoun's *manghal*, his opium grill—nothing since I had heard that young man screaming on top of the rubble burying his loved ones. Three weeks later, I couldn't get him out of my mind.

He lost everyone he loved in a blink of an eye. He would never again feel his mother's warm embrace, the gentle pat on his back from his father, nor hear his little siblings' mischievous laughter. "Why them? Why not me?!" he had cried. I felt his pain. I felt his confusion. I had been asking myself the same question for a long time. Why had my life been spared, twice now?

Why them? Why not me?

Why had God spared me? I was nearly forty years old and had done nothing with my life for about a decade. Day in, day out, I killed time at home by reading, playing solitaire, listening to songs on my Walkman, cooking and cleaning, smoking cigarettes and opium. I felt like a bird trapped in a cage, just waiting for something, for some deliverance.

Why them? Why not me?

I missed Kambiz terribly. The last time we spoke on the phone he was on his way to the U.S., where he was hoping to work in the Iranian diaspora entertainment industry. God only knew if I would ever see him again.

Why them? Why not me?

My marriage felt meaningless, devoid of love. Whatever attachment I had felt toward Homayoun was disintegrating with every slight comment he made. I had nothing to lose. I had no purpose, no future. Nothing. Why was I being protected?

For eight years, I had convinced myself that by staying in Iran I was showing solidarity to my compatriots, showing them that they weren't alone in these dark times. I would cheer myself up by rereading a line from a letter my dear friend and lyricist Ardalan Sarfaraz had written to me from exile.

"Googoosh-e aziz," he wrote, "with your silence, throughout these years, you have emitted the loudest cry."

His words couldn't bring me any comfort today. The silence was deafening. What could I say to end it? Day after day, I had more difficulty recognizing my country. My heart hurt for all the innocent children who had lost their lives in this bloody war, for all the young men lying dead in the battlefield, and for all the families crushed in their own homes. I worried for my child living on the other side of the world. I missed my friends terribly. Googoosh was gone. I no longer knew who I was. I never even dared to sing alone in my own home, for fear of being overheard by neighbors. I couldn't turn on the speakers and listen to music, and let it flow into my soul. No, there was nothing special about me, about my silence.

I put the book aside and got up to take another painkiller, realizing how late it was getting; I missed the sunset through the masking tape covering the windows—a trick we employed to protect the glass from shattering. I tossed the pill in my mouth and washed it down with a glass of water before grabbing Louise Hay's book along with my headscarf and rushing out of the house despite the pain. Homayoun was expecting me at his mother's house.

Just as I was about to open the gate for my car, I noticed a pile of unopened letters that Mansour Khân had kindly slid under the foot of the steel door, sheltered by the rain as well as any nosy onlookers. I hadn't checked the mail in a week or so, but was only expecting the usual utility bills with the letter or two from family or friends living abroad. I would go through them at my mother-in-law's, I decided, as I picked them up before getting into the driver's seat of my car. But as I waited for the engine to warm up, I noticed one of the envelopes slipping out of the pile on the passenger seat. "Googoosh" it read on the envelope. No address. No postal stamp. No return address. It was strange, I thought. Googoosh only received hand-delivered letters once a year: for my birthday. Every February 7 (as per my birth certificate, though Mama told me I was born on May 5), a dozen or so fans would leave flowers and sweets at my gate, accompanied by heartwarming wishes, poems, or lyrics of my songs. But it had already been two months since my birthday. I felt a knot in my stomach, fearing it might be from that woman.

For years now, starting a year or two before the revolution, a young woman would appear at my gate, leaving enigmatic notes and sometimes following me in her car as I ran errands. She was around my age, with a sharp, penetrating gaze that seemed to follow my every move. Her appearance was always messy—her dark, wavy hair looking disheveled even after the mandatory headscarf was introduced, as if she didn't bother to tuck it in properly. Her clothes seemed carelessly thrown on, wrinkled and mismatched. At first, I wasn't worried, thinking she was just another devoted fan leaving poems and letters with Mansour Khân. But then, months after I first saw her, she started acting strange.

She stopped responding when I said hello to her outside my gate or in public places. Instead, she would glare at me with the intensity of a hawk. It was troubling, especially after the popular singer Dariush Eghbali narrowly survived an acid attack by an obsessed fan in October 1977. I was even more frightened after John Lennon's tragic death in December 1980. Since the revolution, I hadn't had fans following me, except for her. There was a girl named Simin, with mental and physical disabilities, whose parents would call and ask to bring her over to me whenever she was in crisis, a pattern that continued for many years. I gladly saw her every time, just to help soothe her with my voice and a gentle caress on her face. But this woman was different; she was a stalker. After what happened with John Lennon, I kept my distance. Finally, six months ago, Homayoun got her to leave me alone; he raised his voice at her and, without laying a finger on her, scared her off. We hadn't seen or heard from her since.

I tore open the envelope and found inside a three-page letter, written front and back. There was no date. I didn't recognize the script, which was uneven and shaky, with some lines slightly slanted, as if it had been written in a hurry. Despite the unsteady appearance, the handwriting was still legible. At the bottom of the last page, it was signed "Ahmad-Reza," a name that didn't ring any bells.

Dear Mrs. Googoosh,

So many times I asked the nurse for a pen and paper wanting to write to you, wanting to tell you everything, all the horrors I've witnessed, the sleepless nights, the brothers I've lost, the heartaches, wanting to tell you how every step of the way I heard your voice in my ear, pulling me out of the abyss.

Ahmad-Reza went on to explain that he was a twenty-seven-year-old soldier from a village near Babol, the "Orange Blossom City," and that he had recently been wounded in combat with a piece of shrapnel lodged in his leg—though he didn't dwell on this matter much more than that. For generations his family had worked the moist land of the northern province of Mâzandarân, he wrote, on local orange farms and rice paddy fields nestled between the Alborz mountains and the Caspian Sea. Ahmad-Reza had also worked the land, ever since he was a child, alongside his father, mother, two brothers, and two sisters. He fondly remembered those days spent with his family, weeding and plowing the luscious rice paddy fields or picking sweet and succulent oranges as well as sour *nârenj* (bitter orange) from the citrus trees. He remembered the neighbor girl, Mahtâb, whom he planned to marry.

As tenant farmers who rented the land, his parents didn't make much, he explained, just enough to put a roof over their heads, food in their bellies, and clothes on their backs. They led simple pious lives, he continued, and with enough sacrifice, they made sure their three sons went to school to learn how to read and write (unlike themselves), and even managed to send both sets of grandparents on a once-in-a-lifetime trip to Mecca for hajj.

"But even though they were deeply religious they never stopped me from listening to your music," he wrote.

He had grown up listening to my songs on the family radio.

Then the war came and he and his two brothers were sent to the battlefront in the city of Khorramshahr. For years Ahmad-Reza made it back to the barracks every night in one piece, unlike most of the young men in his unit, who succumbed to the never-ending shelling, the blasts from Molotov cocktails, rocket-propelled grenades, and land mines, as well as the deadly chemical attacks—he said he could never forget that strong chemical odor. Those who survived like Ahmad-Reza, the "lucky ones," had to carry on with horrific images of their brothers-in-arms torn into pieces, of bodies without heads, without limbs, not to mention the bloodbath seen on the minefields involving members of the *basij*, a paramilitary volunteer militia within the Revolutionary Guard Corps, some as young as twelve.

At night, he and other servicemen tried to distract themselves with jokes and stories from back home. And they secretly listened to music. Music helped drown out the constant ringing in their ears, he explained, caused by the endless rounds of fired ammunition and explosions.

"We were so careful with the volume at first, but quickly saw that no one cared as long as you'd get back on that battlefield," he said. "We listened to your songs on Radio Kuwait—people would call in and ask for Googoosh."

Most of the men in his barracks had memories associated with my songs, memories of better days, of school or first loves, memories they were eager to share with one another, memories that took them far away from that cold, damp, makeshift shelter.

"Your voice and the melodies brought peace to our troubled minds, especially to mine after the sky came crashing down on me."

His two brothers were killed in combat one year apart from each other.

Losing both of his brothers was devastating, he wrote. But his heart had already been shattered into pieces a year earlier, after his mother broke the news to him that his sweetheart had been married off in his absence. He said that the only words he found to describe his feelings came from my song "*Do Panjereh*" (Two Windows), written by Ardalan Sarfaraz in 1970.

Ardalan's lyrics told the story of impossible love; two windows are madly in love, but are forever separated by a wall made out of stones. Their only hope is to find one another after death, in a world where such barriers don't exist. The first time I read Ardalan's lyrics, I wept: "I wish that this wall be destroyed and you and me die together / So that in another world we could reach for each other's hands."

I had felt the windows' pain, their hopelessness, and their despair. At the time I also felt trapped in a loveless marriage with Mahmoud, but even years later, during my happiest days with Behrouz, whenever I sang this song I had to fight off emotions that would close up my throat.

"You felt my pain," Ahmad-Reza wrote. "Your voice echoed my broken heart. And so I knew I wasn't alone. Together we cried, we mourned . . . I knew then somehow I'd survive this, too."

I sobbed as the car's engine began to rattle with impatience. I hadn't cried like this in a very long time, not since Papa had passed away the year before.

Ahmad-Reza wasn't the first soldier to write to me. Over the years, I had received dozens of heartbreaking letters. Each time, I could hardly believe that they would write to me, to Googoosh. How did they get my address? How did the letters make it past the postal censorship? Weren't they Khomeini's followers? Khomeini's followers listening to my music? Didn't they know that Googoosh was *harâm*, that a woman singing was *harâm*?

Each time I read their written words I would think back to Evin Prison, and to that dreadful basement. I would think back to Ali Tehrani, or that greasy-faced Afshoun, who had repeatedly drilled it into my head that I had been wrong all those years. I remembered when the angry mullah in Evin Prison yelled at me for having recorded an upbeat song. "How dare a piece of shit like you decide for others!" I believed them, convincing myself that I must not have really known my countrymen or our culture. But then what about these letters all these years later? Were these soldiers that wrote to me also wrong?

My mind raced.

Why was singing *harâm*? If it was *harâm*, then why hadn't anyone said anything to me earlier when I was a girl? Why did people keep buying my cassettes? Why did they listen to my songs on the radio? Why did they come to the cabarets? And I wasn't the only one, nor the first woman to sing. Qamar-ol-Moluk Vaziri courageously paved the way for us.

Throughout my life I had gotten to know all types of people as I traveled across Iran. Back then everyone could see our differences, even in movies. In the same shot, you would see a woman fully covered in her chador, her face barely showing, walking past a woman wearing a miniskirt. There were also women who wore neither, but earned a living for their families in work clothes. Not everyone saw eye to eye on lifestyle choices, but there was a mutual respect. Staying with Dâyi and Khadijeh Khânoum in Haft Katchaloon as a kid, I went to the *tekyehs* and observed the rituals, the chadors, and the more traditional way of life. When I went back years later at the height of my career, the people there never made me feel like scum, as Afshoun had. They might have disagreed with some of my choices, like the love scene in *Dar Emtedâd-e Shab* or my divorce from Mahmoud, but they never looked down on me as he had.

And what about the guards who snuck out the confiscated cassettes from Mr. Mesbahzadeh's house, or Abolfazl, who secretly waited in the narrow corridor just to hear Marjan and me sing? What about the bags of cassettes Mr. Tehrani took back to his wife? Or what about the Supreme Leader's own relatives who listened to my music? The grandson of Khomeini's brother, Ayatollah Pasandideh, and his wife had invited me over for dinner under the guise of being able to help recuperate the deed to my house and new passport, but were just eager to meet Googoosh, the singer, whose music, in their own words, was loved by all of the women in their extended family. Were they also wrong?

And why would singing be *harâm* when it's found in nature, in birds chirping, whales humming, elephants trumpeting, lions roaring? When it's among the first sounds we react to as infants? When it's used to call for prayer from the mosque's minaret tower, or when it's used to praise, celebrate, and worship God(s) in all faiths and corners of the world? And why would a woman's voice be *harâm*? Why was music even sexualized? Music knows no gender, age, or ethnicity. It transcends them all. Music knows notes, chords, beats, rhythm, melody, and harmony. It knows feelings from melancholy to ecstasy, feelings that we all experience, but don't always know how to put into words.

Music takes our pain and gives us hope, I thought, as I reread the last sentence in Ahmad-Reza's letter. "My only hope is that one day I can write verses worthy of your voice, dearest Mrs. Googoosh, however long it takes."

—

The war officially ended five months later, on August 20, 1988, when both countries signed the UN Security Council Resolution 598. Khomeini famously described accepting the ceasefire as "worse than drinking poison." And so ended the eight-year-long bloody war between our two nations, a bloody war that took the lives of more than a million souls—some say 2 million. Everyone, on each side of the border, has memories engraved in their minds and bodies. Some memories were shared, like the ones of waking up in the middle of the night to the piercing shrieks of sirens, warning us to take shelter, while others were more horrific and traumatic.

When I heard about the signing of the ceasefire, I immediately thought with a heavy heart of all those young soldiers like Ahmad-Reza who had written to me. I wondered if they were still alive. I thought of the teenage boy on Farmânieh Street, screaming frantically for his family buried under the rubble. I thought of all those mothers, whose little twelve- or thirteen-year-old boys never made it back from the minefields.

The nation was still healing from these deep wounds when another monumental event shook us, less than a year after the ceasefire. On June 3, 1989, Ruhollah Khomeini, Supreme Leader and founder of the Islamic Republic of Iran, died from a heart attack at the age of eighty-six or eighty-nine. The moment the news broke out, mourners rushed to his home, defying the government's call for calm. The cameras captured scenes of devastated mourners wailing in the streets while hitting their heads, just like those who had lost their loved ones under the rubble. They shouted, "We wish we were dead, so not to see our beloved imam dead!" All of the channels showed similar scenes happening around the country.

I cried and cried, and cried some more, each time the TV showed his face under that black turban, those thick, black eyebrows arched in a perpetual scowl, that menacing gaze, and that long white beard. This went on for a few days. I went about my daily routines with tears streaming constantly down my cheeks. I would do the dishes and all of a sudden I would bawl. I would read a book, then hear his name on the radio or television and weep. I woke up crying. I went to bed crying. I cried under the shower. I sobbed every time I heard the television playing the traditional mournful songs—like daggers cutting through my heart. I had become hysterical, just like his most devout followers, crying day and night. But unlike his devout followers, I didn't feel like I had lost a loved one. This was the person, after all, who had refused to sign the ceasefire that would have spared hundreds of thousands of innocent lives, the same person who had ordered the execution of thousands of political prisoners—some thirty thousand, according to Amnesty International—a month before the end of the war. I just felt this profound sadness that I had also felt when Fery died.

"What's wrong with you?" Homayoun asked. "You should see yourself! You didn't cry like this for your own dad!"

Everyone around me, Homayoun, my circle of friends and loved ones, here and abroad, were celebrating the news of his death, unlike those mourners. It took me a moment before I was able to explain what I was going through to myself, and then to Homayoun. I realized that I was finally grieving for everything and everyone that this person had taken away from me. I was grieving for myself, my loved ones, and for my country. For nine years, I had kept everything inside, forced myself not to feel a single emotion, even enlisting the help of opium and sleeping pills. And now that he was gone, that I had lost everything, I couldn't keep anything inside anymore.

A part of me was also afraid. We had just found something resembling stability after eight years of war. *But now what? We are plunging back into the unknown. Who is going to replace him? What's going to happen to the country? To the government? To Parliament? To the people? To Googoosh?*

As soon as I allowed myself to feel all this pain, I started to feel better, even lighter.

Then one day, about a month later, Kambiz called. We hadn't spoken in three months, as he was busy trying to build on his singing career in the Persian diaspora music scene in L.A., where he and Mahmoud had moved to. Kambiz had a decent voice and great rhythm, like Papa.

"You would've loved it, Mom," Kambiz said to me about Steven Spielberg's *Indiana Jones and the Last Crusade*, which he just saw at the cinema. "You can't even imagine how amazing the sound and picture qualities were! It's a whole new experience!"

I hadn't set foot in a cinema since 1979, when we had seen *Superman* together in NYC. Just then, Homayoun walked in and over to my side of the bed, close enough to hear Kambiz's voice in the receiver.

"What's that spoiled brat saying?!" he blurted out, loud enough for Kambiz to hear.

A boiling furry swelled inside me, especially knowing that Kambiz had heard him. I snapped.

I dropped the phone and slapped him across the face. He was stunned. Then his face quickly turned red.

"Get the hell out of here!" he screamed from the top of his lungs, his face only a few inches away from mine. "I said, get out! Now!"

I stormed out of his mother's house, leaving all my things behind. I didn't know at the time that I was leaving him for good. I was just livid. But as the days passed, the fiery anger began to fade, replaced by an unexpected sense of relief.

For years we had been stuck in a codependent relationship—the love was replaced with attachment—and neither of us wanted to admit it, let alone do anything about it. That last year was the worst; ever since we had moved into his parents' apartment building, there was barely any affection left, only growing resentment, and the tension was palpable. Without knowing it in that moment, I was saving myself again. Our demons would have finished us off sooner or later, like they nearly had that night on the twentieth floor of that Manhattan hotel.

It was as if I had woken up from a long slumber, yearning for more from life. After a week or so, I decided I wasn't going back to him—I wasn't scared of being alone anymore. Perhaps letters like Ahmad-Reza's had inspired me. Perhaps surviving the war when so many hadn't had changed something within me. I couldn't explain why, but with Khomeini's death marking the end of an era, I felt the need to pick myself up from rock bottom—the need to take care of Googoosh.

Chapter 19

A New Beginning

Spring 1991

There were more than forty thousand verses to go through, but it was there, somewhere. I knew for a fact that it was in Rumi's *Dîwân-é Kabîr*. We had read it so many times at Soli's. As I leafed through the pages one more time, certain that I had missed it, the phone rang. I was running late, having spent the entire morning crouched over the poems, not seeing the time go by.

"I'll be ready," I reassured Maryam on the other end of the line.

The apartment door buzzed fifteen minutes later. I was already dressed in my loose jogging pants and T-shirt, covered under a thin manteau, and my hair concealed under my headscarf. All I was missing was my tennis racket, which was leaning on the wall by the entrance. We were lucky to have a friend who had a private tennis court on his property—it sure beat the only other alternative of playing in an all-women's sports complex, under the mandatory manteau and the headscarf in the heat of late spring.

I was forty-one years old, and yet I felt more energetic now than I had in all my thirties. I played tennis three times a week, swam five times a week, and greatly reduced my daily cigarette intake. I had kept this routine up for the last two years, ever since Homayoun and I had separated. Most important, I was two years clean. I hadn't smoked opium since that night he told me to get out of his mother's home. After all, I had never smoked it without him, just like I had never smoked freebase cocaine without him. It was always with him.

Maryam was one of the few friends from Homayoun's circle who I continued to see. She was the one to retrieve my things from his mother's after I had stormed out that night.

"Any news?" she asked as she slowly steered her car into the usual traffic on Vanak Street, close to Vanak Square, a major intersection in Tehran.

"Nope," I replied.

"After all these years, they're still afraid."

"Afraid of what? That I'd sell my house, burn through my own money, and end up on the streets?" I chuckled.

After I had left Homayoun, I went back to the Ministry of Economic Affairs and Finance, desperate to get them to remove the lien on my house. I was penniless and was considering selling my home in Velenjak. Again, I was sent on the same wild-goose chase from one office to another—it was the same story when I attempted to get a new passport. Seeing that nothing concrete was happening, I had decided to rent out my house in the meantime and to live off the rent money, something I was still allowed to do without the deed.

"I'll never give up, though," I said to Maryam now.

In fact, I was going to meet Youness, who I considered to be as close as a cousin, after our tennis match so that he could help me draft a new letter to the ministry—the second one this month.

"Already, whenever they see me coming from a mile away, they cry to themselves, 'Please, not her again!'"

Maryam let out a boisterous laugh.

In order to rent out the house I had needed to make some necessary repairs. I ended up selling my diamond earrings for much less than I had paid to fix the tin roof in the courtyard, replace the broken windows, and repair the deformed main door, all remnants of the bloody war. My half brother Mehrdad (once called Farâmarz) helped find the right people for the job. Once the house was ready, I found eager tenants from the German embassy, who would pay their rent in U.S. dollars. This allowed me to rent a three-bedroom apartment on Farmânieh Street. After the repairs were done, I still had some money left over from the earrings. So, like anyone who unexpectedly comes into money, I went on a shopping spree—my first in eleven years! I bought new clothes that actually matched the era—high-waisted trousers; bold, colorful silk blouses; and a blazer with padded shoulders—as well as some kitchen appliances. I even bought my very first Persian rug. Mehrdad was kind enough to also help me set up my new place. "I feel like a young bride eagerly decorating her new home," I said jokingly to him. The situation was far from ideal, as I would have preferred being in my own home that I loved so much, but I was happy to rebuild a life for myself.

Two hours later, after our friendly match, Maryam dropped me off back at my place, where I jumped into my newly purchased navy Daewoo—it wasn't an expensive car or a good-looking one for that matter, but it was an automatic, a blessing for when my sciatica acted up. Luckily I was having fewer episodes in the last two years, as though my happier mental state had something to do with it. I had no time to shower or change, so I pressed down on the gas pedal and headed straight to the Hedayat Film studio, where Youness worked.

"They won't budge, Googoosh jân," he said, reading the latest letter from the ministry. "They won't return your deed until you pay them the full balance."

The ministry now claimed that I owed them 6 million toman (officially more than 850,000 U.S. dollars), twice as much as the original claim from before the revolution. For years, I explained to the clerks that if they looked into my file, they would find all of my work contracts and bank statements that would exonerate me. But each time they refused to listen, saying that such a file didn't exist and that I needed to hand over the same documents that I knew they had all along or face a Revolutionary Court. For many, the Revolutionary Court was synonymous with a firing squad. That's how I knew that this was all an excuse. It was just another way for them to tie my hands behind my back and silence me.

"But how many times must I write to them explaining that I handed in all the proof before the revolution? It's bullshit. It's all there in front of them!" I could feel the heat in my flaming cheeks.

"Besides, if they believe a woman's singing voice is *harâm*, then why is Googoosh's income *halâl*?" I said, recalling the wise words of Aghdas, the Azeri prostitute I had met in that basement more than a decade ago.

"Don't work yourself up so much," Youness said to me. "There's no point . . . You know these things take time. But it will all work out. You'll see . . ."

I didn't share his optimism. I couldn't, not after a decade of this.

As he reread the document, the phone on his desk rang.

"Hi, Masoud jân," he said. "I'm fine, thank you, and yourself?"

He then winked at me, as if to say he wasn't going to be long.

"I'm with Googoosh right now, can I call you back in . . ." He paused and looked over at me. "Just a moment please," he said into the receiver. "Googoosh *jan*, it's Masoud Kimiai. Giti's with him and she wants to speak to you."

Giti Pashaei was a famed singer prior to the revolution. Although we were never close friends, we had worked together on many occasions back in the day and got along well. It was a different story between her husband and me; Masoud Kimiai was one of Iran's most notorious filmmakers (if not the most notorious), an avant-garde screenwriter and director who had paved the way for a new wave in Iranian cinema with his movies like *Qeysar* (*Caesar*, 1969), and he disliked me very much.

I was happy to talk to Giti; we had only run into each other twice briefly since the revolution, before she sought asylum in Germany.

"Googoosh jân, please come over," Giti said warmly. "I would love to catch up properly with you before I go back to Germany in a couple of days."

"I would love to Giti jân, but I need to write this letter, and plus I'm still in my workout clothes, and by the time I get home and shower—"

"No need to change! Just come by as soon as you're done with your cousin. It'll be just us."

I hesitated. The thought of dealing with Masoud brought back a memory from 1974. I went to see Behrouz on the film set of *Gavaznhâ*, which was one of Masoud's most acclaimed films, starring Behrouz as the male lead. A few times I caught Masoud looking at me from across the set as if he were thinking, *What the hell is she doing here?* And a few weeks after that cold encounter, when Behrouz had invited him to Velenjak, Masoud barely seemed to acknowledge my existence in my own home. So I ignored him, too. He wasn't the only one. Intellectuals like Masoud didn't like pop stars like me. They looked down on me, just like some of the haughty members of the royal court did. Masoud, like the rest of the intellectuals, was very political, anti-Shah, and anti-monarchy. To him, Googoosh probably represented everything he stood against. I supposed he considered himself smarter—like most intellectuals did—more sophisticated than a sixth-grade-level-educated pop star. It was such a narrow-minded way of thinking, as if intelligence only came from formal schooling. As I saw all around me, real sophistication wasn't just about what you learned in school, but about asking the right questions, about seeking different perspectives and reading all sorts of books. If anything, I felt that my experiences navigating through the entertainment industry and surviving all sorts of personal and political turmoil had given me a deeper understanding of how the world works—an understanding I wouldn't have automatically gained from a university degree, even though I always wanted one.

"Come on," she insisted.

After I finished drafting the umpteenth letter, I drove over, even stopping on the way to get flowers, but no one was home. I was somewhat relieved. I left the flowers with their concierge, along with a note explaining that I had come by and how happy I was to have heard her voice earlier over the phone.

Back in my living room, with a cup of tea in one hand and a pencil in the other, I plunged once more into the mystical world of Rumi—a world of love for the divine, of transcendence, and of celestial music. I was determined to find that one particular poem we would read in Soli's apartment basement in the early years of the war. As soon as I read the beautiful verses from Rumi's "Ghazal 2214"—the part when the two souls unite in a state of heavenly bliss—I heard the song playing in my head, accompanying the rhythm of the poem's meter: ooXX ooXX ooXX ooX. It was an upbeat melody that I hadn't heard before—old poems were usually coupled with *sonati* music. Since waking up that morning, I had this urge to write it down, even though I had never composed or arranged music in my life. I didn't even question it. I just knew I had to do it. And for a moment I even half jokingly thought that if ever I were going to sing again, it would have to be this song.

One of the items I had splurged on with the money left over from the sale of my diamond earrings was a piano keyboard—luckily, Khomeini had lifted the ban on the sale of musical instruments not long after signing the UN ceasefire, most likely to give a boost to the heavy postwar morale. It was nothing like the grand piano I used to have, the one I had gotten rid of during the war, which I used more as a decorative piece than anything else. This piano keyboard was modest, but good enough for a beginner like me, who still needed to learn how to read musical notes and identify the keys on the keyboard. I enlisted the help of a private piano instructor.

I had first taken piano lessons at the age of thirteen or fourteen with the revered pianist Anoushiravan Rohani, but with barely any time to eat or sleep with my schedule, I had to stop after only four sessions. Then upon my return from New York City in 1979, I briefly started up again with a local piano instructor, until I was summoned to Evin Prison.

As much as I wanted to learn how to play the instrument, a part of me also wanted to learn how to compose melodies. I knew I wasn't good at writing lyrics; I was just as bad with words as my father, but I knew rhythm. Now, after nearly two years of lessons, I was able to play some classical songs on the keyboard while reading music (though I was still frustrated by my limited repertoire), and I felt comfortable enough to play around with melodies.

My search finally came to an end when I found "Ghazal 2214." The first lines gave me chills:

> *That moment (is) joyous and blessed when we are sitting*
> *(together) in the veranda, you and I; with two forms and faces,*
> *(yet) with one soul, you and I.*

As soon as I started playing around on the keyboard and writing down some notes, the buzzer rang. Giti was standing outside my door.

She explained that she had stepped out to buy fruit when I had gone by their home and insisted that I go back with her.

"But it's already nine p.m., it's getting late," I protested.

She refused to take no for an answer.

"My place is just a few minutes away from here, I'll drive you back home myself," she said as she grabbed my coat and handed it to me.

We let hours go by as we sat in their kitchen, just the two of us. There was so much catching up to do. Banned from the stage like the rest of us, Giti had decided to channel her creativity into musical composition, which she had studied in her youth, and which wasn't unlawful, since she was only writing the music, not performing it. She was very gifted. In fact, she had composed songs for several of Masoud's films.

"This country!" she burst out. "I studied composition, I put all my heart and effort into my work, and for what? What's the point? They don't understand the value of art here!"

Her work on one of Masoud's films had been snubbed by the Fajr Film Festival several years ago, a festival started in 1983 to commemorate the revolution, while the film itself was being praised and revered by all the critics.

"I had given my all, poured my blood and sweat and tears into that project, and nothing! Why? Because I'm a woman!"

The eight brutal years of war, the mass executions of political prisoners, the economy in shambles, and the uncertainty following Khomeini's death had crushed the nation's morale. The regime was aware of the widespread discontent—a recipe for potential civil unrest. So in the past two years, they tried to boost the public spirit by loosening some social restrictions, such as allowing women to participate in public cultural events, like the Fajr Film Festival, and lifting the ban on music with traditional Persian instruments, male vocals, and themes of national pride and religion. It was all damage control. But despite these tiny cosmetic changes, the system remained deeply rigged against women.

After being ignored at the festival, Giti moved to Germany with their son, Poulad, where she was granted political asylum and continued to pursue music. As for Masoud, his life was here in Iran, so she said there were no plans for him to join them. She explained that she only came back occasionally to check on her properties. I could tell she hadn't been to her home in a while. It looked like a messy bachelor pad with piles of creased shirts, papers, books, and odds and ends scattered all over the place.

"Every time I come back for a visit, I feel more confident in the choices I've made," she said.

Giti also spoke of her cancer treatment. She had been diagnosed with breast cancer sometime after she had moved to Hamburg. She underwent surgery, and she was determined to beat the cancer, just like she was determined to follow her passion abroad, where she would get the rightful recognition for her work. I admired her strength and her good spirit. Not everyone was lucky to be as resilient as she was, I thought.

Homayoun was diagnosed with a type of lymphoma cancer in the fall of 1989, less than three months after we separated. I was devastated when I heard the news; deep down I still cared for him. After all, we had lived nearly thirteen years together. She and Homayoun were facing similar battles.

I told Giti how I saw Homayoun a year ago at Maryam and Hossein's. I had learned about his cancer a month earlier. He seemed thinner, tired, and was coughing more than before. But his attitude and spirit were the same; he wore his favorite handmade shoes and made his smart-ass jokes. Our exchanges were awkward at first—we hadn't spoken in twelve months since our separation. But somehow it got easier. I asked him about his medical treatment, whether he had considered radiotherapy before deciding on chemotherapy. He had. I also asked whether I could introduce him to a specialist I had heard about, to which he abruptly answered no. But I knew the moment the words came out of my mouth that I no longer had the right to ask him such a personal question. Despite our apparent cordial and civilized interactions that evening, it had been impossible for us to escape that strange feeling shared by two former lovers meeting again, that heavy feeling that however intimate they had once been, however well they knew each other's natural perfumes, the different tones of their voices and their different meanings, their fears and dreams, that they were now nothing more than two strangers with fading shared memories.

"Giti?" Masoud called as he entered their apartment.

"I should be going soon," I quickly said to her. It was 11 p.m.

"Don't be silly, I'll cook us something to eat. Masoud, in here!"

Masoud strode into the kitchen, a dark leather briefcase swinging from one hand and a stack of books nestled under his other arm. He was a man of medium stature. He wore one of his famous black fedoras perched atop his full head of dark hair that was now turning gray—his beard had even more silver. His glasses hung on the tip of his nose, giving him the quintessential intellectual look, like an impassioned professor in a constant state of contemplation. In some ways, he looked a bit like the Iranian version of the world-renowned American filmmaker Francis Ford Coppola, even more so in their younger days before the gray had fully set in. Dressed in dark clothing except for the red linen scarf that draped loosely around his neck, his overall demeanor exuded his artistic nature. Unsurprisingly, Masoud bore that same serious expression I had seen so many times before.

"Look who we have here, it's Khânoum-e Googoosh!" he suddenly exclaimed, his voice surprisingly warm and smiling as I got up to greet him. "Wow! How long has it been?"

"Masoud Kimiai!" I said, mirroring his tone, trying not to show my true feelings. "It's been a few years."

"Why don't you go put your things away," Giti said to him before adding, "I'm making *kabâb* for the three of us."

Masoud quickly excused himself to his office, while I remained seated in the kitchen, where all the surfaces were occupied by plates, pots, and pans that seemed to have lost their way back home. Somehow, despite the chaos, Giti quickly found metal skewers she needed to grill the already-prepared minced meat, which was mixed with onions and parsley. The skewers, much like the rest of the house, hadn't been properly cleaned, with traces of dried meat lingering from the last grill. If only I had been more insistent about not being hungry.

It wasn't long before Masoud joined us, this time without the book, the hat, or the leather briefcase. He hadn't changed much, except that his beard and hair were grayer. Masoud pulled up a seat next to me, and again, in a surprisingly friendly tone, he asked me about what I had been up to all these years, about my son, and about my recent contacts with our mutual acquaintances and peers. I was surprised by his whole demeanor, his attentiveness, his warmth. He even smiled—I had never seen him smile before—which made him look much younger, even younger than when he had come to Velenjak in 1974. His dark brown eyes also seemed kinder. It was as though I were meeting an entirely different Masoud Kimiai.

Giti must have had a talk with him, I thought. He asked if I had worked on any new songs.

"No, not since 1979," I responded quickly, though I was slightly taken aback by his question. Everyone knew that I was banned from singing for life along with all of the other pre-revolutionary singers—though some exceptions were being made for certain male classical singers.

I hesitated before telling Masoud how I was wanting to compose a song for Rumi's "Ghazal 2214." After all, he might think to himself, *How dare a former pop star like Googoosh think of getting anywhere near the master's work!*

"I'd love to hear it when you're done," he replied, surprising me once more with his warm tone.

"Yes, absolutely," Giti added.

"Masoud jân, how about you?" I said, changing the subject. "What are you working on these days?"

His eyes lit up. Masoud had continued to make films after the revolution. He was a master of the craft. He wrote the screenplay, the scripts, and directed the films himself. As an anti-Shah intellectual, he never had to atone for his pre-revolution career. He simply learned to work within the new legal framework, around the new set of censored subjects, just as he had before the revolution.

He described his new project to me with such enthusiasm and passion, it was contagious. I always knew that he was an extremely knowledgeable person, but since we had never exchanged more than a few words, I had no idea how deep his passion for cinema and art ran. It was electrifying.

By the time we all sat down to eat, I had forgotten about the state of the skewers, fully immersed in the conversation the three of us were having about our memories of the old days. Back then, I could have never imagined spending an evening like this in Masoud's presence. Perhaps the last decade had changed us.

When I saw the clock dial pointing to 1 a.m., I got up and insisted that I would take a taxi home.

"Nonsense, Masoud will take you," Giti said without checking with him.

I protested, but to no avail. She had her way, just as earlier.

"Googoosh, you should stop by once in a while to see Masoud," she said after we kissed each other farewell. "He gets awfully lonely when I'm back in Germany."

"Sure," I replied politely without giving it any more thought.

The short car drive was a continuation of our dinner conversation as Masoud filled me in on some of his future projects. If only younger me could see me pleasantly conversing with Masoud Kimiai, I said to myself.

It was 2 a.m. by the time I sat back down behind the keyboard with Rumi's "Ghazal 2214" sprawled open in front of me in my living room. As I dove back into the masterful writings, I visualized two souls, one in Iraq, the other in Khorasan, twirling as one to the blissful music under the night sky. Soon enough all the notes were coming together as I pressed down on the piano keys. It didn't take long for me to find the chords and the harmony I heard that day at Soli's. By the time I reached the final note, I felt a sudden pang in my chest, realizing that I would probably never get to sing this song. I called it "*Bi Mano To*" (One Soul, You and I).

Chapter 20

Lachini's Recording Studio

I was on my way back home from tennis one afternoon, a week after that late impromptu dinner with Giti and Masoud, when I found a brown package on the doormat. It had a note.

"I thought you might enjoy these, let me know what you think. —Masoud Kimiai."

Inside were some of his own films, some of John Ford's, and books. I was surprised that he had remembered that I enjoyed old films, and even more so that he went through all the effort to share them with me.

Giti was already gone, back to Germany, when Masoud called a few days later to ask about my thoughts and impressions. He listened quietly, although sometimes I could hear him stroking his thick gray beard, which he seemed to do when he was concentrating. Aside from sharing my love for poetry with Soli and Homayoun, I had rarely voiced my opinions on deeper matters—perhaps because no one ever asked. Like with most celebrities, people seemed more interested in Googoosh's fashion sense and personal life than in what I thought. After carefully listening, Masoud shared his point of view with such enthusiasm, similar to the other night when he spoke of his biggest inspirations. I could almost see his eyes sparkling behind his glasses on his end of the telephone receiver. I was absorbed by our conversation, by the exchange of our two different perspectives, one from years behind the camera and the other in front of the lens. In a way, Masoud was bringing me back, as a former film star, to that magical world of cinema, a world I had grown up in, a world I knew and understood. I couldn't get enough.

Masoud stopped calling after about three long phone conversations and instead began showing up at my door in the afternoons. We would sometimes sit for hours in my living room dissecting a ten-second scene. We would go over everything from the choice of lighting, the camera angles, prop placements, to dialogue. It was magical. I was always curious about the creative process involved in making films.

On one of those afternoons, about a week later, as Masoud wrapped up one of his fascinating commentaries on a particular movie scene, he turned to me, his eyes locking with mine. "You possess such a rare beauty," he said softly, the words hanging in the air between us. I looked away and refilled his teacup, pretending not to hear him. But he pressed on, explaining that he and Giti lived separate lives in different countries and that their marriage was merely on paper. I nodded, swiftly changing the subject. I wasn't looking for anything more than friendship, even though a little part of me was drawn to his magnetic charm.

In an attempt to deter him, I managed to avoid a few visits, but Masoud wouldn't stay away. One day, he called, his voice smooth and inviting, each word carefully measured, carrying just enough charm to make me wonder.

"*Khânoum*," he said to me in that same warm and affectionate tone one typically uses when saying, "my darling." "I'm going over to hear Lachini's latest track for my film, and I'd love for you to join me."

I knew of the composer Fariborz Lachini. He had recently worked on Masoud's highly acclaimed film *Dandân-e Mâr* (*Snake Fang*, 1990). They were now collaborating on Masoud's new project titled *Radd-e Pây-e Gorg* (*The Wolf's Trail*), a film about friendship and betrayal.

My heart fluttered. Not from the subtle playfulness laced with intention in Masoud's tone, but because I hadn't stepped inside a recording studio since the fall of 1979, when Morteza Kan'Âni, my flutist, and I had snuck into Studio Pop to record Zoya's "*Sahneh-ye Khâli*" for the underground, artist-led, antiauthoritarian monthly recording "*Shabâneh*" (Nightly).

Reciting those heartbreaking lyrics over Spanish-style music was my one and only act of defiance against the new regime.

"Masoud jân, I'd love to, but we're celebrating my brother Mehrdad's birthday tonight," I replied, relieved that I didn't have to make up an excuse.

"How about tomorrow?"

"Tomorrow?" I hesitated.

I could hear Faegheh asking Googoosh in her typical worried tone, "But what if you get caught at the recording studio? They'll surely arrest you!" Googoosh, meanwhile, was more concerned with Faegheh's emotional well-being. For years I was unjustly accused of splitting up Behrouz and Pouri. Did I want to go through all of that again?

"I can pick you up at eight thirty p.m.," he insisted.

"Okay," I finally replied.

The thought of returning to a studio stirred something inside me. But I quickly tried to smother it. I knew I wasn't going there to sing. The magic of the recording booth and the microphone, the thrill of hearing my voice deliver those tougher notes through the headphones—that part of my life was behind me.

Don't get too carried away, I kept telling myself the next day while sitting in Masoud's car. *This is just a visit, nothing more*, I thought as my heart skipped a beat with anticipation. I carefully wrapped my headscarf to shield my face from any possible onlookers before getting out of the car. Granted it was already dark outside, but I wasn't going to take any chances. Masoud didn't say a word as we walked toward a house on a quiet residential street in Gisha. As soon as Masoud rang the doorbell, a fair-skinned man with a perfectly groomed beard opened the door and invited us in. It was Fariborz Lachini himself. For no good reason I had imagined him as being older, in his fifties like Masoud, but he was in his early forties like me. He led us straight upstairs, barely leaving me enough time to remove my manteau and headscarf.

The recording studio was a room on the second floor—most likely a former bedroom. It was much smaller than the studios I was accustomed to, but it had all of the imaginable recording equipment (some that I recognized, and others completely alien to me) and instruments tightly packed in with wires running in every direction, barely leaving room for us to move around without tripping over something—it was heavenly! Fariborz Lachini, who went by Lachini among friends, was apologetic as Masoud and I squeezed into a cramped space by his workstation, surrounded by equipment. I quickly reassured him, telling him I felt like a child returning to her favorite playground, and he seemed more relaxed as he poured us some tea. When our legs brushed against each other in the cramped space, I glanced at Masoud. His eyes met mine, and he gave me a soft, confident smile, clearly enjoying the closeness. I looked away, pretending not to notice as the fresh scent of his cologne, subtly masking the lingering odor of pipe tobacco, filled the air between us.

Masoud asked Lachini to play us the film scores he had just finished working on.

"I can't wait for you to hear them," Masoud whispered to me with a gentle smile.

We listened to the compositions, one by one. I closed my eyes and left this cramped room instantly as I imagined scenes reflective of their tones, scenes of pain, anger, and hope. I described my experience after each listen and then finally congratulated Lachini on his fine work.

"He's great, isn't he?" Masoud exclaimed.

"Please," Lachini said rather timidly, running his fingers over his mustache.

After about an hour and a half, it was past 10 p.m. and I was slowly getting ready to tear myself away from this lovely creative environment when Lachini asked whether I had been working on any songs.

"I haven't," I said.

"What about those songs you sang with Soli?" Masoud asked.

In one of our conversations I had briefly mentioned to him about those nights at Soli's, the songs Soli had composed for Sohrab Sepehri's poems.

"I didn't work on them, Soli did. I just sang along while he played his harmonium."

"I would love to hear them," Lachini said.

"Perhaps another time, it's getting late," I replied.

"It's not that late," Masoud said, glancing down at his watch.

"It's never late in here," Lachini added.

"*Khânoum*, we would be delighted to hear you sing."

I was surprised to hear him say that. I never thought he liked my voice. We'd only talked cinema in the past few weeks.

"Yes, if you're not too tired, that is," Lachini said. Then, as though he could hear my inner thoughts, he added, "You can sing your heart out in that booth! The whole studio is soundproof. The neighbors can't hear a thing."

The booth was right in front of me. It was smaller than I was used to, about the same size as those famous red English telephone booths. Butterflies fluttered in my stomach as soon as I laid eyes on the microphone standing there in the middle. I hadn't been so close to one in years. I took off my shoes and got up from my seat—Masoud and Lachini looked at me curiously—and walked barefoot into the booth. I never sang barefoot. Lachini quickly followed me in with headphones and adjusted the microphone before leaving me there alone.

I planted my bare feet on the ground and placed the headphones over my ears. The microphone was only a few inches away from my mouth. My heart pounded. I wondered if the microphone was picking it up. It then hit me how long it had been; I was forty-one years old now and the last time I had stood in a recording booth I was twenty-nine. I took a few deep breaths, but nothing could calm down my racing heart.

I looked ahead. Lachini was sitting at his workstation with his back toward me, while Masoud faced me. He smiled and encouraged me with his kind brown eyes. There was no music, no instrument playing. I could only hear my own rapid breathing through the headphones. I closed my eyes and took another deep breath. I started singing the words of Sohrab Sepehri's poem "*Âbr'â G'el Nakoni*" (Don't Muddy the Water)—a poem that had helped Soli and me, over and over, escape our sorrows, the war, the ban on music. My voice echoed back to me through the headphones. I couldn't believe it. I was hearing myself after all these years. I carefully listened to my breathing, diction, every note, pitch, timbre, pace, and rhythm. I paid attention to every detail, just as one does when getting back on a bicycle after a long time.

At first, I was happy with myself, happy that my voice hadn't changed that much. But then, just as I was trying to reach a high note, something strange happened. It felt as though my voice hit a barrier, unable to rise any higher, like it was colliding with an invisible ceiling. I tried again with the next note, but the same thing happened—my voice pressed against that limit, straining but never breaking through. It was as if I couldn't push past it, and without meaning to, I found myself singing in the same restrained mezza voce I had learned with Marjan in that damp basement.

You can do this, I thought, even more determined to hit the high notes as loud as I could. It was a strange thought for me. I never had to think about it consciously, just like I never had to think about pushing down one pedal after another on a bike.

The moment came, and this time, I managed to sing a little louder, but still not loud enough. Only half of my voice flowed out of my vocal cords. It was as if there was a ceiling over my voice. Again, and again, I tried, but I kept hitting that ceiling.

Why was this happening?

The ceiling moved higher and higher as the song progressed, but it was always there, confining my voice.

"Bravo!" one of them yelled across the studio at the end of the song.

"Fantastic!"

I removed the headphones and returned to my seat, hiding my disappointment.

"It's incredible," Masoud said. "To think, all these years have gone by, yet that voice still commands such power and passion!"

I fought back the tears swelling in my eyes.

"I hope I didn't mess up the notes," I said, putting on my best smile.

"Not a chance!" Lachini said, laughing.

"If you could sing one song for people to hear, and one song only, what would it be?" Masoud asked with a youthful smile I was growing attached to.

I thought hard about it.

"'*Bi Mano To*,'" I said.

I explained to them that I had written the music.

"Why don't you sing it?" they both asked simultaneously.

I was back in the booth, standing on the cold tile with the headphones on. Once more, I took a deep breath and reached for the microphone—this time my hands didn't shake. I concentrated on the words and visualized the two souls as I had done when I was writing at the keyboard. As I began to sing, I felt an energy rush through every single fiber in my body. The words rolled off my tongue and I felt the air building up and bursting through my vocal cords, just as I felt the verses and the melodies echoing inside me. This time I paid no attention to my voice, nor the ceiling, as I became one with the words, one with the rhythm, one with the two souls uniting as one. The world outside Rumi and the sound waves ceased to exist, including me.

By the end of the song, I came back to myself, to Googoosh, to the booth, to the studio. But my heart was now filled with joy and serenity, which words failed to express. I felt alive, as though I had woken from a coma. It no longer mattered that my unexercised vocal cords had developed a ceiling that constrained my voice. It no longer mattered to me what Masoud or Lachini thought. It no longer mattered that this could be my last chance to run free around my playground. What mattered was that I had visited this magical place one more time, even for an instant, and no one could ever take that away from me. Never.

I felt intoxicated with joy when we finally left Lachini's around midnight. I still couldn't believe it. Being back in a studio, singing one song after another into that microphone, had felt like being reunited with a long-lost love. During the entire drive back to my apartment, sitting in the passenger seat of Masoud's car, I kept thinking this couldn't have happened, that it wasn't possible, that it was all a dream. But it wasn't a dream, and it was all thanks to Masoud. I thanked him for the amazing night as he double-parked in front of the main entrance of my building, and just as I was about to step out of the car, he gently took my hand, his touch warm and lingering.

"*Khânoum*," he said, removing his fedora with a slow, deliberate motion, his eyes locking onto mine with an intensity that felt almost palpable. "One day you must return to the homeland of your talent. The stage is your sacred land."

Chapter 21

Being Mrs. Kimiai

Winter 1998

There were less than a dozen cards left unturned. It should have been a swift victory, but I was stuck. It wasn't the first time tonight. I rarely lost like this after years of playing solitaire nearly every day. This was Masoud's fault, with his damn interview.

I lit another cigarette, as though smoking would magically solve everything, before returning to the seven piles and the homeless king of spades in my hand. Then Poulad, Masoud's son with Giti, entered the living room. *It must be already dinnertime*, I thought.

"*Azizam*," I said to him. "I've cooked some *khoresht-e bâdemjân* [eggplant stew], and your father said he won't be back for another two hours. Would you like to eat now?"

Masoud was away day and night in the editing room working on the final touches of his latest film, *Mercedes*.

"No thanks, I'm going over to my friend's place," he said as he grabbed his backpack and coat. "Have you seen my CD player? I can't find it anywhere."

I wasn't surprised. He was as messy as Kambiz was as a teenager.

Thinking of Kambiz tugged at my heart. I missed him so much. He was about twenty-nine now, still living in L.A., newly married to an Iranian woman (whom I barely knew), and about to become a papa to a baby boy. So much had changed since I last saw him, seven years ago, in 1991, when he came to Iran for a visit after being away for six years—Masoud had helped me get Kambiz's Iranian passport renewed and to complete all the paperwork for his return. Kambiz stayed for about eight months before heading back to the U.S., and I cherished that time with him. We talked about movies, new gadgets, and cars—our shared interests. He mentioned that since his singing career wasn't taking off the way he hoped, he was considering getting into the personal security industry—his love for martial arts, Bruce Lee, and self-defense in general, had sparked the idea. But, just like both Papa and me, Kambiz never shared anything deeply personal, and I never thought to pry. Now it was 1998, and my son was becoming a man, and it was tearing me apart not knowing when I would see him again or hold him and his unborn baby boy in my arms.

"It's not in your bedroom?" I asked Poulad.

"No," he replied.

It was nearly impossible to find anything these days with Masoud's books, manuscripts, and notepads covering nearly every surface of my apartment, including the third bedroom we had converted into his home office. It drove me mad, especially since we had hired someone to help clean a few times a week, and despite that, I was still spending most of my time cleaning—I hadn't cleaned this much since I was a child. At least when I was doing all the chores for Mouness, I could escape to the stage each night. Writing music and songs as I was now doing was enjoyable, but nowhere near as cathartic for me as singing used to be.

Looking around the room, the throbbing ache in my lower back returned.

"Are you okay?" Poulad asked, seeing the expression of pain on my face.

No. I wasn't okay. I was forty-seven years old, married (my fourth time) to a man I loved and respected, a stepmother to a teenage boy, and yet, all I could think about was running away to a small remote shack by the Caspian Sea. I was fed up with all the cleaning and cooking. I was fed up with this pain. I was fed up with it all. This was not the life I had envisioned for myself, seven years ago—I had sought a simple, peaceful existence where I wasn't responsible for anyone else. And by the early 1990s, the atmosphere in Tehran had softened since the end of the war—the country, though still burdened by its struggles, seemed to carry a faint sense of optimism, much like the period following the French Revolution's Reign of Terror, when glimpses of hope began to pierce through the grim shadows of the past—and so living alone as a woman wasn't as daunting as it had been for me in the early years after the revolution. But everything changed after that night at Lachini's studio, in 1991, as my feelings for Masoud grew exponentially.

I fought off those feelings as hard as I could, out of respect for Giti, since they were still married, after all—it helped that Kambiz was around. But once Kambiz left, Masoud wouldn't stay away. He kept coming to my apartment, insisting that he and Giti were separated, that she was living her life in Germany with their son, while he lived his in Tehran. Eventually, I believed him, seeing it with my own eyes, confirmed by our mutual acquaintances. I finally gave in to his spellbinding charm that became impossible to resist. We had been married for more than three years now.

"Yes, *azizam*, it's just my sciatica," I said to Poulad while pressing on my lower back. "I'll let you know if I find your Walkman."

"CD player."

"Yes, CD player."

When Poulad left the apartment, the burning sensation in my lower back shot all the way down my left leg. I had to get up. I had to do something about all the clutter around me, which only seemed to amplify my pain.

I lowered the heat under the rice and the eggplant stew before clearing the dining table that was in danger of disappearing under Masoud's books, loose papers, and notebooks.

In that moment, it struck me how clean Homayoun had always been—almost obsessively so. He was a neat freak. In fact, he used to clean as much as I did, maybe even more, when he wasn't high or zoned out by his small portable charcoal grill. My brother Mehrdad had been the one to call me with the news of Homayoun's passing about four years ago, in 1994. I was devastated. We had been estranged and divorced for five years, and our relationship had been a toxic and codependent one. But for thirteen years, he had been the closest person to me—my husband, my best friend, and my lover.

There had been a ray of hope for his recovery right before he went to the UK to meet a specialist. But it turned out the Western doctors didn't know much more than the Iranian physicians. At some point, Homayoun decided to stop the chemotherapy, while the disease continued to spread through his body.

He stayed true to his word. His body was "fucked up" long before the disease got to him. Then one day, Homayoun was no longer captive of his demons. As I got off the phone with Mehrdad that day, my heart rejoiced for a second, imagining Homayoun in the middle of the dance floor of Couchinie, where I first saw him in 1965. His body was once more in unison with the rhythm of the music, his eyes filled with joy and passion, his spirit soaring higher with every beat. *He is free at last*, I thought.

I gathered all of Masoud's things that were sprawled across the dining table and, with some effort, carried the heavy pile to his office down the hall. Of course, his desk was also covered with more books and paper. But I wouldn't touch anything in case he had purposely left that book open or that photograph lying on top of that typed page with crossed-out sentences and margins filled with handwritten notes. I also didn't want to see anything that wasn't meant for my eyes, like Giti's letter to Masoud I had found months after she passed away in 1995.

Giti and I hadn't spoken since 1991, after that one and only impromptu late dinner she cooked. She never tried to contact me, not even after more people in our circle of mutual acquaintances learned about Masoud and my budding relationship. And it felt odd for me to reach out to her, especially since we didn't have much communication before that dinner. I found her strong-worded letter to Masoud on his cluttered desk, under a thick, messy pile of documents. In it, she denounced his betrayal of their marriage and called me a home-wrecker. It hurt me deeply. There was nothing I could have said that would have made it right between us. I could understand that she was upset with him, and I was sorry that she felt this way about me, but to say that I was the cause of their marriage's downfall was both painful and unjust. I wasn't the one who had caused them to live separate lives in two different countries all those years ago.

Part of me wished she knew that I hadn't been the one relentlessly pursuing Masoud, the one who wouldn't take no for an answer. Perhaps she already did—Masoud had a talent for charming his way into people's hearts, a pattern I suspected she had witnessed before. After all, he had been married to another woman before Giti. But in the end, maybe it didn't make any difference. When she moved back to Iran in 1994 with Poulad, I tried to end things with Masoud multiple times, but he wouldn't hear of it, insisting that they were already separated and there was no going back. It was a terrible situation for three lonely people, lonely in their own way.

Poulad was fourteen years old when his mother passed away. Masoud and he moved in with me shortly after. I did everything to help him feel loved and wanted in my home—the opposite of everything Mouness had done—which wasn't too hard, since he was a good kid. At first, I felt I was helping, being a shoulder for him to cry on. But then for a while, I got the feeling he blamed me for everything. His anger toward me disappeared over time as he went through the different stages of grief. And ever since, we maintained a friendly relationship, the kind I wished I'd had with Kambiz when he was a teenager.

The trash overflowed with crumpled papers and I went to empty it. *I can't keep doing this*, I thought.

Among the clutter in Masoud's office, I also found several cups of half-drunk tea and coffee. They were days old. When Masoud got deep into his work, he often forgot about the world outside of the page, including sleep, not to mention beverages. Masoud lived very much in his own busy world. I didn't mind that about him; after all, I was initially attracted to his passion for filmmaking.

But while it was one thing for me to live exclusively in Masoud's world as Mrs. Kimiai, slowly transforming into a cookie-cutter housewife without ever intending to become one, it was another for him to deny publicly that he was married to Googoosh, as he did in his latest interview. He denied that I was his wife, telling the inquisitive journalist that his personal life was nobody's business. I felt betrayed. I felt belittled. He had never hidden his previous marriages, whether it was with Giti or his first wife, Mashid. Was he embarrassed of me? Was I not worthy of being Mrs. Kimiai? It stung in a way I couldn't quite articulate, especially because I knew he loved me—we had a deep connection that I hadn't felt with Homayoun and not even with Behrouz. And he was always encouraging me to sing and write songs. I was stunned when I first discovered in 1991 that he knew how to play all of my songs on the piano without any notes—never in my wildest dreams could I have imagined that Masoud Kimiai had listened to Googoosh, let alone learned the melodies of her songs by heart. So why was he so embarrassed to admit he was married to Googoosh? Why did he refuse to acknowledge me as his wife, while I'd given so much of myself to him, adapting to a life I never thought I'd lead? I wouldn't bring it up to him, of course; that would have been even more humiliating. Besides, the interview wasn't the only reason I was feeling down these days.

I had known these feelings since childhood, feelings that snuck up on me and gripped their hands tightly around my neck even at times when I should have been the happiest, like when Kambiz finally came for a visit in 1991, after years of us being apart. This was my lifetime dance with depression. It didn't help that my sciatica was starting up again. Lately, the slightest physical discomfort or even a word could trigger these feelings. Masoud simply mentioning his work could do the trick. But I would never let it show; I kept it all bottled up inside.

If not for my depression, I would have truly enjoyed listening to Masoud talk about his projects. He often asked for my input on his writings, and I was always happy to contribute. In a way, I got to live my passion for cinema through him, through his work, through our dissection of films—only a month earlier, we watched a Gary Cooper movie ten times in a row just to study his acting style. But recently, as soon as he talked about his work, distant memories flooded my mind and left behind an aching hole in my heart. I remembered film sets, locations, the people I worked with, including some of the directors and their peculiarities, or some of the laughing fits my costars and I had while the camera was rolling. I even remembered some of the more embarrassing moments with a lump in my throat, like when I smashed my elbow against the floor during the already-awkward filming of the infamous love scene in Parviz Sayyad's *Dar Emtedâd-e Shab*. The bang was so loud that my brothers and Zoya heard it from the room on the other side of the two-sided fireplace—that scene was anything but sensual!

As I took Masoud's days-old, half-drunk cups of coffee and tea back into the kitchen, I heard the key unlocking the main door. It was unlike him to come home early at this last stage of a project. Perhaps he knew I was upset. Perhaps he was coming home early to try to make up for it.

I pretended everything was okay, greeting him like I would any other night, urging him to take a seat at the dinner table for another freshly cooked home meal.

Masoud looked tired with the dark bags under his eyes, but you couldn't tell just by listening to him. He barely even touched his plate as he spoke excitedly of the progress he was making, chattering like an eager child, while I debated on whether I should go for my second serving. It was typical of him. His mind never stopped working; he had written *Mercedes* while he was still shooting his last project, *Soltan*.

Once we moved to the living room after dinner, Masoud pulled out a notepad from his leather briefcase.

"*Khânoum*, I wrote this for you," he said, handing me the yellow notepad.

"What is it?"

"Have a look."

It was a poem.

"When did you have the time to write this?"

He smiled as I grabbed my reading glasses.

The title was "*Zartosht*" (Zoroaster), which was the name of the ancient Persian prophet whose teachings led to Zoroastrianism, the official religion of ancient Persia before Islam.

"It's beautiful," I said with a lump in my throat as I finished reading these lines that had captured something within me, something buried deep down.

Since when is singing a crime?
Zoroaster planted this land while singing hymns.
He planted this land while singing hymns.

"I thought maybe you could write a song for this, and that one day, you will sing it for the public."

As soon as he said that, I forgot all about the interview. After all, ever since that day at Lachini's studio, Masoud had relentlessly encouraged me to be more proactive in the realm of music. He was like Mahmoud in that sense (and only in that sense!); they both believed in my musical talent and wanted me to pursue it regardless of the obstacles placed by the external world. Masoud had introduced me to the composer and songwriter Karen Homayounfar, who gave me piano lessons. He would even go as far as to say, "*Khânoum*, one day you'll star in one of my movies." "I would love that," I often replied, even though deep down I had accepted my fate that I was never going to return to the screen, just like the stage. This was why I couldn't understand his public denial of our marriage, and why it hurt me so deeply. Perhaps it was simply difficult for the intellectual in him to publicly admit he was a fan of a pop star like Googoosh, let alone that he was married to her.

"Masoud jân, you know very well that they're never going to let me sing in public again. I don't want to waste my time on dreams like this."

"*Khânoum*, you never know," he said, wiping his thick glasses with a cloth. "Just play around with it and then keep it under your pillow."

Despite his cynical views on society, Masoud had an optimistic side that I came to know over the years, just like his hidden musical talent—he was a great piano player, he knew most of the worldly classics. He was hopeful like many that reformist president Mohammad Khatami, elected on May 23, 1997, would stick to his promises of social reform, including lifting some of the draconian restrictions around music and film. But even if Masoud and the many others were right, I knew I would never be allowed to sing again.

"Maybe," I said, unconvinced. "But I love this poem, thank you."

"Once you're done, maybe you can play it for Karen and see what he thinks."

Since when is singing a crime?
Zoroaster planted this land while singing hymns.
He planted this land while singing hymns.

Chapter 22

1998 World Cup

Beads of sweat trickled down my neck beneath the headscarf, all the way to my drenched shirt under the manteau. Bustling, affluent Jordan Boulevard—renamed Africa Boulevard—was as crowded as ever despite the scorching heat, with people rushing in and out of the many shops. I should have come much earlier, I thought, as I made my way to the produce shop to buy some fruits. It was 4 p.m. and about 38 degrees Celsius—even the shade couldn't protect you. I couldn't help but envy men in these moments. At least they didn't have to melt under a mandatory dress code, while every woman I saw walked sluggishly under their layered garments. How many would take them off if they could? I wondered. But despite the heat and my irritatingly heavy attire, I was happy to be out on Jordan, happy to be out of the hospital bed and back on my feet.

It was a short walk to the produce shop, the same one I had first shopped at a year ago after Masoud, Poulad, and I had moved into this three-bedroom apartment on Nahid-e Sharghi Street, right off Jordan. I usually enjoyed watching people go about their day as I imagined who they were and wondered about their stories, their pain, dreams, and aspirations. But it was too hot for such mental exertion. Besides, I was taken by the music blaring from one of the cars stopped in traffic just a few feet ahead of me. My heart rejoiced every time a car passed with the volume of its speakers up, even though I still looked around to make sure there weren't any morality police nearby, since listening to such music still constituted an offense. Ever since Mohammad Khatami had won the 1997 presidential election, the city seemed to be in a state of euphoria, especially the youth, who could be seen smiling, listening to rhythmic music blasting once more in the city. Qualifying for the 1998 World Cup (the second time in our country's history!) had also helped lift the mood, with millions of people pouring into the streets of Tehran last November to celebrate. And in just a few days, on June 14, we were scheduled to play our opening match against the Federal Republic of Yugoslavia in France.

I couldn't recognize the pop song, nor its Iranian singer, booming from the car's speakers. I knew it came from L.A., though, as pop music was still banned here. The driver and the passengers were all young men with their heads turned toward a Peugeot, stopped on their right. In it were veiled, but equally young women.

"What's your number?" the front passenger shouted over the music to the loosely veiled female driver and passenger of the Peugeot. "My friend can burn you a copy of this album. Who knows? Maybe we can all listen together!"

"We already have it," the driver retorted before increasing the volume of her car's stereo system.

The girls both laughed.

This had recently become a common sight among Tehran's youth. Banned from socializing with the other gender in public, young men and women had learned to go around the system; they piled into separate cars and cruised on Jordan, socializing with each other in traffic or at stops at the intersection with music flowing into the street. As soon as they spotted Revolutionary Guards or police, they lowered the music and pulled up their windows. They were so quick in their maneuvers that it almost looked choreographed. It was heartening to see that, despite everything stacked against them, these kids still found a way to have fun, just like their peers in other, freer parts of the world.

My clothes were soaking wet under my manteau by the time I reached the produce shop. But it was worth it. They had an incredible selection of mouthwatering fruits, including ruby cherries that I had bought a week earlier, which Masoud and Poulad also greatly enjoyed. I left the shop with two full bags of seasonal fruits.

Less than a minute into my journey back home, I was struck by regret. *I shouldn't be carrying these heavy bags*, I thought. Only two weeks ago I was released from Tehran Clinic, the same one where I had visited Papa after he had his second heart attack. They couldn't release me until they were convinced that my intestinal bleeding had stopped. It was the second time in my life that this had happened to me, the first back in 1975, when my manager showed up at my house at 2 a.m. in a state of shock and bloodied from head to toe after being attacked by a knife in his own neighborhood. He said he didn't want to alarm his wife, so he had driven all the way to my house in Velenjak, hoping I would take him to the hospital. That was when I collapsed. Behrouz must have driven us both to the hospital. The doctors explained that I had a stomach ulcer and that the shock of seeing my manager in that state must have triggered the internal bleeding. But this time, the symptoms had appeared more gradually over the course of a year, starting with bad stomach acidity followed by increasing pain that made it barely possible for me to stand up straight. It wasn't triggered by a shocking incident. It was stress—the same stress that made me suffer from frozen shoulder syndrome (both of my shoulders) for twelve months the previous year.

The truth was, I was finding this life of the "perfect" housewife and stepmother unbearable, constantly cooking and cleaning, staying up all night with Masoud while he wrote, or waiting up for Poulad to come home from a night out with friends. I was also angry at myself for being weak and smoking opium again after years of being sober. Masoud enjoyed smoking from time to time (nowhere near as much as Homayoun) and so I sometimes accompanied him.

While I was in Tehran Clinic for treatment, I told Masoud over the phone that I couldn't go on living like this, that he and Poulad needed to leave and move on. And after about two weeks there, I came back home feeling rested, hoping that Masoud had heard me. But he and Poulad were still there, as though nothing happened. I knew it was up to me to accept my life as it was or make a big change. Either way, I needed to think of my health, first and foremost.

I stopped by the curb and dropped the heavy bags.

"Taxi!" I called out to a driver passing by.

He didn't stop. Nor did the taxi driver after him, nor did the taxi after that. I walked a few more steps before stopping again. To hell with it! I waved at the oncoming cars. I had never hitchhiked before, but I had seen it done in many films. It couldn't be that hard.

Cars rushed by without looking my way. Then, a Patrol SUV approached. There were two young men sitting in the car. I heard music pouring from the speakers. As the car got closer, I recognized the rhythm and the voice. It was my song "*Gharibeh Ashena*" (Familiar Stranger)! It was the beginning of the chorus:

Oh familiar stranger, I love you
Take me with you to the land of fairy tales
Take my hand and place it in yours

It was the first time I had heard my hit record (written by Ardalan Sarfaraz, music composed by Hassan Shamaizadeh) in more than two decades. I waved heartily at them as though to say, "It's me, Googoosh!" I continued to wave with great enthusiasm and a big smile as they got closer. I couldn't wait to see their reaction. When they were about ten yards away, the passenger pulled down his window. He was young, like the driver, in his early twenties, with his hair slicked sky-high with gel, right on trend, paired with fashionable sunglasses.

"Get lost!" he yelled over the music, barely looking at me.

As the car sped away, I heard the chorus again, my own voice. I burst out laughing. Here I was, standing with my grocery bags, smiling and waving at these young fellows listening to my music, expecting them to recognize me. *At least the car's tailpipe didn't blast smoke in my face*, I thought. I chuckled the entire way home, forgetting the heat and the heavy bags pulling on my hands and shoulders.

June 21, 1998

It was nearly midnight, and like millions of other Iranians all over the world, we waited anxiously in front of the television.

Eight days had gone by since we lost the match to the Federal Republic of Yugoslavia, 0–1, yet nobody cared anymore. This match was more important. It was going to be the match of all matches: Iran versus the USA. Even the president of the U.S. Soccer Federation was said to have called it "the mother of all games." But it was more than the World Cup. It was going to be the first time in more than twenty years since the U.S. embassy hostage crisis that our respective governments would put their political differences aside for the whole world to see, on a soccer field, in the French city of Lyon. People who couldn't stand watching sports were following this game.

The Iranian media's coverage leading up to the match was a mix of national pride and sportsmanship. They framed the match as an opportunity to showcase the Islamic Republic's strength against the U.S., often referred to as the Great Satan by officials. But most people I knew didn't care much about the media's narrative—they were just excited to see our country as part of something uplifting for once, instead of wracked by war and turmoil. And you could see it on the faces of those lucky enough to be inside the stadium. It brought tears to my eyes, seeing Iranians with their faces painted red, white, and green, standing side by side with American fans with their faces painted red, white, and blue, both proudly waving their flags. The image was a beautiful reminder that, despite our government's desperate efforts to teach us to hate Americans, even having our young children chant, "Death to America" at school, we wholeheartedly rejected that demonization. What we wanted was peace.

Adrenaline rushed through my veins as the two teams entered the bustling arena, Iranians in red jerseys and Americans in white. The two opposing captains made their way across the field toward each other. This was the moment we were all waiting for. How were they going to greet one another? The day before the game, the Supreme Leader, Ali Khamenei, ordered our players not to shake hands with their American counterparts. And yet, against the Supreme Leader's official directive, the two captains looked at each other with warm smiles and shook hands. *I can't believe it*, I thought as tears welled in my eyes.

"They did it!" Masoud exclaimed.

The captains exchanged flowers and gifts. The rest of the players followed suit with the same level of enthusiasm; our players even handed their American counterparts white roses as a symbol of peace. They were so brave, I thought. After all, no one dared to defy the Supreme Leader due to a valid fear of imprisonment or, worse, a death sentence. My jaw dropped as players from both teams joyfully posed side by side, with arms around each other's shoulders, for the ceremonial picture.

As the cameras panned across the audience, I was also thrilled to see some of my compatriots holding banners on a global stage calling for freedom in Iran. It was powerful to witness our women standing there, most with their hair uncovered, especially knowing that women were barred from attending sporting events back home.

I could barely sit still on the couch. For the longest time the ball kept going back and forth across the large impeccably groomed green field, without ever getting near the net on either side. Every time a player, from either team, got close to the goal area, my heart skipped a beat. I felt like I was there, in Lyon, intoxicated by the collective energy pumping from all sides of the stadium filled with thousands of screaming fans.

Then the ball passed the center mark down the right flank to the corner, and midfielder Hamid Estili was fed a beautiful lob to the top of the box that he headed just past the goalkeeper's reach and into the top left corner of the net.

"GOOOOOOOAL!" I yelled as I jolted up from the couch and clapped my hands like a fanatical soccer fan.

By the time the players were back on the field after halftime, Masoud and I were equally energized (with the help of the sweet cherries that did wonders on this warm Tehran summer night) and ready for the second half. *Anything could happen now*, I thought to myself, trying my best not to get my hopes too high. I sat on the edge of my seat until the eighty-third minute of the game, when Mehdi Mahdavikia broke free near center field and took his defender one-on-one before sending the ball past the keeper, scoring another goal.

"GOOOOOOOAL!" I yelled and jumped once more.

Just as I was getting ready to celebrate our victory, the Americans scored their first goal. It was a reminder that it wasn't over until it was over. I lit a cigarette, hoping to calm my nerves. But even nicotine was no match for my adrenaline.

When the referee finally blew his whistle for time, I leaped out of my seat and pumped my fist in the air in celebration like they did in the stadium.

"Let's go outside!" Masoud said.

It was nearly 2 a.m., but we weren't going to miss out on this once-in-a-lifetime celebration. We had missed out on the unforgettable night in November when Iran qualified for the World Cup. Thousands of people had gone out in the streets of Tehran, with car speakers blasting banned pop music, men, women, and children dancing and cheering—many women had even removed their mandatory headscarves. I even heard that some people were openly drinking bootlegged alcohol in their cars, an action that could have cost them prison time in addition to the lashings. All while the morality police and the Revolutionary Guards stood back and did nothing! They must have been celebrating, too.

Masoud agreed to take the car for a quick spin on Jordan. It would have been easier to walk, but Masoud had hurt his back, and with my sciatica, the car ride seemed our only solution.

As soon as Masoud steered the car onto Jordan, we hit some light traffic and saw more people walking along the sidewalk. Vehicles around us, and on the other side, began honking to the tune of victory, while their occupants waved the national flag and yelled out enthusiastically, "Iran! Iran!" We weren't the only ones in a celebratory mood.

By the time we reached the next block, less than a five-minute walk away from the apartment, the traffic came to a full halt with cars lined up behind us. The opposite lanes of the wide boulevard, divided by a concrete barrier, were just as jammed. I could hear loud rhythmic music playing from every direction—although it was a cacophony of different songs that were hard to tell apart, they were all new Iranian pop songs that been recorded by old and new singers now living in L.A. People danced in their cars, while some stepped out to move and dance more freely in the street. I couldn't believe it. I kept looking for the Revolutionary Guards; surely they were prepared for this scenario, with units patrolling busy streets like Jordan after everything that had happened last November. Perhaps a motorcycle brigade was on its way.

As the honking grew louder and more dancers congregated in between the lanes, the sidewalk on my right grew more crowded. I pulled down on the top of my headscarf as well as the sides to cover my face some more, while Masoud readjusted his hat.

"Thankfully, we're only a block away," I said, trying to reassure Masoud and myself.

We decided that we would take the next exit on the right, which was an entrance to the freeway, and make our way back home from there.

Fifteen minutes passed, and we hadn't moved an inch. Meanwhile we could no longer distinguish the street from the sidewalk; the sidewalk had become so overcrowded that people had to walk in between the vacant cars, often stopping to join former passengers in the street dance party. We pulled up the windows to be as discreet as possible.

Another fifteen minutes went by, trapped in this unbearably warm car. As I prayed for the traffic to pick up just enough for us to take the next exit, a young man walking in between the lanes paused in front of Masoud's window and stared right at him with a twinkle in his eyes; he recognized him.

"Guys, look!" the young man yelled out to those around him. "It's Iraj Ghaderi!"

My heart nearly stopped. It didn't matter that he had mistaken Masoud for Iraj Ghaderi, a well-known actor and film director; it was only a matter of time that others would come for a look and then actually recognize Masoud and me. I tried to look down, avoiding all eye contact.

"We've got to leave the car now and walk back home," Masoud said rather calmly in his soft voice, turning his gaze away from the young man. "We'll never make it back like this."

He was right. At worst, our car would be towed. But just as we were getting ready to make a quick exit, a boy came up to my window. He was no older than ten or eleven. Although it was dark, I recognized him. He was my brother Adel's nephew (his wife's nephew, to be exact). He knocked on my window with a big smile. I discretely waved back with a smile and then motioned for him to keep quiet. He nodded.

"Guys, look!" he turned around and shouted. "It's Googoosh!"

He showed me that big smile of his again before bolting out of my sight. As soon as he yelled that, the people nearest tried looking into our car, from both sides. Masoud and I stared down into our laps to avoid all eye contact. That little devil was lucky I couldn't run after him!

"It's her!" a woman yelled, drawing more curious eyes to our car. "Googoosh!"

I calmly tried to cover my face a little more with my headscarf.

"It's Googoosh!" another person shouted a few seconds later.

My heart thumped against my rib cage. *We're never going to make it out now*, I feared as more people flocked over to our car, curious of the growing buzz around us. I kept looking down into my lap, though I could hear different voices shouting from every direction.

"Googoosh!"

"I can't believe it's you!"

"I want to see her!"

"It can't be!"

"Show us your face!"

"I love her!"

"Googoosh!"

Before we knew it, Masoud's massive Mercedes-Benz sedan was swaying from side to side, then lifted up and down. I looked over at Masoud. He was equally terrorized. Just then my door flung open.

"What the hell are you doing here?!"

It was Poulad.

"Get out of the car now!" he yelled as he grabbed my hand.

"Googoosh!"

"It's really her!"

"Forget about me!" Masoud said to his son as he tried to get out of the car. "Take her home!"

Poulad and his three friends, all in their late teens, encircled my open door, making sure no one could reach me, and then formed a U-shaped chain around me with their arms.

"Let's go," Poulad ordered.

Poulad and his friends pushed through the crowd, while I followed in the middle. We were only about a quarter of a mile from home, less than five minutes away. I put my head down, hoping to get less attention, but it was futile; people reached over the boys' arms and pulled on my clothes, my headscarf, my arms, my shoulders, on anything that they could get their hands on. We had just made it to about ten feet away from the car when someone yanked on my headscarf, and incidentally my hair! It was so painful that I immediately looked back and saw a woman's hand with red-painted fingernails.

"Googoosh, let us see you!" she cried out. She was easily in her forties.

"What's happening! Who is it?" an approaching onlooker asked.

"Googoosh!" someone yelled back from behind us.

The onlooker and a few others immediately tried to get closer to me for a look, but Poulad and his friends held them back using their arms. This pattern kept repeating itself, with more people joining the enthusiastic crowd around us, almost like the crowd chasing Elizabeth Taylor's character and her cousin Sebastian Venable in the film *Suddenly, Last Summer*.

We tried to walk faster, but it was impossible. Not only was it difficult to push through this growing wave of people, it was even tougher to do so going uphill. My legs trembled. I was sure my knees were going to buckle at any moment, but Poulad and the boys kept pulling me. Just as we were reaching our street, I prayed that the crowd would lose interest and go on with their celebrations. But the wave of people continued to follow us. Unlike Jordan, though, our street was empty. Poulad turned to me and yelled, "Run!" As soon as our security guard saw me running toward him, he motioned me to the underground parking entrance and closed the gate behind me while I collapsed on the floor. Once I stopped hyperventilating, I started crying hysterically. And for the longest time, I couldn't stop. It was a mix of fear, pain, and relief.

Twenty-four hours later I still couldn't understand how I had managed to sprint those seventy yards to my building. Some higher power must have protected me, having sent Poulad and his friends our way, I thought. I couldn't have imagined what would have happened had they not been there that moment. The adrenaline certainly helped. By now we were able to laugh about the whole thing, Masoud, Poulad, and I. Masoud comically described how he climbed up the busy block, holding on to the wall for support while he watched the crowd swarming around us like a school of fish.

"Imagine," he said, "some people out there are now boasting, 'Not only did we beat America last night, but we also saw Iraj Ghaderi with Googoosh!'"

Then it hit me. All these years later they hadn't forgotten me. They hadn't forgotten Googoosh.

Chapter 23

Hatami

Late spring 1999

It was nearly 6:45 p.m. and Tehran's peak rush hour was as bad as in any other capital around the world. The invitation had specified that the doors would close at 7 p.m., though everyone knew that meant 7:15—as a people, we Iranians are always fashionably late. I was just minutes away from Shahin's home on Kayhan Street, where I was picking her up, but I knew it was going to take us some time to get to Hafez Street, where the concert hall was. Besides, we had agreed that it was best for us to arrive at the very last moment, minimizing any risk of my exposure.

As usual, Faegheh worried about Googoosh's reputation, always thinking a few steps ahead and erring on the side of caution, but this time Googoosh's resolve was unwavering.

Shahin and I were going to attend Khatereh Parvaneh's long-anticipated concert (with orchestra leader Ophelia Parto). Khatereh, a renowned traditional Iranian singer who hadn't performed in more than two decades, was set to become the first female performer—and the only one from the pre-revolution era—to be granted permission to sing before a strictly female audience. It felt like a hopeful sign—perhaps 1999 would finally be the year of change that President Khatami had promised. Until then, and since the early 1990s, the ban on singing had only been lifted for male performers—including those from before the revolution—allowing them to perform select, preapproved pop songs before audiences that weren't gender-segregated. We still had a long way to go, as state restrictions continued to weigh heavily on women; our singing voices were still considered sinful, deemed sexually provocative in nature, and therefore strictly forbidden in front of a male audience.

Although Khatereh Parvaneh's concert organizers had obtained permission from the Ministry of Culture and Islamic Guidance, it still felt as though we were attending an illegal gathering. Everything about it was hush-hush, with invitation-only entry and zero advertisement. The reason for the secrecy was simple; other official departments, not the Ministry of Culture and Islamic Guidance, were known to shut down artistic events and arrest everyone, including spectators, arguing that they were the rightful ones to grant permissions. I was willing to take the risk to watch a live performance after more than twenty years. As I waited for Shahin in my nine-year-old Daewoo parked at the bottom of her building, I imagined the concert hall called Tâlâr-e Farhang on Hafez Street, the stage, the live instruments, the acoustics that would soon vibrate with Khatereh's powerful voice. My heart fluttered in anticipation.

Shahin hopped into the passenger seat, visibly as excited as me, her beaming smile accentuated by her scarlet-red lipstick, the same shade as her recently painted fingernails. Shahin was always cheerful despite the struggles she faced in life as a widow and mother of two, something I always admired about her ever since we met some fifteen years before. Our bond grew even stronger through our mutual love for music. A professional violinist, Shahin's entire life had revolved around music until the revolution decided her passion and life's work was sinful and forced her to sit at home like the rest of us. Over the years, she resorted to giving the odd violin lesson here and there, but like every musician living in this country, she dreamed of the day, much like today, where instruments would be heard playing once more in Tehran's old concert halls.

We made it through the doors just as the female ushers were getting ready to close off the entrance. One of the young women grabbed our invitations without even a glance at us and led us quickly into the packed concert hall. My heart raced as we rushed down the aisle toward the front row. It had been twenty years since I had attended a musical performance. I'd missed this, the energy, the anticipation, the thrill, the enthusiasm of the spectators and their chatter as they awaited the performer. Sitting in the front row, careful to keep my head down, careful not to attract any attention, I wondered how Khatereh was feeling. I imagined stepping into her shoes for a moment and feeling the sorts of emotions she must be feeling backstage, all of the excitement, joy, and stress. She must be afraid, I thought, afraid of not living up to the audience's expectations, of not living up to their memories. After all, everyone vividly remembered her grandiose voice from the seventies, but nobody knew what that voice would sound like some twenty years later. But I knew she was going to be as great as ever, otherwise she wouldn't have decided to get in front of the audience in the first place.

It was seven thirty and Khatereh Parvaneh was going to make her entrance at any moment. The atmosphere was electric with some 250 to 300 eager guests tittering in their seats. I found myself taking a few deep breaths to calm my nerves, as though I were the one standing behind the curtains. Then, just as Shahin leaned into whisper something in my left ear, I heard someone mentioning my name somewhere nearby. Shahin froze like me.

"I'm telling you, it's her," the voice continued.

"It can't be Googoosh," another woman said.

It sounded like they were sitting behind us.

"Look for yourself!"

Moments later, as I was pretending to examine my fingernails, pretending I hadn't overheard the conversation behind us, I saw a woman approaching me from my peripheral vision. I tucked my feet under my seat, imagining that she might just be trying to get to her seat farther down our row—we were sitting near the center. But she wouldn't move.

"Googoosh?"

I pretended I didn't hear her. I could feel Shahin nervously fidgeting in her seat.

"Is that you?" she insisted.

When I finally looked up, I saw a distinguished looking woman in her seventies with perfectly coiffed blond hair under a loosely fitted maroon headscarf.

"It's you, I can't believe it!" she cried, before I could even react. "Googoosh, where have you been all these years? What have you been doing? You know, I first saw you sing when you were this little," she said, pointing to the height of her knees. "You were so little—I remember you even peed onstage that night! Do you remember?"

I smiled and nodded, hoping it was the end of our interaction. But then others came rushing in behind her.

"Googoosh!" another woman yelled, loud enough for everyone in the back to hear, adding to the growing brouhaha.

"It's Googoosh!" someone shouted in the back.

"I want to see!" another person replied.

"Please let us see your face!"

Just when it seemed like half of the guests were rushing toward the front row, Shahin and I leapt onto the stage in our heels. We ran toward the backstage, searching for a place to hide. I could hear some of the guests not far behind us. One of the organizers magically appeared—she had been watching the chaos unfold—and swiftly steered us toward the exit. She must have realized she couldn't, on her own, hold back the flood of guests eager to catch a glimpse of Googoosh. Thankfully, no one had followed us outside, where Shahin and I, both past our prime, sprinted like young Olympians toward my car.

We huffed and puffed as I turned on the ignition and steered the car into traffic. As soon as she caught her breath, Shahin started with her cheerfulness.

"*Khânoumi* [missy], did you see that? They were all so happy to see you!"

I couldn't hide my smile, though I was disappointed to miss Khatereh's concert.

"Had there been half as many, I'm sure we could've stayed and enjoyed the concert," she continued, as though she could hear my thoughts.

"Half?" I laughed.

Just as our adrenaline subsided and our heart rates stabilized, a noisy unmarked motorcycle pulled up to my window in the middle of ongoing traffic and started honking. I knew right then it was a Komiteh agent—we still called them that, even though the Komitehs had been officially dissolved years ago, their enforcers absorbed into other repressive branches of the government. No one else ever behaved this way. They were always dressed in plain clothes, using unmarked vehicles and motorcycles, blending into the chaos of the city.

When I pulled over, the Komiteh agent made his way to my window, still on his bike, with his rifle strapped to his back. I knew what we were in for the moment I saw his angry face.

"What were you doing over there?" he said aggressively, barely articulating his words. "Don't play dumb with me! I know who you are! Who told you to go there? To that concert place!" he barked.

"I was invited," I answered, fighting the urge to knock the smug look off his face.

"The hell you were!" he shouted as he gave me a nasty look. "Stay away, and pray that I don't find you!"

He gave me one long, disgusted look, the same burning animosity in his eyes as Afshoun had decades prior, before he sped off.

"But how did he know it was you back there?" Shahin asked, as shaken and upset as I was. "We were running so fast . . ."

A part of me wondered if he had followed us from the start.

A few weeks later, after I returned from a weekend by the Caspian Sea with Shahin and her daughters, she called me on the phone, her voice tight with unease. She explained that shortly after we left, some agents visited our friend who had hosted us. They demanded to know whether I was there that weekend, what we discussed, and what I was up to these days. It seemed highly unlikely that a curious onlooker could have alerted them to my presence, as we had arrived late at night and spent the entire day on the property, staying mostly on the patio, where we were shielded from any public view. And even if someone had seen me there, why did my visit matter so much? It wasn't a crime. I was never told I couldn't travel within the country. I had been going up there for years like this, staying with friends. So why did this trip warrant an interrogation? Something didn't feel right.

Late September 1999

Nearly four months had passed since the concert, and a lot had changed. Most of my friends stopped coming over to my apartment following the incident with Ladan. It was early June when she called me in a panic—less than an hour after we'd had afternoon tea—saying that unidentified regime agents had stopped her just outside my building as she was leaving. They threatened to harm her thirteen-year-old son if she didn't answer all their questions about me. "Just when one of them told me I was free to go," Ladan continued, "the other one said that I needed to persuade you to write your memoir."

It was terrifying, especially that they had threatened her boy like that. And all for what, Googoosh's memoir? I felt unnerved and worried for my loved ones. It felt eerie when, just a couple weeks later, the news broke about the death of Saeed Emami. On June 19, 1999, to be exact, Saeed Emami, the former deputy minister of intelligence, had allegedly committed suicide in his jail cell. Masoud had unknowingly encountered him at a cultural event just a year earlier. He didn't realize at the time who Emami was—just another senior government official who walked into the room as if he owned it. Emami (still an active minister then) approached Masoud and, without introducing himself, insisted in an authoritarian tone, "Googoosh must write her memoir." Masoud replied politely that, as my husband, he didn't want me to do that. It was only months later, after Emami's arrest and with his face broadcast across every news outlet, that Masoud recognized him. I felt shaken at the time when I realized that this man who had demanded my memoir was one involved in the orchestration of the Chain Murders.

The so-called Chain Murders were a series of assassinations over roughly a decade, where more than eighty people in and outside of Iran—writers, poets, journalists, and political activists who were openly critical of the regime—were systematically murdered in stabbings, shootings, car crashes, and unexplained fatal medical complications. Among those hunted by agents of the government was the beloved TV host, poet, singer, and writer Fereydoun Farrokhzad. On August 8, 1992, German police found Fereydoun murdered on his kitchen floor in Bonn, Germany, with dozens of stab wounds on his face and body. He was discovered by the police after neighbors complained about his two dogs barking for five days, day and night.

I felt sick to my stomach every time I thought of Fereydoun's butchered body stretched on the kitchen floor in a pool of blood, thousands of miles away from his family and homeland. Until his very last breath, Fereydoun's thoughts were back here, with his family, his friends, and his people. He took every opportunity to criticize the government of the Islamic Republic, as well as to encourage his compatriots to rise in the face of the injustices. His very last act was to invite three people whom he had taken for Iranian refugees over to his house for afternoon tea, believing their false promises that they could smuggle him back into his homeland, never once suspecting that they were paid assassins.

The systematic targeting of artists and intellectuals was in full force by 1996, when there was a failed attempt to derail a bus carrying twenty-one Iranian writers and poets on their way to a poetry conference in Armenia. There were also the horrific assassinations of prominent political figures, such as Dariush Forouhar and his wife, Parvaneh Eskandari, along with several writers and activists, including Mohammad Mokhtari and Mohammad Jafar Pouyandeh, which sparked widespread public outrage and international condemnation. Under mounting pressure, the government looked for a scapegoat. Emami was killed just like his victims.

His death didn't appease anyone. Everyone knew Emami wasn't a lone acting agent, and his death didn't bring back any of the victims. I, like everyone around me, was still filled with rage. Artists, musicians, writers, and poets were targeted for expressing themselves and speaking their minds. They were not criminals, yet they were hunted down and treated like war enemies, as though their words, melodies, and voices were more dangerous than any weapon.

Three weeks after his dead body was found in his jail cell, the country descended into turmoil—the biggest since the revolution. Peaceful protests, with university students at the forefront, erupted after the government forcibly shut down the reformist newspaper *Salaam* on July 7, accusing it of "confusing public opinion." The newspaper had published an old memo written by Emami, while he was still in power, to the Intelligence Ministry chief, Qorban-Ali Dorri-Najafabadi, outlining plans to further restrict press freedom.

On the night of the 18th of Tir—July 9—a violent raid was carried out on the male student dormitory of Tehran University by plainclothes paramilitaries who called themselves the Ansar-e Hezbollah, the Comrades of Hezbollah. Young male students were brutally beaten, with some even thrown from their dorm room windows—at least one student was reportedly killed this way. The bloodshed at the dormitory ignited mass protests from the streets of Tehran to other major cities, including Tabriz, Mashhad, Shiraz, and Esfahan. What started off as a protest in defense of freedom of the press quickly escalated into a broader movement against the government and its repressive forces. Many protesters were physically assaulted or killed by regime forces across the country.

For days, Masoud and I, like millions of Iranians, tuned in day and night to BBC Persian, as well as to illegal Persian-speaking satellite channels broadcasting from abroad—using our illegal satellite dish we had installed five or six years earlier like most Iranians had—since our state media refused to cover the protests. It was devastating to witness our children—the hope for our future—targeted so violently, assaulted, beaten, and even killed. The entire country felt the weight of this tragedy. All our hearts ached as we saw one horrific image after another. The cover of *The Economist*, showing a young man carrying the bloodstained T-shirt of a fallen fellow protester, was burned into my mind.

For the second time in my life, I found myself deeply concerned with politics—only this time, I was sober. I was reading every newspaper I could get my hands on, poring over every page, trying to understand more about the government's decision to close *Salaam*, the student movement and their demands, and the ruthless crackdown they faced. I had never heard of *Salaam* before, but now it felt like it was more than just a reformist newspaper—perhaps a symbol of everything we had lost.

Although the protests were violently quashed in less than a week by official and paramilitary forces, the collective anger and grief lived on—we were now in late September and the country was still unofficially mourning. It seemed that all of the optimism and hope ushered in by President Khatami's election had vanished, replaced by long faces and despair, just like during the war. I was feeling even more hopeless than I did during the war, seeing our kids forcefully arrested, savagely beaten, and killed by our own government for wanting nothing more than to protect their fundamental rights. It was on days like this that I wondered if I was still in my country, the one that I had loved for better or for worse and had stood by all these years.

As I was wrestling with these dark thoughts on this early autumn afternoon, the phone rang.

"Mrs. Atashin," a man said with a deep voice.

He presented himself as Hatami. I knew just from his tone that he was some government agent—you got a sense of these things after years of interacting with them. He ordered me to present myself at a specific address the next day. My heart began racing. What if it had something to do with the 18th of Tir? After all, arrests were still being made of supposed "enemies of the state." And the last time they had interrogated me was sixteen years ago, in the summer of 1983, after the Shah's last appointed prime minister, Shapour Bakhtiar, had called from exile for people to carry out civil disobedience against the regime by getting in their cars, turning on their headlights, and honking while creating traffic jams up and down the country. At the time, I was held at the Komiteh station in Daryâ Kenâr for several days of questioning, before being transferred to Evin Prison. There, I endured another full day of being blindfolded and interrogated. The questions at both places were repetitive, rehashing the same old inquiries I had answered years ago—about royal gatherings and parties where I had performed, and about this or that famous person. It felt like Prime Minister Bakhtiar's call for resistance had simply given the regime agents a fresh excuse to harass Googoosh.

This time, I was summoned to an office on Saltanatâbâd Street, in the former headquarters of SAVAK. I recognized it. I had been in this same office once before, long before the revolution, to pick up a paycheck from Ardeshir Amirghassemi, who was in charge of organizing the official entertainment for visiting heads of state that required high security. Ayatollah Khomeini's portrait now hung where the Shah's portrait once had, and behind the desk, below the portrait, sat Hatami instead of Mr. Amirghassemi. And here I was, less than a year from turning fifty, dressed in a long manteau and my hair covered by my headscarf, standing where that twenty-six-year-old pop star had once stood.

Hatami, or whatever his real name was, looked just as I had imagined him over the phone: early forties, dressed in the ill-fitting dark suit and mandarin-collared shirt like the many government agents I had encountered, his lower face covered with the unofficially mandated four-day stubble.

"Have a seat, Mrs. Atashin," he said, pointing to the empty chair placed a few feet or so across from his desk.

As soon as I sat down another man similarly dressed, with the same facial hair and stern expression, entered and took a seat next to Hatami, behind a smaller adjoining desk. The man didn't introduce himself and he began writing on a document Hatami placed in front of him.

"As I mentioned over the phone," Hatami continued with his deep voice, "we've got important questions that need clarifying."

My heart began to hammer against my chest.

"Tell me, you know Bahram Beyzai, what is he working on these days?" Hatami asked.

Bahram Beyzai was a heavyweight in the art world as an acclaimed playwright, theater director, and influential and innovative film director. He was a good friend of Masoud's.

"I don't know, I've never met him," I replied, rather dumbfounded.

"You don't know," Hatami said mechanically. "But your husband must know. He must share some things with you, as men sometimes do with their wives behind closed doors."

"I don't know what Mr. Beyzai is working on," I repeated. "And my husband is far too busy and focused on his own work to talk to me about others like that," I added with a slightly frustrated tone.

Both men's eyes slightly widened.

"Yes, I'm sure he's very busy," Hatami then replied, narrowing his eyes at me, before going on. "And how do you know Rasoul Mollagholipour?"

Rasoul was a film director, who in addition to his critically acclaimed films had directed several documentaries about the Iran-Iraq War. The press was shocked when I had showed up to one of his film premieres a few years ago, although they didn't report it, since it was forbidden for them to write about me. I was surprised myself when I received his invitation. After all, we had never met and it wasn't obvious as to why a film director who covered the war would want to associate with Googoosh, a persona non grata. It all made sense when we finally met in person at the premiere. Not only did we share a common Azeri background and mother tongue, but he was a music aficionado and grew up listening to my records. Of course, I wasn't going to tell Hatami any of this.

"You were close to Marzieh," he interrupted me before I could reply.

Marzieh was our treasured traditional *sonati* singer whose singing voice had been compared by some foreigners to those of Maria Callas and Edith Piaf. I had been a fan of hers ever since I was very young. I listened to her music trying to emulate her style, just as I had with Delkash and Pouran. We were never that close personally, only close enough to have caught up over the phone maybe a handful of times since the revolution, as well as in person maybe once or twice, including at the wonderful and impromptu seventh-day commemoration of Papa's passing.

"Have you heard from her recently?" Hatami asked.

I wasn't surprised he was asking me this. The regime was probably worried that former performers such as myself would follow in Marzieh's footsteps and join the much-detested Sâzmân-e Mojâhedīn-e Khalq (People's Mujahedin Organization, MEK), just as she had in exile in France in 1994. Though the MEK initially fought hand in hand with Khomeinists in overthrowing the Shah, it was banned by Khomeini in 1981 for political differences (leading to the mass arrests and executions of MEK members throughout the 1980s). The MEK went on to join forces with Saddam Hussein during the Iraq-Iran War, something that millions of Iranians have never forgiven them for.

"No," I replied.

I told him that I must have last spoken to her a year or two before.

"What did you talk about? What did she say?" he asked.

I explained that I couldn't remember the exact conversation, but that we would have likely had a brief, cordial exchange about each other's health.

"Nothing else?" he persisted.

"Not that I can remember."

"She didn't mention her plans about leaving the country?"

"I don't think so," I replied.

There was no need to mention that we must have also expressed our common woes about the state of our homeland, as well as our woes from the deafening silence of the empty stages and concert halls. Nor did I explain to him that people didn't reveal their plans over the telephone, knowing that privacy didn't really exist inside the Islamic Republic.

He briefly paused before resuming. "You don't think so." Then with a hint of a smile he went on. "Say, are you sure your father was your father?"

"*Hajji*, her father's dead," the man at the smaller desk interjected in a sympathetic tone, as if to say, "We don't speak ill of the dead."

"Who's ever sure that their father is their father anyway?" I quickly countered, showing Hatami that he hadn't broken me.

His smile faded away, but so did his harsh tone as he went on to the next question. I felt as though I had just passed some sick test of his by not letting him sully my father's honor.

The interrogation went on like this for several hours, with Hatami doing the questioning, while the nameless man silently jotted down notes. The questions were all the same. So were my answers.

I became hopeful that our session was coming to an end when the nameless man began checking his watch more frequently.

"There's one last thing," Hatami finally said. "Now more than ever is a good time for you to write your memoir."

There it was, the memoir they had threatened Ladan to get me to write, the same one that Saeed Emami insisted to Masoud that I write. They called it a "memoir," but they didn't actually want my life story. They wanted to slap my name on some made-up confession, or some endorsement I wasn't willing to give. They did this in 1997 with Parvin (Pari) Ghaffari, a beautiful actress known for her pre-revolution roles in films like *Mou Talâi-e Shahr-e Mâ* (*The Blond Woman of Our Town*, 1965) and *Tunnel* (1968), and famously rumored as being one of the Shah's girlfriends. Thousands of printed copies of a book carrying her name appeared in every bookstore across the country, without any information regarding a publisher. What made readers more skeptical about her having anything to do with this alleged memoir was that there were not many personal stories, except for the somewhat graphic descriptions of her intimate encounters with the Shah. The Ministry of Culture and Islamic Guidance allowed explicit passages in this "memoir" to be published, while prohibiting other writers from depicting married couples kissing on the cheek or simply sitting on the same bed. This led many to believe the book was written to serve a political agenda rather than offer a genuine personal account. Also, beyond the few racy passages—tame by Western standards—it read more like a collection of political essays, in which "she" mostly denounced the Shah and praised the Islamic regime. Some passages even resembled a political prisoner trying to appease a kangaroo court.

"But I'm not a writer," I replied to Hatami.

"You don't have to be a writer; we'll find someone to help you write your book."

"But then it won't be my book, will it?" I pushed back. "It will be the writer's book, sort of like Pari Ghaffari's memoir."

He knew what I meant. Government censors would never allow Googoosh to publish her book in her own words.

"No, nothing like her book," Hatami shot back. "We'll find the right person for you so that you can finally tell people everything."

Everything? Like how the Islamic revolution destroyed my life? Or how it has been destroying our country, day after day? Plunging us into an unnecessary war that claimed so many lives? Sending innocent little boys to clear minefields? Throwing college students out of their dorm windows in the middle of the night and killing others in broad daylight for exercising their God-given right to speak their minds? Or executing homosexuals for simply loving the person they love?

"Mr. Hatami, you want me to say everything?" I insisted, my heart pounding. "Like how after Mr. Khomeini died, I cried for seven days and seven nights and I couldn't understand why—why would I cry hysterically for this person who had taken everything from me, my career, my friends, my family, my child? Then, I realized I wasn't mourning him—"

"You see," Hatami abruptly interrupted, "we've successfully erased Googoosh from the minds of more than half the people. But there's still some young folks out there who know you and listen to your music. So you should use your name to help stop them from repeating your mistakes. It will be a good cautionary tale for everyone."

Mistakes. Cautionary tale. I was right. They weren't interested in my story. They wanted a book in which I would repent for my "mistakes" of singing, dancing, and performing for the monarchy. It wasn't enough that I had kept my head down all these years. Now they were insisting that I use my voice to promote their propaganda by publicly condemning Googoosh and everything she stood for.

After my interrogation on Saltanatâbâd Street, Hatami started systematically calling moments after Masoud stepped outside the door, like clockwork. It was as though he had a set of eyes and ears in our apartment.

Masoud's friend Bagher Parham was even detained twice in a month after leaving our place, just like Ladan. And only a few days ago, while Hatami had me on the phone for more than an hour, which was normal at this point, my brother Mehrdad quietly entered our apartment not making a sound. Hatami asked, "How's Mr. Mehrdad doing?" The calls were cut short whenever Masoud returned home, with Hatami sometimes stopping midsentence and saying that we would pick up the conversation later.

I felt scared and paranoid; Masoud and I were constantly censoring everything we said and did in our own home. I felt violated. Was someone watching us through our windows? Had bugs been planted in our home unbeknownst to us? Or was our cleaner reporting back to Hatami? Maybe the building doorman? And how long had this been going on? Long before the Khatereh Parvaneh concert? Masoud tried to keep calm, but even he couldn't hide his increasing irritability and restlessness. No one could, given these circumstances. I retreated into my own bubble; I wasn't talking to loved ones on the phone, brushing them off, telling them I was busy, nor was I going to them, for fear of getting them into trouble. I was barely sleeping, even with sleeping pills. I couldn't focus on anything. I felt as though I had been sent back into Mr. Mesbahzadeh's basement, where instead of silencing me, now, twenty years later, they were trying to compel me to give my voice to their purposes.

Then one day, during one of our phone conversations, I stalled and kept Hatami on the line until Masoud walked in. I handed him the phone. Masoud knew how to speak to men like Hatami. After years of dealing with the Ministry of Culture and Islamic Guidance and their broad brush strokes of film censorship, he had learned how to carefully navigate these murky waters with some success. It also helped that he was a man in the Islamic Republic, where the life of a woman is legally worth half that of a man. He patiently listened to Hatami, who laid out the reasons for me to write a memoir, just as he had to me in person, and then when the time came, Masoud calmly explained in his soft voice that he didn't want me, his wife, to expose herself to the public with her life story. He didn't have to remind Hatami that he, too, was a public figure with a large following, large enough to create problems if he were to speak out openly against the constant harassment. Hatami said he understood and hung up.

He stopped calling. But I wasn't going to let my guard down. I knew they were never going to let Googoosh out of their sight.

Chapter 24

A Door Cracking Open

Early May, 2000

It was almost 8 p.m. and the sun had not yet fully set, a sign that summer was just around the corner. Masoud and Morteza Shayesteh were still busy discussing their latest project in the living room, so I lowered the heat of the stove to a minimum, careful not to burn the rice and overcook the stew. I was used to these long work sessions when Masoud was collaborating with Morteza. Morteza was a film producer and a shareholder of Hedayat Film, the very same studio Youness had worked for. He was a younger man, in his early forties, dynamic and easy to talk to—on one occasion, not long after my stress-induced intestinal bleeding, I even confided to him about my growing impatience with life as a housewife.

As I prepared another hot batch of tea for them to go with the barely touched dried dates and confections already placed on the coffee table, I decided that I was going to invite Morteza to stay for dinner. It was getting late after all, and I could hear Masoud was only now discussing his new idea for a film inspired by Phyllis Hastings's book *Rapture in My Rags* (1954), a thriller about an English countryside girl and her scarecrow that comes to life.

Just as I placed the hot ceramic teapot of cardamom-infused tea on the table, thinking I was going to have to wait for the right moment to interrupt them, Morteza stopped midsentence and turned to me.

"How would you feel about playing in Mr. Kimiai's next film?" he asked with a smile.

I smiled back, knowing he was kidding.

"I'm serious," he said.

"I would love to, but you know very well that will never happen—they would never allow it."

"What if I told you not to worry about that?"

"But how? They'll never—"

"Don't worry about that part."

I looked over to Masoud, thinking I would find a puzzled face similar to mine, but his eyes glimmered with enthusiasm. He had always told me how he wanted me to act in his films.

"Of course, we won't film in Iran," Morteza continued. "There would be too many obstacles here with you in front of the camera. We'll film abroad this summer, come back for the editing, and then I'll work on securing its release."

He was serious.

"But how can I leave the country without a passport?" I asked in disbelief. "They've refused to grant me one for the last two decades."

"Don't worry about that, either," Morteza said.

Then it struck me how several renowned pre-revolution actors had recently made their comebacks. On top of that, Ata'ollah Mohajerani, the current minister of culture and Islamic guidance, had stopped by our home, unannounced, one afternoon, about three months ago. Masoud left his tobacco pipe in his office after a meeting, and I found it peculiar that Mohajerani would take time out of his busy schedule as a high-ranking official to come to our house and return it. But then I realized from our brief exchange that he was more curious about Googoosh than returning the pipe to its rightful owner.

"What do you say?" Morteza asked with that same enthusiastic smile.

"Of course I want to act in Masoud's film!"

Masoud added that I would play the lead role, who would be older than the original character in Hastings's novel. Then the two of them suggested we do four films together, given the opportunity of being abroad. And no one doubted that Masoud could write all four screenplays in no time.

"Mrs. Atashin, while we're abroad, how would you feel about singing?" Morteza asked. "We could easily put together a world tour," he added, while Masoud calmly poured tea into our guest's empty glass. "A concert in each key city around the world."

"It's the year 2000 and the world is ready for a Googoosh comeback," Morteza added with a bright smile. "But the important question is, are you?"

Masoud looked at me, his eyes smiling.

"What do you say?" Morteza asked again.

"Of course I would like that," I finally said, "but it's impossible! They made me sign a paper and—"

"It's possible as long as you want to," Morteza interrupted enthusiastically.

Maybe it is possible, I thought. After all, I knew that Morteza had important powerful political associations, running a big film studio like that—you couldn't do anything in the Islamic Republic without the right connections, and without greasing some palms along the way. But then, what about Hatami, all that surveillance, the daily calls, and the interrogations he put me through? I hadn't forgotten what he had said to me less than a year ago, about how they'd tried everything in their power to erase me. Why would Morteza think they'd give me a passport now and let me go on a world tour?

"All I need is a yes from you," he said. "Then I'll go ahead and draft two contracts, one for the films and another for the tour."

June 14, 2000

It was 4 a.m. and Masoud was sound asleep next to me while I lay awake with my sciatica in full force, staring out the window. As I watched the pink and purple hues creep across the previously dark sky, I remembered those cool summer nights at Dâyi and Khadijeh Khânoum's house in Haft Katchaloon, when we all slept on the rooftop, under the bright stars. I must have been eight years old and Fery six and a half. We were so happy there, Fery and I, lying side by side on the mattress, under the mosquito net, as the same warm-colored hues danced above us.

If only you were here beside me now, I thought.

I had been thinking of Fery a lot these past few days. I missed him terribly. I learned that at times like this it helped to talk to him, as though he were with me.

> Fery, do you remember the big Persian mulberry tree in Dâyi's garden? How we used to spend hours running around it with Simin? How big it seemed to us back then . . . Or remember how many rounds of *yeh-ghol dô-ghol* we used to play? How we had to first find five of the roundest pebbles that would be easiest to catch midair? And remember how we used to wait outside in the street for that vendor to show up with the large wooden crate filled with toys that he carried around on top of his head? We waited hours just to buy those little handmade *ferferes* (pinwheels) and windup toys, like *vagh vagh sâhâbs*, with the little pocket money Dâyi and Khadijeh Khânoum would give us. And what about that time our older cousins dared me to go begging in the street dressed in a chador? It all feels like yesterday. I turned fifty this year, can you believe it? And you would soon be forty-nine . . .

He wasn't supposed to go before me. He wasn't supposed to leave me that soon. I've often wondered if he would still be around if we had stayed at Dâyi's and not lived under the same roof as Mouness. But I know what he would say, he would tell me not to go there, he would tell me not to look back . . . And maybe he would be right. It's just that I missed him so much.

It was still hard for me to talk about him, even after all these years. He was the gentlest and most generous soul I'd ever known. As if he were an angel loaned down from heaven. One time, when we were little and living at Dâyi's, I remembered how upset he got when he realized I had tricked him into buying me an ice cream, while saving my own pocket money. But just as quickly, his frown turned into a smile, and he went back to enjoying his own treat. He always knew how to let things go—he was always the bigger person.

Even though he was quiet growing up, he knew how to make people laugh. He used to poke fun of his lower lip because it was thicker. He used to roll it up with one hand and talk as if everything was normal. Then one day a bee stung it. Instead of screaming or cursing like any other teen would do, he saw the humor in the situation and started running around, playfully holding his lip with both hands, laughing, and yelling, "What should I do with this?" He was great at imitations, just like Papa. He always cracked me up with his chimpanzee walk. I always felt good around him.

Some of my best days were spent visiting Fery in Paris, right after Mahmoud and I separated. He showed me so many hidden gems there, but also in Naples, Capri, London, and Beirut. I had never been on trips like these before, with a lot of sightseeing and no one to please. We walked everywhere together. We joked and acted silly, like we used to as kids. Any worries I was carrying would vanish.

If only he had listened to me, if only he had given that Texan professor a chance. Maybe the surgery could have successfully repaired his heart, and he would still be here . . . But he wanted to live a life without constant medical supervision, and I needed to respect that. Even though his doctor asked him to stay away from emotional and physical excitement, he lived his life to the fullest and married the woman he loved. At his funeral, my heart filled with so much love and sorrow seeing how many lives he touched. He forgave those who had hurt him, even Mouness, and never once looked back. I wished I could do the same. Though I could forgive, I could never forget.

It took me until Papa's passing to forgive him for not protecting us, for not protecting Fery. It took me even longer to forgive myself, to understand that I was just a child, too, back then, and that I had done everything in my power to protect him. But Fery never looked for someone to blame. He would say that pain is life, that pain is what strengthens us and makes us grow, and that pain is what makes us love and forgive. Pain prepared me for everything life had thrown my way. Without all that pain, I might have gone mad after they took music away from me. Without it, I wouldn't be here now, about to embark on a new journey in nineteen hours.

Nobody knew, not even Kambiz, but if all went as planned, I would be flying out of Tehran tonight and heading to Canada, where I would embark on a world tour. If all went as planned, I would finally meet my grandson, Daara, who was turning two—he looked as adorable as Kambiz at that age. I would also surprise Fariborz and Adel, who were living in Toronto. But for now, it was all hush-hush. All I had to do was sneak through the most crowded airport in the country, past the armed Revolutionary Guards and immigration officials, and get into international airspace. Easy, right?

It all happened so fast. One minute I was asked if I wanted to sing, and the next I was getting my professional headshots taken after decades, working on a new album and sneaking into a makeshift home studio in the middle of the night, with walls covered in egg cartons, for a secret recording session. So much had changed! I was so distracted by all the screens and buttons that I couldn't even sing the way I wanted to. Nothing came out right, so after a few hours we called it quits and decided that we would do all of the recording in Canada. But what if the same thing happened to me there? What if I couldn't sing like I used to? What if my voice had changed? What if the ceiling I felt over my voice in Lachini's studio was still there? And what if my sciatica got out of control and I couldn't stand up straight, let alone dance onstage? And what if people had forgotten me after all those years?

Now I knew exactly how Papa must have felt as he was getting ready to go back onstage in Istanbul after nine years—I got goose bumps just thinking about it! But then, why was it that every time I imagined getting on that plane, I felt a sinking sensation in the pit of my stomach, just like when Fery's wife called me that early morning or when Uncle Nader called about Papa? For two days, I had been drinking glass after glass of water from the kitchen sink, even when I wasn't thirsty, telling myself I needed to memorize its sweet taste.

Nothing felt certain—they probably wouldn't even let me board that plane. But what if they did? What if I made it to Canada? Would I be able to return? Would they arrest me when I came back? I had been thinking a lot about Bahbah and her painful life in exile, far from her beloved homeland. Could I survive as long as she did? And what if I didn't go? Could I survive another twenty-one years like this, in deafening silence?

> Fery, I wish you were here to tell me what to do, though a part of me already knows what you would say. You'd tell me that I should never let anyone or anything stop me from having a fulfilling life. You'd tell me to go on without looking back. What I wouldn't give to see you now, Fery, to see those reassuring innocent brown eyes and that sweet baby face of yours . . . I've told myself that you're off traveling and exploring the world. It's been easier that way. So until we meet again, my dearest Fery, go enjoy the rest of your travels.

—

A blaring car alarm hollered in the distance. *Ignore it*, I thought as I pulled out a cigarette from a half-empty pack of Marlboro Lights, my second pack of the day. But neither the cigarette nor the antianxiety pills the doctor had prescribed me could help, as with each loud beep my heart pumped faster and the ache in my lower back grew stronger. Just as I managed to get up to shut the window, the buzzer rang. The knots in my stomach tightened. It was almost 9 p.m.. It had to be Morteza, I thought, as I struggled to close the window, the same window I had seamlessly closed hundreds of times before.

It was too late to back out. I had signed a legally binding contract and had even spent nearly five and a half million toman (roughly thirty thousand U.S. dollars) of my advance to finally pay off that erroneous pre-revolution tax bill, which the Ministry of Economic Affairs and Finance held over my head all these years as an excuse to keep the lien on my home, and to prevent me from applying for a new passport.

"Please come in," I overheard Masoud saying as I finally locked the window latches.

"Thank you," Morteza replied.

"Thank you," another man said.

I recognized his voice. I turned around to greet them and found, as I had suspected, Morteza's business associate standing there in a dark suit with a black shirt, his forehead glistening with sweat.

"Mr. Mohammadi has kindly come up to help with the luggage," Morteza said.

Mr. Mohammadi was in his thirties, tall, and bulky. I had first met him a few weeks earlier when Morteza asked him to accompany me to the Ministry of Economic Affairs and Finance, followed by another government office to take care of my new passport. I was taken aback by the way he handled those power-hungry administrative officials. One was at their mercy, but not Mr. Mohammadi. He smoothly argued back and forth with them using their language and their expressions, and he even talked them into dropping their last-minute late fee that would have doubled the already-disputed tax bill. It was clear as day that Mr. Mohammadi had powerful political associations, given his confidence and his way of challenging the officials. That didn't surprise me. But what I found strange was how comfortable Mr. Mohammadi seemed among those people, as though he were in his element. No one ever felt comfortable around officials, as they were all part of the Islamic Republic's own version of a royal court.

"Thank you, but you really didn't have to," Masoud said. "Poulad is going to help."

Mr. Mohammadi insisted as he wiped the newly formed sweat beads off his temples.

"Is this all?" he asked in a surprised tone, pointing to the two suitcases and carry-ons.

If only he knew how long it had taken me to pack my one suitcase, I thought as I put on my manteau, careful not to further agitate my already-aching lower back. I had spent days packing and unpacking, questioning every item, wondering whether this color or that cut would be problematic for my return—that is, if I got on that flight in the first place—in case I were filmed or photographed. In the end, I settled on several neutral-toned long-sleeve tops and trousers that wouldn't be too intolerable to wear in Toronto's summer weather (though definitely more tolerable without the mandatory manteau in Tehran's scorching heat).

"Shahrokh is already in the car," Morteza said, referring to Shahrokh Reihani, a concert promoter based in Canada who he was collaborating with for the concert in Toronto.

We were all traveling together, minus Poulad, who was going to join us in a month or so, sometime before the concert.

"And there's been a small change of plans," Morteza added in a solemn voice.

My heart sank.

"I won't be coming with you—at least not in the beginning," he said.

"Why not?" Masoud asked, appearing as stunned as me.

"It would create too many problems for the studio," Morteza replied in a regretful tone. "I can assure you that you'll be in great hands," Morteza continued. "Mr. Mohammadi is taking my place."

My mind was racing. When did the plans change? Why hadn't he said anything sooner, like on the phone this morning or in person yesterday or the day before? And why was Mr. Mohammadi coming with us when the contract I signed was with Morteza?

"You're too kind," Mr. Mohammadi replied with a smile, "and if I may, I'm sorry to rush anyone, but we must go now."

I didn't have time to voice my concerns or frustration, as Mr. Mohammadi ushered us quickly into a large luxurious van whose engine was already running. Following Mr. Mohammadi's order, the driver stepped on the gas pedal, and we were on our way.

"We're almost there," Masoud whispered to me less than twenty minutes later as the driver sped southwest on an empty Parkway toward Mehrabad Airport.

My stomach churned as I remembered the last time I was there. It was nearly twenty-one years ago, on Sunday, November 4, 1979. We didn't know it at the time, but students of the Imam Khomeini Line had besieged the U.S. embassy in Tehran earlier that morning—they held fifty-two U.S. diplomats hostage for 444 days. Homayoun had spent weeks trying to convince me to go back to the U.S. for a short stay, where I could hide my remaining jewelry at his sister's house—he was worried the Komitehs would march in one day and find it. I finally agreed and sold some of my collectible gold coins to pay for the plane tickets. This was before I was summoned to Evin and Mr. Mesbahzadeh's basement. I also felt secure knowing that Bahram Emadi (the Revolutionary Guard who had followed Masoud Fardmanesh's orders in letting me walk out of Mehrabad a free woman just months earlier and whom I had befriended afterward) would be there.

On that Sunday in 1979, Bahram asked me to stay in the car while he and Homayoun went to retrieve our passports—you had to hand over your passport to the airline officials twenty-four hours before the flight for Passport Control and check-in. I knew something was wrong when he marched back to the car several minutes later.

"You're on the list," Bahram said with a worried tone. "They've kept your passport."

"List?"

"*Mamnoo-ol-khorooj*, you're banned from leaving the country," he replied as he glanced back at the airport entrance. "Homayoun went through, so did your suitcase. But you can't go in there. Go home until we figure this out."

All of a sudden I felt like a character in one of those science-fiction movies, as though some liquid creature was crawling up my body, restricting my legs, arms, hands, and finally my head. I couldn't move. I couldn't even think of what it meant that Homayoun and my suitcase with all of my jewelry were getting on a plane to the U.S. without me.

"Don't worry," Bahram added, seeing my reaction. "It might take some time, but you'll get your passport back."

It took twenty-one years, I thought as Masoud, Shahrokh, and Mr. Mohammadi continued their polite small talk. I thought back to all those times I had wondered what it would feel like to escape, and every time I heard Faegheh in my head insisting that Googoosh wasn't something illegal to be smuggled out like that.

The truth is, I secretly came to believe the mullahs, Mr. Tehrani and Afshoun, and everything they had to say about Googoosh, just as I came to believe every cruel word Mouness ever uttered to me. And when they condemned Googoosh to a lifetime of silence, I tried to bury her.

A big part of me believed this trip to the airport would turn out to be just as pointless as the one in 1979. They didn't let me leave then, and they wouldn't let me leave now. I knew it. Masoud knew it. Even Morteza knew it; that's the real reason why he didn't come.

The howling sound of a siren suddenly appeared out of nowhere. Just as everyone held their breath, an ambulance flashed passed us on the other side of Parkway.

When our car finally pulled into Mehrabad Airport, Mr. Mohammadi moved quickly with the luggage to check-in, while we waited in the car, just I had done all those years ago.

I could barely follow what Masoud and Shahrokh were discussing, though I could tell that Masoud was also nervous, stroking his beard and scanning the airport doors. Morteza's last-minute change of plans had also shaken his confidence.

I glanced at Masoud, forcing a smile, trying my best to appear calm. He did the same. As I watched passengers walk in and out of the terminal, just as they did twenty-one years ago, I saw Mr. Mohammadi walking toward us, waving something in his hand, though I couldn't see what it was in the dark.

He opened my door and leaned in.

"We're ready to go," he said, holding passports with tickets tucked in the middle. They had issued all of our exit stamps.

I pulled on the top of my headscarf, trying to cover as much of my face as I could without looking suspicious to wandering eyes.

"We're going to move quickly," Mr. Mohammadi said as he opened the heavy car door for me. "Follow me as closely as you can, and if anyone comes up to you, let me handle it."

I did as he said. I took bigger steps in an effort to keep up with his fast pace, while Masoud and Shahrokh followed behind. I avoided all eye contact as we entered Mehrabad Airport.

"This way," Mr. Mohammadi said as he turned left, avoiding a number of passengers stopped in the middle of the path with their carts and luggage to watch the large computerized panels with departure and arrival times.

I kept my gaze fixed on the floor tiles, possibly the same from back in the day, barely registering how much the airport had changed over the years. I couldn't afford to be recognized now. But the few times I dared to look up, I noticed that the vibrant chaos I remembered, all the chatter, laughter, and spontaneity, was gone. Sure, it was late in the evening, but I suspected that energy was gone for good, replaced by a sense of surveillance and silent authority, ever-present at all hours, regardless of the time.

"Please come with me," Mr. Mohammadi said, sounding slightly winded.

I couldn't feel my legs, though they somehow continued to follow Mr. Mohammadi into the mostly empty line. I was so desperate to be on the plane already that I barely recognized Babak, standing there with his guitar case—Babak Amini was the young talented musician I had been working with for the last month and whom I had hired to lead my future orchestra on the tour—next to a similarly young woman, whom Mr. Mohammadi quickly introduced as our tour photographer. I nodded and discreetly smiled back at them.

"Next!" the controller called to the couple ahead of us.

The controller was younger, despite his deep frown lines that made him look angry. I looked to Masoud for some comfort, but his eyes were also fixed on the controller.

Mr. Mohammadi shuffled through the passports, as though he were looking for something, as his temples dripped with sweat. He carefully reordered the passports, checking that the right ticket was tucked in on the picture page. When he was done, he grabbed a crumpled tissue from his coat pocket and wiped above his brow.

"Next!" the controller shouted, looking straight at us.

My mind froze.

"Come with me," Mr. Mohammadi said, gesturing me to walk by his side, while Masoud and Shahrokh followed behind.

Mr. Mohammadi greeted the controller with the same confidence I had seen at the Ministry, while the controller muttered back. Mr. Mohammadi handed him our passports, starting with mine.

This was it!

The controller opened my passport, flipping quickly through the first few pages. He paused for a moment on the photo and then glanced up at me, studying my face.

He then looked back down at the page with his frowned expression for what seemed like an eternity before inspecting my face again.

Without uttering a word, he looked back down again, while my heart thumped stronger and stronger against my rib cage. Just as I thought my heart was going to stop, he flipped through my passport, looked over the exit stamp issued earlier, and returned it to Mr. Mohammadi with the ticket tucked in the middle.

"We've got ten minutes to boarding," Mr. Mohammadi said as our group made it past the passport control checkpoint.

My mind was still frozen as I followed Mr. Mohammadi closely. The gate was in eyesight, but as we approached, a unit of three Revolutionary Guards appeared not far ahead, almost out of nowhere. Each step they took closer to us with their rifles strapped over their shoulders made my stomach tighten. As they looked around the different gates, one of their eyes caught mine.

But then his eyes turned to the young female photographer, before walking away without a second look. Just as I was about to sigh in relief, an announcement came over the loudspeakers: "We have an announcement to make. Would the following travelers report to the nearest gate agent: Mr. and Mrs. . . ."

Masoud also seemed to freeze beside me.

Luckily, they were looking for another couple. By the time we reached our empty boarding gate, another message came through, this time announcing that boarding for our flight was about to close. *They'll never let you on that plane*, I told myself again while Mr. Mohammadi got ready to show our tickets.

"Come with me," Mr. Mohammadi said.

The airline host seemed as young and as disgruntled as the passport controller. Just as he was about to take our tickets, his phone rang. The caller's muffled voice sounded agitated as the airline host gruffly shuffled through printed sheets with names listed in a long column. After giving a few telegraphic responses over the phone, the host looked straight at me for the first time. His eyes widened.

He hung up. His face softened.

"Right this way," he said to me with a mixed smile of recognition and disbelief.

I couldn't believe it myself.

Masoud and I took our seats in the first-class cabin, careful not to rouse the attention of the other passengers already seated. Minutes went by without any sign of Revolutionary Guards storming the plane. Then, just as the cabin doors were about to close, I saw a red light start flashing on the main panel's phone close to the cockpit. The cabin steward answered the call.

The call was brief, and soon enough the cabin doors closed, and the engines started to hum.

As the plane started moving, flashing lights from indistinct vehicles caught my attention.

Here they come to stop the plane.

But these were maintenance vehicles.

The plane accelerated down the runway strip and the whole cabin shook as the front wheels lifted off. I felt each vibration that pulled us away from the ground, away from my beloved homeland. As the plane climbed higher in the sky, I felt a huge lump growing in my throat.

A few minutes later the pilot made an announcement, "Ladies and gentlemen . . ."

I was sure the control tower had asked him to turn around and land the plane.

"Please stay fastened in your seats, as we are about to reach thirty thousand feet . . ."

Any minute now they were going to send fighter jets to intercept and escort us back to Mehrabad, I thought as seconds, minutes, and then nearly an hour went by.

"Ladies and gentlemen," the pilot interrupted again, "I would like to inform you that we've just left Iran's airspace."

Masoud turned to me with a smile. I tore off my headscarf and breathed an immense sigh of relief. Then I thought of Kambiz as I fought back the tears welling in my eyes. I couldn't wait to call him from Amsterdam and tell him I was on my way.

Chapter 25

The Comeback

Toronto Suburbs
July 29, 2000
1 p.m.

The car was going to pick us up at any moment. My stomach churned—it hadn't stopped churning since the press conference about two weeks ago. To make matters worse, I only learned yesterday when they brought me to the Air Canada Centre to see the venue, that they had sold seventeen thousand tickets. Seventeen thousand people were coming to see me. I panicked. I had never done anything like this. I had performed in state-sponsored cultural programs and military entertainment events, reaching at most a few thousand people. Nothing even close to an audience of seventeen thousand. How was I going to pull this off? How was I going to manage a crowd that size, after all these years? I had built my career in cabarets, singing to intimate crowds, where I could feel a deep connection with the audience. Even at the peak of my fame before the revolution, I had never performed in an arena of this magnitude. This was something totally new, a different style from anything I had ever done.

I was already anxious about living up to the standards I had set all those years ago, but this brought new fears. Would I still be able to feel the audience's energy? Could I convey my emotions in such a vast, impersonal space? And what if that ceiling came to trap my voice again? Even the

Iranian reporters at the press conference quietly wondered, in between questions, whether I still had a voice after all these years.

Part of me still felt like I was dreaming. When we went to meet my grandson, Daara, at Niagara Falls, shortly after our arrival, I was reminded of the movies that were set there, including Henry Hathaway's film noir *Niagara* (1953), starring Marilyn Monroe, a movie I saw as a young girl. I couldn't believe I was there, by those majestic waterfalls, thousands of miles away from Tehran. Seeing Daara for the first time felt even more surreal. My daughter-in-law brought him alone that first time, as Kambiz couldn't join them—he was waiting at his home in L.A. for his U.S. immigration status to be adjusted. I could barely hold back my tears. Luckily, Daara helped me calm down when he ignored me and refused to come into my arms. I felt a twinge of disappointment in that moment, a little hurt by his rejection. But I quickly brushed it off—after all, he was only two, and I was still a stranger to him. A group of people were throwing coins into the waterfall a few steps away. I copied them and managed to grab Daara's attention. Soon enough he was in my arms, tossing a coin down the immense waterfalls. In that instant, it felt as though I had always held him, ever since his birth, and that, if anything, being away from him had been just a bad dream.

I had lived a bad dream for twenty-one years. And here I was, now, across the world, reuniting with family, recording a new album (*Zartosht*) in a high-tech studio in broad daylight, and about to step onstage again.

My band was already at the venue, or so I was told. There were fifteen musicians gathered from as far away as Venezuela and Iran. They must have thought I was crazy; in rehearsals I nearly damaged my vocal cords by singing my heart out for three hours nonstop for three days in a row. I could see them wondering why I was using up all of my energy just days before the concert. I couldn't blame them. It was reckless of me, just as it would have been reckless for someone preparing to run a marathon to sprint twenty-six miles just before the big race. But I couldn't stop. I needed to make sure that I could do it, that I could stand for more than two hours and sing in front of a live audience after all these years. With each song I felt like I was tearing off large pieces of that ceiling until my voice was finally freed.

I went over the set list in my mind while I gathered all my things from our bedroom in this rental house in the suburbs of Toronto. Mr. Mohammadi urged me to stay away from my fast-tempo hits and romantic ballads, songs he believed would be problematic for our return to Iran, where dancing was still illegal. Initially I wanted to remind him that Googoosh was a pop singer, but then I remembered the concerts were going to be filmed. I didn't want another call from Mr. Hatami, another interrogation session at Evin, or something worse. So I carefully chose twenty-three slower-paced songs, with the exception of one notable fast-paced love song, "*Hamsedaye Khoobam*" (My Good Sympathizer), which I would dedicate to my dearest Daara.

Ten days ago, I sat in a large hotel press room, in front of large cameras, with my hair uncovered. I chose every word carefully as I spoke to the Iranian diaspora reporters, telling them how I had spent twenty-one years sitting on my couch at home. I left out any mention of Mr. Mesbahzadeh's basement, the shrieks, the pain, the drugs, the hopelessness, the interrogations, the surveillance. But I wasn't being careful just for the cameras. Ever since I spotted a different last name—Khoshzaban—on Mr. Mohammadi's passport during our layover in Amsterdam, I had been watching my every word around him, too.

My suspicions about him grew when I learned a few days after our arrival in Toronto that we were going to be staying together in the same house somewhere in the suburbs while the concert was being organized. I couldn't understand the need for such close proximity, especially since there was clearly the budget for Masoud and me to have our own separate space. And why were we leaving downtown Toronto, making us so dependable on Mr. Mohammadi for everything? Masoud was also concerned.

The situation became even more awkward and unsettling with Morteza not coming to Toronto as promised, leaving us with this person we barely knew. There was no longer any mention of him joining us on the tour at all. I couldn't understand why. Was Morteza now afraid of being associated with Googoosh and the tour? Was he worried about how this might affect him or his film studio? When Masoud reviewed the contract I had signed, we noticed something even stranger—Morteza's name was nowhere to be found. It was only me and Mr. Mohammadi—the name exactly as it appeared in his passport. How could I have missed that? All the uncertainty and these unexpected twists gnawed at me, adding to my feeling of insecurity and growing stress. But I knew there was nothing I could do but go on with the tour. Whether I liked it or not, this was my one and only chance to get back onstage after all these years. So I decided to bite my tongue and keep my suspicions to myself.

As I put on my shoes, the two voices in my mind—Faegheh and Googoosh—picked up their debate over the smallest details of the upcoming concert. How would I greet the audience? Would I say hello in Arabic or Persian, *salâm* or *dorood*? Faegheh was worried that if I said "*Dorood*," they would punish me back home for evoking a pre-Islamic Iran. And would I bow to the audience? Googoosh was determined to do so, even if the gesture could sometimes evoke the monarchy and, by extension, the Shah. I would have never even wondered about such things twenty-one years ago, having improvised all aspects of my performances aside from the set list. But I couldn't afford to improvise now, not even with a simple hello. I prepared my introductory speech down to the comma with Masoud's help, which would include some words about the devastating passing of our national treasure Ahmad Shamlou, a poet and someone I was honored to call a friend.

Are you sure the dresses aren't too revealing?

Faegheh, they're fine.

Mr. Rahmanian, an Iranian haute couture designer in Toronto, was mindful of my concerns about returning to Iran after the tour and the risk of facing trouble for not dressing modestly onstage. He carefully incorporated these considerations when designing my two long-sleeve stage gowns, using the fabrics I personally selected.

"Okay," Faegheh said reluctantly.

"Are you talking to me?" Kambiz asked. He had fortunately arrived three days ago.

It took me a second to realize I had spoken out loud.

"No, *azizam*," I replied.

I didn't have time to explain to him that Faegheh was speaking to Googoosh.

"The car is here," Mr. Mohammadi shouted from the main door.

Everything was already in the suitcase, including the dresses, my hair products, my notes, and the printout of the set list. As I grabbed my purse with my cigarettes and sunglasses, Masoud turned to me.

"*Khânoum*, do you have everything?" he asked in a sweet tone.

He had been so much warmer to me in the past few days. It had taken him some time before he finally forgave me for the gaffe I had made at the press conference—while trying to defend him in the face of silly rumors about him using my comeback tour to promote his upcoming films, I told reporters that he was a "pioneer, for himself" in the Iranian film industry.

"For myself?" he exclaimed. "What the hell does that mean?"

What I had tried to say was that he was a pioneer in his own right. But I knew it wasn't as much about the gaffe as it was about Googoosh overshadowing him for the first time in our marriage. After all, for years I was just Mrs. Kimiai. Even though he knew how much I loved him—I even bought him a high-end reflex camera—I was still going to have to do a fine balancing act of preserving his ego while being back in the spotlight, just as I had done in all of my marriages.

Perhaps he realized that he had overreacted and was making up for it now. Masoud had spent the entire morning sitting with me and discussing the script he was working on. For hours we dove into his project like we used to back in Tehran, discussing plot and character development, as well as my role. He probably knew it was somehow liberating for me to focus on something other than the concert.

"Yes, *azizam*," I replied, and we headed to the door.

Air Canada Centre, 6 p.m.

"All done," the young Canadian makeup artist said as she put on the finishing touches to my makeup.

She had done a great job highlighting my features and hiding my wrinkles and the dark rings under my eyes without making me look like I had too much makeup on. It was exactly what I had asked her for—a chignon and neutral-toned makeup—since I was going back to Iran at the end of the tour.

"Mom, would you like more tea?" Kambiz asked.

I still couldn't believe how grown up he was, even compared to nine years earlier when I saw him last. He was now a father—a great one—and a husband. He had come so far from the teenager who secretly spray-painted the band name "KISS" on the back of my leather jacket and then got stopped by the morality police in Iran for wearing it over ripped jeans. I was so proud of him, but I didn't know how to tell him. A part of me was scared he would say that I didn't have the right to be proud, that I had been absent for more than half of his life. Perhaps he would tell me that I was barely there for him even when I was present. He wouldn't be wrong. There was no point in going there, I thought, especially not today. But I knew I had to make it up to him in the days, weeks, and months to come. And in the long term, if he was willing, we could both work on building a healthier relationship.

"Can I get you something else?" he asked, pointing at the large table along the wall behind me, covered with all kinds of snacks, fruits, vegetables, and beverages, warm and cold, sparkling and still.

"Only tea with some honey please, *azizam*," I replied, just as I felt another wave of nausea approaching.

I had never seen a dressing room like this before, as big as a hotel suite. I was used to the small hallways and tiny changing rooms backstage in the cabarets and theaters in Tehran, space that I shared with other artists, set decorations, and wardrobes. It was impressive. Then again, it took very little to impress me these days. Going to the local flea market in Toronto felt as exciting to me as walking into Dior or Yves Saint Laurent in Paris. Of course, it was my first time in Canada, but even something as simple as walking down the street without a headscarf and manteau was an amazing new feeling. I felt like a little child discovering the world. I had that feeling a couple of weeks earlier while watching Ridley Scott's *Gladiator*. It was my first time back in a movie theater since I'd attended one of Rasoul

Mollagholipour's film premieres in the early 1990s. I couldn't believe my eyes or ears, all the sharp and crystal clear images, the vivid colors, the battle scenes with all that precision and movement, or the loud clang of swords and daggers clashing while the cries of thousands of Roman spectators vibrated throughout the theater room. Watching this movie set in antiquity in that theater room ironically felt like a futuristic experience.

For twenty-one years I had been far from everything. The illegal satellite dish we had installed less than ten years ago provided me a small window into the outside world via Turkish, Italian, and German channels. But it was a small window, and so I had been clueless about global trends, whether social, technological, or in music and fashion. I was like a fish out of water in some sense. I even asked our local guide in Toronto if there was a national holiday, since all the cars were driving with their lights on in broad daylight. I had no idea that there was such a thing as mandatory daytime running lights.

Kambiz was already pouring me tea when my diaphragm tightened again. I'd never felt this way before a performance. I reached the bathroom just as the contractions grew violent and stomach acid clawed at my throat. I went to vomit, but there was nothing much for my stomach to purge besides several cups of tea and two packs of Marlboro Lights.

8:25 p.m.

The door opened and closed, blurry faces came and left, as I paced back and forth between the walls of the dressing room. An hour went by like this in absolute silence, as though there was some unspoken rule that I was to be left alone. As I tried to take a puff of my cigarette, I realized it had gone out, just as the other unfinished cigarettes laying in the ashtray. Then, as though the un-mute button had been pressed, I heard someone say, "The orchestra has started." Everything went silent again. My stomach churned.

Several tall men entered the room. Someone motioned that I follow them. As soon as I stepped out of the dressing room, the deafening silence was replaced by a humming noise that increased with every step I took. I couldn't hear anything else, not the men or our footsteps. I followed the uniformed men through a long hallway with countless doors on each side. I felt like Alice in Wonderland. There were large pictures with blurry faces hanging on the walls. I wondered who they were and if they, too, had heard the humming noise when they walked down this hall. It got darker when we exited the hallway, but I could make out the shape of a staircase up ahead, in the backstage area. As we approached the stairs the humming noise started to sound like a roaring giant, a giant that I both feared and loved. As the giant roared louder, I realized we were steps away from meeting. *Is this really happening?* I wondered.

I was escorted all the way to the bottom of the stairs, but I knew that I had to climb them alone. The floor was vibrating, and I felt my heart about to burst from terror and joy. I looked down at my feet, careful not to miss a step or stumble on my dress. When I reached halfway up the staircase, I saw light illuminating the tall pillars—replicas of the majestic Persepolis columns, remnants of another era—that stood proudly along the back of the stage. Every nerve in my body tightened. Suddenly, the noise hit me. I heard all seventeen thousand people calling me. "GOOGOOSH! GOOGOOSH!"

It had been twenty-one years since I last heard their voices. Twenty-one years since I last heard their cheers, their cries, their love, and their energy. My hands shook and I felt a lump growing in my throat as I reached the stage. "Deep breaths," I told myself, fighting back tears. I tried desperately to clear my throat. My body moved forward in a trancelike state, summoned by a sea of familiar voices. I couldn't see much; the spotlights were almost blinding. The crowd took the form of a wave, stretching all the way back to the other end of the arena, as seventeen thousand people clapped, stomped, and chanted all at once.

Tears streamed down my face. All I could do was bow in front of all this outpouring of love and emotion. Just as I got a hold of myself and the crowd sounded like it was calming down, their cheers doubled, sending chills throughout my body like an electric shock. I turned to Babak and the other musicians, wondering whether they were also experiencing this. They all seemed similarly shaken by all of the love.

I took a deep breath.

"In the name of Iran and Iranians, *salâm*. 'Salutations to the day of friendship's delight,'" I said, quoting Hafez, while the stage trembled under the energy of the crowd's excitement. "My God, how I wish all Iranians and Persian speakers, Tajiks, and Afghans were here with us tonight. I bring you warm greetings from Iran, from all your mothers, fathers, brothers, and sisters—I think they would allow me to be the messenger of their greetings and best wishes for you all—and I wish that one day we find ourselves reunited in Iran." I fought back the tears and continued. "I would like to ask of you a minute of silence in honor of the father of all poets, writers, and intellectuals of Iran, the greatest poet and modern-day Hafez, the late Ahmad Shamlou."

Seventeen thousand people sat in silence for sixty seconds in his honor. Not one word.

Then the music started. First the violin, then the piano, drums, and flute, all began summoning me. The song was "*Hejrat*" (Emigration), written by my friend Shahyar Ghanbari with the music by Nasser Cheshmazar. As soon as my cue arrived, I was choked up again and I could barely get the first line out. Same with the second line. And the third. And the fourth. And so on. The lyrics of the song had become too real: "Your departure hanged the pitch of my voice / on a bough (I can't speak or sing anymore)." And the more I panicked the more my throat tightened up. I could hear myself in the earpiece. I had no control over my voice, and everything sounded off-key. It felt like I was living a slow-motion train wreck. I felt as though my mind had been invaded by the tragic lyrics. *Get it together, you cannot be this emotional*, I thought.

But just as I reached the chorus, I regained control over my breathing, which allowed me to take back control of my pace, pitch, rhythm, diction. I closed my eyes for a few seconds and then my throat opened up and the air flowed freely through my vocal cords. With every new word, every new line or verse, I felt more empowered.

Just as I was starting to get into the groove, I felt a tremendous surge of energy coming toward me from the audience—I could hear the heartbeat of every single person in the crowd, along with every single foot stomping the ground. It felt like there was a giant octopus with tentacles spreading all over the massive space, causing a wave to form, a wave of energy that grew exponentially as it rushed toward the stage before hitting me and the musicians. Even the non-Persian speakers in the orchestra looked like they were being swept away. The waves came one after another, nearly knocking me to the ground each time. I panicked. *How am I going to make it to the end of the show? I can't give up now.* Then, as the next colossal wave was about to hit, I leaned directly into it and took control.

With each song I traveled back and forth through time and space. I saw Papa balancing himself on a tightwire with his trademark ease. I saw Mama smiling at me from across the street. I saw Fery at his wedding. I walked through the hustle and bustle of Lâlehzâr Street. I saw Nahid holding her boyfriend tightly as they escaped on his motorcycle. I returned with the audience to the homes they had left behind in Iran; together we visited their mothers' neatly decorated rooms, their fathers' offices, their old school chums, their crushes, their long-lost lovers. We saw scenes from movies we had watched together in the theaters all those years ago. We traveled all the way south to Abadan and then all the way north on the windy roads of Châlus. We felt the humidity of Shomâl and the aridity of the Alborz mountains and smelled the sweet scent of Babol's orange blossoms.

Standing in the middle of that stage, in that large arena, thousands of miles away from Tehran, I was finally back home. We all were.

Epilogue

They say old habits die hard. It's true. I still talk out loud to my plants, and the trees, here in Los Angeles, just as I used to in Tehran. Friends still laugh at me for babying my *nârenj* and pomegranate trees, and for sweet-talking unapologetically to the Persian jasmine, all of which I had planted here in my garden more than a decade ago. Luckily, my two dogs have accepted the shared attention (however reluctantly at first). I love walking around my little green haven, watching the flowers bloom and the trees grow taller, year after year, under the Californian blue sky. It's incredible how quickly they anchored their roots in the ground and made themselves at home—if only it were as easy for us humans. I sometimes think of my coniferous trees, the weeping willow Papa gifted me, and the sweet-scented roses I left behind in Velenjak. Did anyone tend to them? Are they still there?

I never went back to Iran. Friends and family urged me not to because of all of the international headlines I made with my comeback. It was one thing for Googoosh to get back on stage, abroad, and to sing for the Iranian diaspora, but another for her to speak to CNN with her hair uncovered. They warned me that I would be arrested. But that didn't scare me, not after everything I had gone through over those twenty-one years. I stayed back because I couldn't sign away Googoosh again. I knew I wouldn't survive this time.

I was able to buy an apartment in Toronto at the end of the world tour, in 2001, using the money I earned. Rumors ran wild that I made many millions being whisked around the world on a private jet to more than thirty sold-out shows. But the truth was far from that. I didn't earn that much compared to what Mr. Mohammadi and some of the promoters made. But it was enough for me to start my life over again.

Masoud returned to Iran with Poulad. He would go back and forth, while I remained in Toronto—fortunately, Fariborz and Adel lived somewhat close by. For a while, we pretended that the long distance wouldn't change much, but in reality, our relationship had already shifted. The rift between us grew steadily after the press conference. It didn't help that he felt he had been strung around the world for twelve months with the false promise of making a film. He had spent months scouting for locations across Canada and Cuba, rewriting the screenplay, the script, and contacting different Iranian actors. But nothing ever seemed to work. The locations were not approved, the actors he wanted were suddenly unavailable, and Hedayat Film seemed generally less interested in the project. At some point, his location manager gave up and flew back to Tehran. Masoud was visibly irritated and I was disappointed that I wasn't going to act in his film. He believed that he had been used as a pawn to get Googoosh to do the tour. "It was always about Googoosh," he said.

When Masoud came back to Toronto for his final visit in 2003, he confirmed my suspicions.

"Back home, everyone knows me as Masoud Kimiai," he said, "but here, I'm just Googoosh's husband."

I could understand his frustration. He was, after all, one of the most renowned Iranian filmmakers. But as his wife, who had supported him all those years from the sidelines, I wished that he had felt a little less insecure about being Googoosh's husband.

We were granted a divorce in 2004; it was amicable. When I look back at our marriage, I will always remember the endless hours we spent in front of the television, blissfully dissecting frames and scenes together. I learned a lot from Masoud during those eleven years, from his intellect and his artistic vision. And most important, I am forever grateful to him for taking me to Lachini's studio that night, and for encouraging me all those years to never give up on Googoosh when it seemed everyone else had.

The world tour had brought the stage back into my life, but it also reunited me with friends and family. Every one of those concerts was unique and unforgettable, but my show at the Zénith Paris was particularly special. Many of my closest and longest-standing friends, whom I hadn't seen in more than two decades, were in the crowd that night—including Sâghi, Amir Javânshir, and my dearest friend of many years, Parto Dehlavi. Having them be a part of my comeback journey was an incredible feeling, but also hard to believe. I had previously convinced myself that they were all gone forever—it was easier to deal with the pain that way. And yet, there they were, singing and dancing along with me like we had never been apart. I didn't sleep much that night, nor did they. The revolution may have kept us apart for all those years, but the beauty of true friendship is that neither time nor distance can destroy that kind of bond.

I've been very fortunate to reconnect with so many dear friends, too many to name. With each passing year, I find that there's nothing better than to laugh with a friend to help deal with life's hardships. I am also thankful for the extra time I was given with some of my dearest friends who passed away too soon, including Amir, and Bijan Saffari.

I've also visited the Shahbânu—who remains Iran's biggest patron of the arts—several times in her home in Paris. I'm reminded each time why I've always felt so much love and admiration for her.

There were those who I kept close to my heart, but never saw again, like Marjan. Sitting in Mesbahzadeh's basement, we had promised each other that we would meet again outside. But that never happened. We lost touch. Maybe it was easier on us that way, easier to forget that dingy room and the haunting echoes of shrieks down the hall. There were many times I wanted to reach out to her, but life kept getting in the way. Marjan left Iran a year after me and reportedly joined the MEK, like Marzieh had done before her. Sadly, she passed away in 2020 (months after the start of the COVID-19 pandemic), at the age of seventy-one. Whenever I hear her songs, that soft soothing voice, I remember how lucky I was that she was with me in that tiny room. I remember the other women, their strength and courage, and how, in the darkest moments, music can still provide light and hope.

I also didn't get to see Mama before she died in 2003, in L.A. As my mother got older, she grew very depressed and withdrawn. By the time I had my comeback concert in L.A., in 2000, she wasn't feeling well enough to meet me in person. We once briefly talked over the phone. In Mama's case, it helped me immensely that I had already said all my goodbyes to her when she left Tehran in the late 1980s. I've held on to our happier memories—though I'll never forget that time, during the Iran-Iraq War, when there was a blackout in the middle of her planned hysterectomy, and I had to hold up the flashlight for the surgeon to carry on with the procedure. I like to imagine that somewhere, up there, Mama is once more singing along with Papa.

I'll never forget when Daara agreed to come in my arms that day we first met, at Niagara Falls. Papa must have felt the same way when he first embraced Kambiz. It was also one of my life's greatest joys to hold my granddaughter, Mya, shortly after her birth in 2003. I moved to L.A. around that time, to be closer to Kambiz and his family. And although my relationship with my son is still far from perfect, my love for him and his beautiful grown children is unwavering.

It took time to get used to living in L.A., or as many have rightly dubbed, Tehrangeles. Here, I am both a nobody, and also Googoosh. When I walk into my local grocery store, there is a 50 percent chance that I can shop with complete anonymity and a 50 percent chance that I will run into an Iranian American who doesn't hesitate to remind me of who I am. This strange kind of dual existence was disorienting at first. One evening in the early days, while Roya, Joseph, his wife, and I were waiting for our table at a trendy Beverly Hills restaurant, Mel Brooks walked in.

"Look who's here—it's dearest Mel Brooks!" I exclaimed playfully as if greeting an old friend, flashing a broad smile and throwing my arms up like a magician unveiling the grand finale of a trick.

The loud room went dead quiet. It dawned on me that I knew who he was, but he hadn't a clue in the world as to who Googoosh was—just like everyone beyond our little party of four. I was about to burst out laughing, but controlled myself, for fear of appearing as though I were mocking him. So I kept up my big smile and my arms in the air. He smiled back, a little awkwardly, to this extravagant fan with an accent.

Today, I consider L.A. home, or more precisely, my home away from home. And although every country has its own set of problems and challenges, I am forever grateful to my adoptive country for all the freedoms I enjoy here in the U.S. Not a day goes by that I don't appreciate the fact that I can walk outside with my hair uncovered, or that I can sing, dance, and speak my mind in front of an audience of men and women.

I've spent the last twenty-five years trying to make up for all the lost time. Year after year, I've performed in front of packed audiences around the world, including in historical venues like the Hollywood Bowl here in L.A., and New York's Madison Square Garden, the Royal Albert Hall in London, and the Sydney Opera House. I've recorded new songs and albums, exploring all kinds of themes, old and new, about love and resilience. I've made music videos that I would have never imagined possible back in Iran, whether it be the use of cutting-edge technology or showcasing the love between two women in "*Behesht*" (Paradise). I've collaborated with so many talented artists, too many to name, from beloved Iranian musicians to globally adored Ed Sheeran. I've even served as head judge (and head of the academy) on the hit TV talent show *Googoosh Music Academy*, broadcast on the London-based satellite Persian channel, Manoto, allowing me to appear back in people's homes in Iran—I even got to perform once again live on TV after more than thirty years. In many ways I've been able to pick up where I left off in the summer of 1978, thanks to the internet, satellite broadcasting, and social media.

Indeed, after twenty-one years away, I finally returned to the homeland of my talent. In exchange, I've had to assume a life in exile. I don't regret my choice—I am healthier now with the sober lifestyle I have led since leaving Iran. But like anyone living in exile, I regret having been forced to make this choice. As a friend put it, "It's like being asked to choose which leg you don't want amputated."

I wake up in the morning, I think of Iran. I go to bed at night and my mind is still there. Anyone who comes to my house, nestled here in the hills of L.A., knows that at all times of the day (and night), my iPad is tuned in to one of the many diaspora radio and television channels. I listen to the latest songs (mostly recorded and released out of Dubai because of the ongoing governmental restrictions on pop music), I watch the television shows and, of course, I follow the news. It's not that I don't enjoy American television and music (I also tune in religiously to shows like *America's Got Talent*, the Grammys, and the Oscars), or that I don't care about the local news. It's more that Iran is part of my being. You can take Googoosh out of Iran, but you can't take Iran out of Googoosh.

For thousands of years, poets and philosophers from all over the world have beautifully described the woes of exile for which there is no known antidote. I can only echo their lament: I miss everything about my homeland, just as I did when I lived in Paris, and then in Rome. I miss the gray shores of the emerald Caspian Sea, the snowy caps of the Alborz mountains, the delightful singing of the sparrows, and even the bustling streets of Tehran. I miss my house in Velenjak; the government put a lien on it again sometime after I spoke at a rally outside the United Nations in July 2009 following the violent state crackdown of the Iranian presidential election protests. I couldn't just sit at home as I had during the 1999 student protests. It was impossible to stay silent now that I was so far away. Like millions around the world, I watched in complete horror at the moment, captured on a camera phone, when Neda Agha-Soltan died from a fatal gunshot wound to the chest. Neda was only twenty-six years old, and she happened to be an aspiring underground musician. Her life was cut short by regime forces, just like nineteen-year-old Sohrab Arabi and many others that summer. Since then, countless young lives have been lost, including during the 2019 nationwide protests. In 2022, twenty-two-year-old Mahsa Amini died shortly after being arrested for allegedly not wearing her headscarf properly. Eyewitnesses reported that she was severely beaten by the morality police. Her death ignited widespread unrest and led to further tragedies—like nine-year-old Kian Pirfalak, who was shot and killed by regime forces on November 16, 2022, during the crackdown. And there have been many more since.

My heart aches just as deeply with each new gut-wrenching report of another political prisoner's execution. In 2024 alone, the government executed more than nine hundred people, the highest number in more than a decade, with many victims being dissidents, protesters, and ethnic minorities. This cycle of brutality must end. I plead for the voices of the silenced to be heard and for justice to prevail.

What could only give meaning to all these tragedies is the enduring bravery of those who faced them. As I write this, I am reminded of Nahid and how she fought relentlessly at just fifteen years old, in that basement, for her fundamental rights. Her courage, like that of Neda, Sohrab, Mahsa, and the countless political prisoners, shows that our youth possess the remarkable strength to carry out extraordinary political acts, even under the crushing weight of the theocratic regime's oppressive boot.

From afar, all I can do is try to be the voice of the voiceless and shed light on the ongoing violence through social media for the world to see. I try to remind my compatriots back home that they are not alone. I wish I could do more. I still feel helpless watching everything from a distance. This is the most difficult part of life in exile. Perhaps there's some level of survivor's guilt.

In the hardest moments, I've turned to music. Just after the violent crackdown began on the peaceful protesters in June 2009, I went into a music studio in L.A. and recorded the song "*Man Hamoon Iranam*" (I'm Still That Same Iran)—I was filming its music video the day Neda Agha-Soltan was tragically killed. The song expresses both the angst and pain of what goes on in my country as well as our undying hope for better days.

There is always hope. As a people, Iranians don't give up easily, whether it's our Persian language after the Arab invasion centuries ago or the traditional customs of Nowruz, to the dismay of the Islamic Republic. Some of the most memorable moments of my years in exile have been watching the videos sent to *Googoosh Music Academy* directly from Iran. Here were these children, adults, young and old, singing their hearts out (with their backs facing the camera, or their faces blurred to avoid being identified and arrested). No matter how hard this corrupt regime has made their lives, whether by mishandling the economy, imposing vast personal restrictions, creating environmental disasters, or crushing peaceful protests, they continue to sing. The videos of little girls and the young women singing were particularly meaningful to me, and I couldn't help but get choked up witnessing their bravery. They are the true embodiment of courage and resilience. To this day, women are still not allowed to record a song or sing solo in front of a male audience.

As I'm finishing this book, I'm performing my farewell tour, traveling to cities across the world. In Persian, we have a saying that goes "A writer puts the pen down before the pen puts the writer down." I am quitting the stage before it quits me. I gave it my all for the last twenty-five years, ever since that extraordinary night in Toronto's Air Canada Centre. I treated each and every show as my first and possibly last, dancing and singing my heart out. I tried to innovate every step of the way, to continuously surprise my audience and keep them on their toes. If it were up to Googoosh, I would never stop. But Faegheh is right, as always when she's looking out for Googoosh. My body no longer moves the way it used to, and I can't push my vocal cords around as hard as before. And though my heart breaks a little knowing that I won't be performing one last time at home, I feel blessed that I have been able to perform again, and now for four generations.

I am forever grateful to my audience, and my fans, starting from the theaters on Lâlehzâr to the sports arenas around the world, for all of the love and support over the last seventy years. You are everything to me. Even recently, I had this incredible experience at the Queen Elizabeth Theater in Vancouver, Canada, where I took the stage anxiously, barely able to speak due to laryngitis. As soon as I felt the positive energy emanating from the audience, I somehow freed my voice and gave the best performance possible. I could have never done it without you!

I will continue to make music as long as I can. I will record uplifting songs to provide a moment of relief in people's busy daily lives, songs that speak to the untended wounds of the heart, as well as songs that shine light on the injustices that people currently face in Iran. I will try to help connect the younger Iranian diaspora to our beautiful Persian culture. And as I embark on this new chapter of my life, I am excited for the next projects on the horizon, the kind that take me out of my comfort zone, like this book.

As a child, my cruel stepmother would tell me to stay quiet, not to say a word to my father about her abuse, just as the Islamic government forced me into silence, away from the stage. I've spent the last eight years looking back as far as I can and digging as deep as possible with the hope that my story can help break down the silence that surrounds my people's plight, especially our women. I pray that very soon, they, too, will have reclaimed their voices.

Acknowledgments

"Googoosh must write her story—a cautionary tale," they said in the late 1990s. But I refused, having no intention of delivering my memoir to the agents of the regime. Besides, writing had never been my refuge, especially when it meant confronting memories that brought more pain than solace.

Over the last twenty-five years, friends, writers, and acquaintances from literary circles urged me to write my book. Yet, between the demands of my career, the unrelenting pace of performances, and the distances that separated us, the idea remained just that—an idea.

Eventually, however, I came to see it not as a choice but a duty. My story, the story of my people, needed to be told. Not just for myself but for those who might find meaning in it. And to honor what was once the land I have always loved. So, in late 2015, with the unwavering support of my cherished friend from youth Parto Dehlavi and her brilliant, curious, and deeply beloved daughter, Tara Dehlavi, we finally began writing. Today, I take joy in knowing that Tara's persistence and dedication have helped me bring this book to life, allowing me to convey my long-held aspirations and messages: social, political, and above all, artistic. I have been, am, and will always be grateful to her.

I would also like to thank my wonderful agent, Thomas Flannery, who championed this project from the beginning with great care and conviction, ensuring it ultimately reached the right hands. Your belief in this book and enthusiasm carried me forward.

I am also deeply grateful to the extraordinary team at Gallery Books—including Natasha Simons, Jennifer Bergstrom, Aimée Bell, and Sydney Morris—for their professionalism and dedication to bringing this book into the world. To my editors, Paul Choix and Mia Robertson, thank you for your thoughtful guidance, sharp instincts, and encouragement through every draft. And thank you Rob Sternitzky and Jamie Selzer for your meticulous copyediting, which helped shape the final text with care and precision.

And to Brian Bowen Smith, thank you for capturing in your photograph the spirit of this story with such grace.

And last but not least, thank you to my fans—without whom I would have never had a story worth telling.

THE LOST EMPIRE OF EMANUEL NOBEL

ALSO BY DOUGLAS BRUNT

NONFICTION

The Mysterious Case of Rudolf Diesel

FICTION

Trophy Son

The Means

Ghosts of Manhattan